AESTHETICS IN PERFORMANCE

AESTHETICS IN PERFORMANCE

Formations of Symbolic Construction and Experience

Edited by

Angela Hobart

and

Bruce Kapferer

Berghahn Books

NEW YORK • OXFORD

Published in 2005 by
Berghahn Books

www.berghahnbooks.com

© 2005 Angela Hobart and Bruce Kapferer

Library of Congress Cataloging-in-Publication Data

Aesthetics in performance : formations of symbolic construction and
experience / edited by Angela Hobart and Bruce Kapferer.
    p. cm.
Includes bibliographical references and index.
ISBN 1-57181-567-8
    1. Aesthetics. 2. Experience. 3. Symbolism. 4. Ritual. 5. Performing
arts—Philosophy. I. Hobart, Angela. II. Kapferer, Bruce.

BH301.E8A38 2004
111'.85—dc22

                                                    2004056002

British Library Cataloguing in Publication Data

A catalogue record for this book is available from
the British Library.

Printed in the United States on acid-free paper

CONTENTS

ILLUSTRATIONS

FIGURES

ACKNOWLEDGEMENTS

We wish to acknowledge the Cross Cultural Centre Ascona (Centro Incontri Umani Ascona) for hosting the workshop on Aesthetics in Performance in April 2001. The orientation of the Centre is to promote understanding, respect, and peace internationally. The Centre is located in Ascona, on Lake Maggiore, on the border between Switzerland and Italy.

We also wish to thank Dr. Giovanni and Laura Simona for helping to organize the workshop and Berghahn Books for their editorial assistance. Above all, we want to express our gratitude to the participants of the workshop, which we found exciting and stimulating. Their papers form the basis of this book.

Angela Hobart
Bruce Kapferer

AESTHETICS IN PERFORMANCE

INTRODUCTION

The Aesthetics of Symbolic Construction and Experience

Bruce Kapferer and Angela Hobart

The essays in this volume address aesthetic forms and dynamics with particular reference to performance. Performance itself is considered aesthetically, that is, as a process that continually forms itself before reflection, engaging those embraced in its dynamic field to its constructive and experientially constitutive force.

Broadly, our use of the concept of aesthetics applies to created symbolic genres, or dynamic structures within which human experience, meaning, and value are constituted or emergent. This orientation accounts for the concentration on performance in many of these essays. It is through performance that the capacities and qualities of what may be described as aesthetic genres, styles, or forms are generated and realized.

Conventionally, the study of aesthetics has concentrated on art forms and the issue of aesthetic judgement. Kant is the commanding figure who begins the major discourse that still dominates concerning the relation between subjective and objective (rational scientific) knowledge and understanding. This is not to ignore other major thinkers in the field of aesthetics where Western thought dominates, such as the towering figure of Hegel and his various critics including Kierkegaard and Nietzsche, whose ideas have been seminal in more recent post-structuralist and postmodern thought. These latter scholars have been important in the shattering of the grand totalizing theoretical schema, for example, that characterize so much modernist thought; this has never been more magnificently epitomized than in Hegel's still grandly

---

Notes for this section are located on page 21.

stimulating phenomenology as represented by his *Aesthetics: Lectures on Fine Art* ([1835] 1975). Developing from within Kantian ideas, Hegel arranges various aesthetic genres in accordance with objective criteria of value that he establishes and, furthermore, in a great historical and cultural sweep that remains unequalled today, attempts to show the progression of aesthetic form in terms of his theory of the dialectical unfolding of Spirit and the Absolute. Hegel, of course, is Eurocentric, but no less so than most scholars in the field of aesthetics even in these post-Enlightenment and postmodern times. However, what is perhaps most difficult in Hegel from our perspective is the thoroughgoing subordination of aesthetic judgement to his own overriding totalizing conceptual and theoretical scheme. This reduces the capacity of what we will present as aesthetic processes to reveal their own force and import in the practice of human beings, aside from Hegel's concern for the developmental process of the self-realization of human being.

We will begin our discussion with Kant, whose ideas are still widely debated in the field of aesthetic understanding. This is not to say that key thinkers like Hegel are excluded. The hierarchy of judgement and value that Lévi-Strauss establishes in his *Mythologiques* (1964) regarding music, myth, and ritual is self-evidently Hegelian, as it is Kantian. Anthropologists (all the contributors to this volume would understand themselves as engaging in an anthropology) routinely return in their analyses to Kantian aesthetics, although, in our opinion, rather too narrowly in terms of an anthropology of art.

Anthropological discussions of aesthetics, perhaps because of a focus on art as aesthetics, become bogged down in definitions of beauty. The apparent anti-Kantianism of some recent discussions by anthropologists (see Weiner et al. 1993) replays a time-worn anthropological relativism in an effort to deny universalist categories. While Kant was concerned with establishing universals of judgement and morality in his aesthetics, he also placed concepts such as beauty beyond definition in an effort to explore the creative forces engaged in aesthetic creation. Here is a key difference between Kant and Hegel, for instance, the latter refusing the Kantian implication that individual creative energy might lie outside the human processes of conceptual reason. For Kant, as with Hegel, aesthetics does not merely concern art but rather lies at the heart of the critical understanding of the human project as a whole. We open with this interpretive significance of Kant's work in mind, for likewise we argue that the field of aesthetics is at the center of understanding of all human endeavor and practice.

The discussion then extends into a reappreciation of the contribution of such scholars as Cassirer and especially Susanne Langer, who expand Kant in this direction (indeed go well beyond him) in ways relevant to many of the themes explored in this book.

Kant, Aesthetic Beauty, and Beyond

Kant affirms that aesthetic judgements, such as what constitutes the beautiful, its modes of appearance to and effect through the perceptual senses, are through and through subjective. This subjectivity, however, is already largely grounded in preexisting conceptual schema. However, for Kant, this central commitment in his work is problematic, for he indicates that there is much that is intuitive and prereflective in subjective and aesthetic experience. This is the source of the creativity of aesthetic processes and also of potential universals (e.g., regarding the unmediated intuition of ethics, justice, etc.).

The subjective sensory or embodied nature of aesthetic judgements is, for Kant, no less a valid form of human knowledge than scientific knowledge. Of course, in Kant the distinction between objective (rational, disembodied) knowledge and subjective (embodied, sensory) knowledge is by no means absolute. This is apparent in his development in *The Critique of Judgement* (1987) of the concept of the sublime, in which Kant recognizes the two forms of knowledge as embodied and sensory. These are at the root of imagination and intuition, which are at the font of all knowledge. It is the embodied ground of knowledge that establishes the horizonal limits of knowledge or what Kant describes as the sublime. In the interpretation that we give here, the sublime is both prior to the schemes of reason (the sensuous ground upon which reason builds) and the furthest limit of reason where the categories of reason are ultimately exhausted. This apex of reason is also sensuous, thoroughly embodied, a corporeality of reason (see Deleuze 1995 for a development of this position).

Elaine Scarry (1999) pursues this argument in Kant, developing upon its Platonic antecedents (but one could detect something similar in Dante's *Divine Comedy*) to demonstrate that truth and justice are brought to realization through a confrontation with beauty and perfection (the apices in a hierarchy of aesthetic judgement). The encounter with beauty and perfection is an engagement with a kind of aesthetic sublime, a lived sensuous ideal that discovers its integrity at the edge of reason but not against it. It is a limit that when reached motivates a reassertion of a realm of order and reason that, in the interpretation pursued here, is both encompassed and provoked by the sublime. Scarry uses the example of the shipwrecked Ulysses' encounter with the beautiful Nausicaa near his home in Ithaca (in effect on the far shores of reason), who leads the way to the restoration of the order of his kingdom (one based in furious judgement). In Scarry's excellent discussion, beauty exists beyond definition, something that appears immediately to the senses as such. Its nature is prereflective and conceptually unmediated, already immediately given to perception. (This view is basic to Scarry's attempt to develop a universal notion of justice somewhat similar to Kant's universalist ethics.) It is a glimpse or, to escape the dominance of the visual in the discussion of sensory experience, a visceral encounter with a particular composition of form that is before or beyond reason, at the generative edge of reason.

The deep cosmological and religious undercurrents should be noted in this perspective, undercurrents that are further developed in Christianity (e.g., the Scholastics) but far from exclusively so. The force and potency inherent within an aesthetic judgement, and its thorough intimacy with the sensing body (integral to intuitive knowledge), are part of the Archimedean excitement of objective knowledge, vital in the realization of such knowledge. The forms and schemes of reason, even in their apparent abstraction or transcendence of the body, are aesthetic in their composition and have their potency realized in their appeal to a feeling as much as to a rationating body. Reason is no less capable of emotional production as that which seems to stand outside reason. Indeed, it is the feeling, intuiting body that is vital in the very production of the schemes of reason and in the creation of abstract, objective knowledge.

Jacob Burckhardt expands this observation in his wonderful opening chapter "The State as a Work of Art" in his path-breaking *The Civilization of the Renaissance in Italy* (1958). Here he argues that the creative artistic outpourings of the period refract a particular rational calculus (for example, epitomized by the political treatises of Guicciardini and Machiavelli) that was integral to the political orders and schemes engaged in the structuring of the Italian city-states. These established the conditions stimulating artistic innovation, which simultaneously produced the enjoyment or pleasure in the reflection upon Renaissance works. The implication of Burckhardt's argument is more than art reflects life or that it achieves its specific generative thrust in particular social, economic, and political conditions. He recognizes (in a particular way similar to Hegel's general conception) an aesthetic unity between artistic creations and their world. That is, the everyday world in its structuring dynamics, in its emergent symbolic forms, is aesthetic and, most importantly, manifests or objectifies (in architecture and the arts) the forces engaged in its composition, which are thus made available to aesthetic contemplation or reflection. In common with the potentiality of artistic creations, the constructions of the practices of everyday life, conceived as aesthetic formations, (re)orient human beings brought within their dynamic emotionally and mentally to their realities, constituting their subjectivities and opening them to new possibilities and sensibilities of action and understanding. (We have in mind here, in relation to the aesthetic, Bourdieu's [1977, 1990] argument regarding the generative potencies of subjects differentially positioned in the habitus.)

Beyond the Aesthetics of Artistic Work

Such an approach to the aesthetic, of course, underpins numerous anthropological perspectives towards culture. Effectively, culture is approached as a complex aesthetic, a composition upon which to reflect (a view most explicitly expressed by Clifford Geertz), a changing and differentiated collection of symbolic formations and processes constructed by human beings within which they passionately objectify themselves and come to be directed into diverse realities, the lived schema of their composition and making. In different ways anthropologists, regardless of their theoretical pigeonholing as functionalists, structuralists, or poststructuralists, for instance, have adopted what we outline as an aesthetic attitude to culture as a symbolic ordering that is constitutive and motivating. It is furthermore a formation of reality whose compositional dimensions—dimensions that condition particular intentionalities—must be investigated in their terms in order to gain understanding of their potential distinction and particular potencies. This we maintain is an aspect of Radcliffe-Brown's study of the Andaman Islanders (e.g., where the emotions of mourning cannot be grasped independently of a culturally mediated set of expectations), as it is fundamental to Lévi-Strauss's structuralist understanding of shamanic cure. We note the centrality, if problematic, of Lévi-Strauss's use of musical form in his understanding of mythopraxis (and vice versa) and in his establishment of the identity and difference between mathematical and mythic abstraction. Lévi-Strauss indeed follows Kant here, demonstrating the inseparable intertwining of subjective and objective processes—an approach already developed in both Cassirer and Langer's potentially more dynamic perspectives. Cassirer (1957) (echoing Hegel), for example, stresses that each moment of human symbolic action as an aesthetic process is one that both continues and differs from established compositional traditions.[1]

The aesthetic, therefore, is not in our usage exclusively the domain of what, regardless of specific convention, is defined as art, a concept that has mainly been shaped in recent and contemporary modernist and postmodernist discourses. As we have made explicit, the Kantian problem of aesthetic beauty and the notion of the sublime extends well beyond art towards a more general and unified approach to the understanding of human being. In other words, art or what is defined as art engages aesthetic processes but is not their necessary or ultimate expression. The aesthetic is primary. In our treatment the aesthetic is what ties art (as all other human endeavors) to life. The aesthetic and its compositional forms are what human beings are already centered within as human beings. This is to say that human beings are beings whose lived realities are already their symbolic constructions or creations within, and through which, they are oriented to their realities and come to act within them. To concentrate on the aesthetic is to focus on the dynamic forces and other processes engaged in human cultural and historical existence as quintessentially symbolic processes of continual composition and recomposition.[2] If the aesthetic is to be equated with art, then art is life, an attention to its aesthetic processes being a concern with its compositional forms and forces in which life is shaped and comes to discover its direction and meaning.

While we state that aesthetics is not reducible to art, many, perhaps most, of the issues relevant to an aesthetic focus emerge through discussions of art forms or objects. The way these engage the senses and constitute or produce experience (exert force or power) is a major concern in the work of a diverse field of scholars in the humanities and social sciences oriented towards general understanding of the human condition. One example of this is the philosopher Susanne Langer who, extending from Kant, Cassirer, and Whitehead, not only explores the shaping of human experience as this is revealed through a study of art forms (*Philosophy in a New Key*, 1957; *Feeling and Form*, 1997) but also, in her major synthetic work *Mind: An Essay on Human Feeling* (1994), attempts to grasp the aesthetic unities and differences engaged in all existence within which human existential and creative uniqueness is emergent. In her neo-Kantian orientation, art, as a dynamic organization of symbolic form, is the key that opens the door to human distinctiveness and potentiality in all areas of human practice. That is, art, or attention to created forms in their aesthetic process, accentuates the symbolic qualities critical to developing an understanding—as much philosophical as scientific in Langer's terms—of human practices that does not separate the logical and the objective (what appears to be disembodied) from the subjective (embodied), the mental from the material and the sensual.

Although Langer's approach does extend an understanding of a variety of art forms, this is not her primary objective. Rather, it is through art (as a relatively autonomous product)—that the symbolic (as a differentiated unity of the sensual, mental, and material) is revealed in its force and dynamic. Langer explores the nature of a variety of "pure" artistic forms defined by the principles governing their appeal to the senses and, among other aspects, the material conditions integral to their particular constructive/creative force (e.g., stone as against canvas, or suppressions or extensions of physical potential as in the elimination of the aural or voice in mime and dance and the simultaneous elaboration of physical movement). One major aspect of Langer's approach is that the different arts manifest what might be described as a transcendence of their particular limitation, filling out or generating critical aspects of their symbolic force or potency as a property of what a more recent Lacanian perspective would call their lack. Critically, in Langer's perspective, the different artistic forms manifest in particular and intensely distinct ways the force of the symbolic nature of human being, the symbolic as integral to what Cassirer describes as "entification" or the effective reorigination of human being as a creature re-created in the symbolic that is nonreducible to other forms of existence.[3] This is the import of what Cassirer and Langer place upon the symbolic that, in different ways, is shared by many other thinkers (through structuralism to phenomenology). It is a strong view of the symbolic best exemplified in the notion of mythic consciousness. That is, it is through human symbolic creativity that human beings not only reoriginate themselves but achieve total distinction from other forms of life with which they are continuous but also, and most significantly, discontinuous. This powerful symbolic vision that is integral to the aesthetic orientation we present here demands attention to all human practice or work (and not merely that characterized as art or artistic) as embodying mythic potency, a poiesis or power to bring forth. What this potency may be is the chief problematic of the aesthetic orientation that we suggest.

The Compositional Processes of Aesthetic Representation and Symbolic Constitution

It should be evident by now that our aesthetic approach is not bound by such traditional concerns as the problem of beauty or taste, which has caused some to eschew an aesthetic perspective. Bourdieu, echoing many others (e.g., Adorno 1970; Lukacs 1979; Williams 1971), attacks positions that refuse the fact that notions of beauty and taste are the products of historical, cultural, social, and political processes. The symbolic artifacts of human creation achieve their power over the imagination and their virtually magical potency through this fact. Nationalist art and representations (see Kapferer 1988, and Handelman this volume) exemplify this. However, in this perspective symbolic forms and processes are reduced to deriving their meaning and potency either in the nonsymbolic—in the factuality of reality somehow outside the symbolic—or in the capacity of the aestheticized symbolic to ideologically obscure or invert the true force and meaning of objective realities, as in various materialist orientations (e.g., see Eagleton 1990, for a summary).

While the importance of such perspectives is never to be denied, aesthetic and symbolic processes generally are locked firmly into subjectivist/objectivist oppositions. The aesthetic and its symbolic organization or process is widely treated as facilitating expressive activity, something to which human beings respond rather than something that actively, through its compositional dynamic, constitutes the very action that is expressed. In aesthetic processes subjective and objective dualisms are dissolved, aesthetic forces especially in the context of performance constituting the realities—in embodied experience—that they may otherwise reflect. Subjective articulations are integral to the aesthetic object, vital in the conjunction that aesthetic forms and processes establish with subjects. What we emphasize is that aesthetic processes highlight not merely that realities are symbolic constructions but that life exists in these constructions that commands or demands or calls forth ways of living the realities the aesthetic as a symbolic composition may be conceived as objectifying or representing. Immanent in the compositional symbolic dynamic of aesthetic construction is how human beings imagine and form their existential circumstances to themselves and to others. It constitutes both the reality and the emergent possibility of the worlds they come to live. Ranciere (2002) effectively reiterates this hard, effectively material view of the symbolic formation of the aesthetic, which we describe as central to the work of Cassirer and numerous other scholars, specifically in relation to artistic production: art (and the symbolic generally) as potentially both an in itself and a for itself, a process that has the capacity to make real that which it constructs. As a consequence art and other symbolic constructions do not merely represent externalities but act as moments of rupture and of reconstruction or reconceptualization, changing and transforming the worlds in which they are produced. Aesthetic processes, dynamics of symbolic construction and composition, manifest their potency certainly in the internalization of what is already external (frequently transforming or transmuting their import). They may also externalize that which is originally internal or immanent within them effecting, in this way, reformations of those symbolic realities, their meaning and import, to which they extend.

How it is that aesthetic formations effectively relate to their larger symbolic universes of action and meaning should be an enduring empirical issue and not be assumed. What we have referred to essentially as the weak view, aesthetic and symbolic processes as determined by processes outside them, is apparent in certain expressivist and representational orientations. Thus, the criticism made by the art historian Erwin Panofsky (1955) shortly after his exile from Nazi Germany of the "art appreciation" approach he encountered in America. Panofsky recommended a rigorous approach to art that he maintained should be no less exacting than that expected of a physical scientist. He opposed dominant schools of art appreciation that he viewed as merely reducing the meaning of an artwork to the independent emotional response of the viewing subject (a practice congruent, of course, with the modernist egalitarian ideology of pragmatic individualism). This refused the autonomy of the art object as constituted within a particular historical symbolic regime following specific compositional orientations and rules, even in their transgression. To overlook this is to ignore the processes underlying the formation of the work of art and the nature of its articulation with its wider realities. Understanding this articulation expands a grasp of how a viewing subject at the time of the work's production might have emotionally or subjectively responded to it. Panofsky was effectively denying a universal (and ahistorical) emotionality or subjectivity that underpinned the American school of art appreciation (that reduced all art to the viewing subject conceived of as universal and without history). He also indicated how the approach deprived the work of its intrinsic potency to form its emotional response.

Panofsky was strongly influenced by the school of the so-called Vienna structuralists (see Wood 2000). These insisted on a close investigation of the internal compositional dynamics of aesthetic or symbolic formations initially independently of assumptions often grounded in the historically or ontically constituted subjectivity of the analyst. The method was closely allied to the phenomenological recommendation of bracketing (e.g., Riegl

[1900] 2000). One example from the Vienna school concerns the exploration of Egyptian monumental art that uncovers a particular space/time dynamic of composition that suggests a reformulation of an understanding of Egyptian cosmological orientations hitherto subordinated to Western notions founded in a different history (von Weinberg [1933] 2000). The approach effectively insists on discovering through the exploration of symbolic artifacts and processes the way they articulate in their own terms with a political and social environment. In addition the aesthetic formation or symbolic process explored in itself may provide original understanding of the world in which it is already embedded. Moreover, it is an approach that is opposed to untested and over universalized assumptions that often lie at the center of contemporary materialist and subjectivist orientations. These alienate to their own independent interpretive consciousness the import, meaning, and existential potency of symbolic processes that, in our view, is an overly reductionist and weak view of the aesthetic and of the symbolic.

The weak orientation to aesthetic and symbolic processes denudes them of their particular interventional force that they may have on the life worlds to which they are oriented. What is especially at risk is the causative and instrumental effect that symbolic objects and processes might have upon the realities to which they are directed as a function of their own compositional order and process. A contemporary attitude to art and the aesthetic is that their value is in their afunctional, nonpragmatic features. Yet in the orientation we pursue here, it may be precisely the pragmatic functionalism of aesthetic processes that both conditions their composition and yields to them interventional capacity and their potency to act on their environment.

The Aesthetic as Agency

The approach we stress is that symbolic forms and processes in themselves have agency. They do not only represent (i.e., manifest the potencies of their larger context) or represent in the stronger performative sense as perlocutionary causation, as developed by Austin ([1954] 2004) and those following him (e.g., Rappaport 1999, with reference to ritual acts). Symbolic forms are active in the creation of their realities and have effect or bring about changes in the circumstances of existence through the aesthetic dynamic of their composition. This observation has long been made, for example, by students of comparative artistic forms.

Thus, Heinrich Zimmer ([1928] 1972) notes the distinct way the statue of the Greek Zeus relates to his world as contrasted with that of the Buddha. Zeus is full of ego, demanding to be looked upon and admired. The Buddha, however, usually appears totally impervious to his surrounds, unaware of an audience. These statues are active in creating their realities, in constituting their context and making what might appear as outside them internal to them through the potency of their symbolic formation. The Buddha actively refuses to be looked at in the way that Zeus demands, or, rather, the Buddha in the particular nonaction of his built form shuns the Self. The point can be expanded. The agency of the statues, their particular dynamic, structures the way they are perceived. We hazard that this structuring of perception, vital to their constituting force, occurs independently of whether or not human beings are culturally predisposed to perceive/ conceive them in a particular way. This is a suggestion that we will return to subsequently.

Ethnographers present a wealth of evidence concerning symbolic potency, the power of things, and symbolic processes. The magical fetish is a clear example. As Devisch (2002) has demonstrated through his Congo materials, the power of the fetish acts on the consciousness of victims through the manner of its internal composition whereby it is transmuted into a highly dangerous organization of bodily and social transgression. Gell (1998) has explored the point more generally, showing how social realities are built into objects yielding to artifacts their capacity to have causative effect. These scholars are adopting a strong aesthetic symbolic perspective in which objects, for example, are not merely representations of their realities but particular condensations or organizations of processes within them that, furthermore, give them an autonomous force, even mythopoieic power, in the environment or world in which they are operated. The fetish apparent to the consciousness of its victim has the potentiality to alter completely the victim's orientation to reality actively bringing about his death.

Aesthetization, or making things and processes into art, as this is usually conceived in modernist or postmodernist terms, is widely referred to pejoratively not only because it decontextualizes objects and processes but also because it often removes from them their agentive, functional, and instrumental-technical (techne) properties integral to their composition and vital to their aesthetic. This, of course, is a problem with which many contemporary galleries and museums deal. A recent example of aestheticization is Damien Hirst's exhibition of an African trap as a work of art. He aestheticized it. While he might have invested it with a new postmodern force (e.g., after Duchamp), he divested the trap of central tensional dynamics of its compositional form that were critical to its raison d'être. The trap was presented unset, devoid of its intentional tension to snare game. It was deprived of its compositional and integrative aesthetic function central to its "trapness" and the time/space dimension by which it was oriented in a potentially violent and changing relation to reality. A larger import of this example concerns our orientation to the aesthetic critical of that aestheticization that refuses what may be described as the life of symbolic forms and processes and essential to what we regard to be their aesthetic functionality intrinsic to their formation.

Performance and the Dynamics of Symbolic Construction

Much of our discussion can be expanded in the context of performance. Most of the aesthetic or compositional symbolic processes explored in this volume only exist in the fullness of their formation in performance. It is through performance that the compositional dynamic of aesthetic forms is set in play. Therefore, an understanding of performance (itself an aesthetic formation) is crucial. We define performance as similar to what is routinely described in the social sciences as action or practice. It is fundamentally symbolic in that it embeds orientations to existence that are meaningful, that is, they are human constructions even if they are not immediately available to the reflective human consciousness of those participants who bring about a performance. This is what conventionally distinguishes action or practice from behavior, which has no necessary meaningful content. (Hence a distinction between behaviorist psychology, which seeks to explain phenomena outside a frame of value, and most sociology, which is value-laden.) However, in our discussion performance is also more than action or practice in that the participants in performance are thoroughly conscious of their action or practice as a performance to be witnessed or participated in as such. We add to this the idea that performance is not mere enactment or the materialization of a preexisting schema or text. This indicates that the text precedes the performance, which of course it often does in some memorized or written form. However, what is stressed in our usage is a notion of performance as a nonreducible emergent phenomenon, a symbolic formation sui generis. In this perspective, what might be regarded as the text is created in the performance and is only available through the performance rather than preexisting it (see Kapferer 1997). This, of course, is the case with aesthetic processes, which only achieve their distinctive character and potencies in their performative practice and the way they are made to appear to and through the senses.

Ritual is a particular class of performance; that is, it is a symbolic formation that is self-consciously performative. It is a domain of practice that has been conventionally treated as the primordial space of the symbolic: where human beings are immersed in mythic consciousness and reoriginate themselves as distinct from other beings. Here scholars have followed on from what is often explicitly asserted in ritual action (e.g., in a host of life crisis rites, see Van Gennep 2004; Hubert and Mauss 1964). Langer (1997) argues that rite is the source of language. For her, ritual, as language, is a symbolic process that effectively makes present what is empirically absent, discursively engages in the creative materialization of the abstract, and simplifies existential complexity. Her suggestion is that the formation of language involves the production of a gestural and vocal economy (dance is given preeminent place in her discussion) that is the emergence or evolution of symbolic simplicity from the sensory complexity of concrete existence. Ritual is the bridge into the symbolic, both discontinuous with the thorough teleology or closure of existence (the in itself), whereby the human being becomes for itself (the separation of self and other and their mutual production) and yet still continuous with the presymbolic. That is, ritual insists on the embodied unity of human being in existence (its grounded roots and integration with other forms of life) yet also the distinctiveness of human being. Ritual performance, for Langer and Turner, is the source of aesthetic forms such as music, dance, and drama. Moreover, it is rit-ual-performance that can highlight these aesthetic forms as manifesting particular organizational processes (e.g., of dynamics of temporality and spatiality, volume, motion, etc.). Ritual—especially those of heal-ing—may also be a context for the demonstration of the differential effect (affect) of aesthetic processes (see e.g., Kapferer [1983] 1991; Friedson 1997). The arts, postmodern and premodern in Langer's con-ception, contain the generative symbolic traces that are more profoundly present in rite.

Langer, as we have already indicated, has been highly influential in anthropology: for example, in Geertz's (1973) general approach to culture and most especially in Victor Turner's early analyses of ritual. We note her critical position (along with Freud and Jung) in Turner's highly important *Chihamba, the White Spirit* (1962), which established the ground for his general approach to ritual. For Turner, the ritual roots of what can be called the performance arts, or arts in performance, contribute to his development of a general sociological/psychological theory for the un-derstanding of human being and its self-generative, creative capacity.[4] Like Langer he strove for a unity of art with science, which is clear in his later work. (Langer argues for a unified approach, of feeling with form.) He also attempted to break free from the kind of Kantian stultification that he identified in Durkheim and structuralism moving in the neo-Kantian direction of both Cassirer and Langer (approaches far more attuned to process and change). In effect, Turner as with Langer developed what amounts to an aesthetic perspective and theory on human being. For this reason they are important for grasping some of the directions taken in the essays in this volume, which are influenced by them even if many of the authors take different paths.

There is a primordialism in the approach of both Langer and to a degree Turner with regard to their perspectives on aesthetic processes in ritual performance. To some extent, such a primordialism persists in recent approaches to ritual (e.g. Rappaport 1999). Such primordialism aside, ritual and other aesthetic regimes (musical and theatrical perfor-mances, for instance) are vital in expanding an understanding of the power of symbolic processes, not usually understood in terms of the aes-thetic, in the constitution of human experience and the production of human knowledge.

Earlier we discussed the importance of function and intention in aesthetic processes. Function, we suggested, is integral to symbolic composition and dynamics: the aesthetic includes a function (a purpose) and the intention (consciously or unconsciously) of an effect (affect) in the specific organization of symbolic form that, through its formation in and to the senses, marries feeling to cognition and meaning. Ritual performance makes the functionality of the aesthetic explicit and might be said to put specific aesthetic compositions of the symbolic, as these may structure experience and cognition, to the test. Rituals worldwide place a diversity of symbolic processes, what are identified as music, song, dance, drama into complex interrelation and intermixture and reveal the potentiality of their force. The density of certain aesthetic genres or forms (of drumming, for example, or of masked dance, of chanting or verbal dialogue) at specific moments in the complex unfolding of a ritual project are not there merely to represent processes but are concerned to directly and immediately constitute the realities, factually and experientially, that they present. In this they can demonstrate not only the reoriginating potency of the symbolic (why some ritual can have the semblance of primordiality) but also the specific force of particular aesthetic processes.[5] Such force is revealed both in the efficacy of their function or purpose (as defined in the ritual project and participant experience) and in the structural tension that is manifested in their interrelation or intermixture with other aesthetic processes (see Kapferer [1983] 1991; Friedson 1997; and Friedson, Kapferer, Hobart, and Handelman in this volume).

We stress the capacity of symbolic compositions to materialize experience. This has been described in relation to emotions or moods. Langer writes of feeling forms or the capacity of symbolic processes to mould as a property of their form an existential state in participants within the structures or dynamics of aesthetic performance. In this way the constructed reality of the symbolic process becomes thoroughly integral to participants so that they are completely one with the formed experience. The occurrence of trance states corresponds with this argument. Demonic possession in Sinhala rites (and similarly elsewhere in the world), during which victims and ritualists fully experience the invasive presence of the demonic are apparently produced at intense moments of drumming (see Kapferer [1983] 1991; Kapferer and Papigny 2002).

There has been considerable debate concerning the power of drumming and other musical forms to produce trance states. The broadly accepted argument is that it is not the music in itself that produces the existential state but what the music signs and symbolizes (see Rouget 1986). The point is Kantian. Thus, in the Sinhala example the musical structures of the drumming are part of a culturally and historically established set of lived conceptualizations. The body is belief and effectively predisposed to the demonic meaning pattern of the music, the body becoming demonic in accordance with the demonic structure of the music. This kind of understanding is

confined within a circle of meaning and overlooks the potential of symbolic processes to create existential circumstances, material realities, independent of conceptual or interpretive frameworks. Friedson (1997; also
this volume) demonstrates such a possibility in the context of his trance-
dance ethnography among healers (*nganga*) in Malawi. He shows how a
particular patterning of drum rhythms creates an intensely felt experience
of an external agent entering within the body and then moving around
inside the body as if it were an independent life force. Friedson argues that
this effect is a musical illusion akin to but nonetheless distinct from the illusion of visual perception created, for example, by the psychologist's Necker
cube. The illusion is not unreal but real in its experiencing (along the same
lines as *maya* or illusion, which is a factuality of consciousness in the Buddhist or Hindu sense). The experience that Friedson describes is repeatable
by means of a rhythmic structure quite independently of any meaningful
conceptual frame. Non-Malawians, in other words, when engaged in this
aesthetic process or particular compositional form will encounter the same
physical effects independently of any cultural predisposition. The importance of Friedson's work in the context here is that it indicates how symbolic
processes can constitute the ground of experience beneath a framework of
meaning—and indeed how these processes can provide the material basis
upon which specific meaning frameworks can build (thus, drumming creates the effect of something concrete and alive entering the body that then
can be culturally interpreted as spirit possession). Furthermore, he demonstrates the significance of attending to the dynamics of performance structures as far more than processes of representation, rather as formations that
can powerfully intervene in situations radically organizing or reconstituting the conditions of experience. We have concentrated on the example of
music (see Beeman, this volume), but the argument can be expanded to
include other aesthetic forms as scholars in the field of the plastic arts have
shown (e.g., Panofsky 1991; Arnheim 1974).

Much of the work on aesthetic performance concentrates on audience
effects or the way nonspecialist participants are conditioned through performance. This is so with Langer's orientation and other very similar perspectives (e.g., that of the important phenomenological work of Mikel
Dufrenne 1973). The emphasis by and large has not articulated thoroughly
enough the conceptual/technical logics whereby performance specialists
understand the production of their work and especially their understanding of the relation of technique to effect. Some of the essays in this volume
aim to correct this neglect (see Shulman, Kersenboom, and Friedson) and
also to address what some might see as the hegemony of what may be
glossed very broadly as Western aesthetic traditions.

One attraction of Langer's work is that she is sensitive to cultural variation and, as we have said, strives through a close attention to processes of
symbolic composition to arrive at general understanding. Nevertheless, a
closer attention to constructive principle and technique may indicate more

cogently not only important culturally based distinctions and similarities but also other constructional bases of symbolic formation that may break new ground in the understanding of how it is that human beings constitute and come to act in the worlds of their creation.

Overall, the essays in this volume attempt to open out to an understanding of aesthetic processes that has general implications for the exploration of the nature of human action. While the essays are by and large grounded in the detailed analysis of ritual practices or specific aesthetic or artistic genres, they are intended as a general contribution to the comprehension of the symbolic forces alive in social and political life and in other knowledge practices. They are oriented to the grasping of aesthetic processes in a general sense, processes that are present in all areas of human activity and extend in their implication beyond the restriction that would confine the discussion of aesthetics to the realms of art.

The Essays

The book opens with essays concerned directly with particular aesthetic and art forms, proceeding to the concern with aesthetics of ritual forms directed to the problematics of everyday life (in worship and healing), and concluding with the aesthetic organization of practices in public secular settings (carnival, circus, political gatherings). There is a shift, if you will, from a concern with the life of art to a discussion of the art of life.

Beeman's contribution is the most generalist in the collection. Exploring the problem of why song can provoke intense emotional response, Beeman examines human physiological reaction to specific structurings of sound. He is thoroughly aware of cultural variations in the organization of sound in song but is directed to the effect of certain qualities of pitch and tone, for example, on human responses that may be independent of cultural conceptualizations or categories. Thus, he makes an intriguing link between singing and the crying of a baby. Both have intense affect on listeners despite themselves and, perhaps, despite the meaning frames whereby they may place interpretations upon the emotional dimensions of song or crying. Beeman addresses the power of aesthetic practices to reach human beings across cultural and social differences. He is concerned, in other words, with a question that lies at the heart of the discussion of aesthetics certainly since Kant—the power of aesthetic forms to appeal to universal subjectivities, to break through the categories and limits of reason.

The chapters by Shulman and Kersenboom enter into more culturally specific arguments. They point up the deep historically and culturally layered dimensions that must inform any discussion of aesthetics and performance. But far more important, both contributors demonstrate how other theories of aesthetic performance (using examples from India) expand understanding of such processes. They break out of the confines of a predominately Western-focused consideration of aesthetic processes, suggesting possibilities not merely relevant to Indian materials but perhaps also critical in the exploration of aesthetics anywhere.

Shulman, taking us beyond the relatively familiar *rasa* theorists, concentrates on music as emergence, linking it with language and especially poetics. Working from Sangadeva's *Sangitaratnakara*, written in the thirteenth century, Shulman examines music, that particular "unfolding of sound into form," as impelled in that inner physical desire to speak and building from that subtle buzz or drone from which ultimately the world itself is born. Through this orientation to the construction of music, Shulman extends towards a grasping of the musical experience and its inseparability from performance in which the listener is a crucial participant. As Shulman beautifully elaborates, the excitement of a musical performance (and, perhaps, in much performance generally), as well as poetry, in the Indian traditions he explores comes not from their expressiveness in a Romantic sense but from what they can bring forth from the vast reservoir of what is already empirically there: in the case of music, to make audible what is already humming beneath the surface.

Kersenboom also leads the reader through the complexities of southern Indian musical performance and into a further consideration of the aesthetics of performance. She seeks to build a bridge between, on the one hand, the orientation developed by Victor Turner, who stressed performance as founded in experience (extending from Wilhelm Dilthey's phenomenology), with ancient Indian traditions, on the other hand. Turner opposed what he conceived to be the stasis of abstract philosophical systems or debates about cosmology, which refused a concern with the pragmatic struggles in existence. Turner's is a voice for freedom against restraint that is directed to uncovering the energies of human creativity, hence his stress on the arts and the dynamics of performance. Kersenboom argues that the notion of performance is an ancient category and that what Turner discards—such as convention and rules, the exactitude of which underlies the performances, especially in southern Indian music and dance—is far from antithetical to the creativity and expressive qualities of performance. The care in performance is at the root of its praxis to which the abstraction of theory must be enduringly subservient. The poiesis of performance, its bringing forth of that which is deep within the existential ground of human being and made manifest in its cosmological production or, more accurately, repeated cosmogenesis, is vital in the memory or embodied knowledge that enables the repetition of performance, which in its repetition always creates something new and different. Here Kersenboom joins with Shulman in opening up properties of performance that the Indian materials point towards so acutely.

Bastin, still in the context of South Asian materials, explores the cosmological dynamic implicated in the built-form of Hindu temples, their vital architectonics. Developing from the work of Dufrenne, whose phenomenology of aesthetics perhaps remains unsurpassed, Bastin effectively conceives of the temple itself as an active force, a dynamic ritual structure that directs the opening up of human imagination to reveal the potentiality of the images that the temple contains and organizes. The temple orients participants or worshippers towards the diversities of their creative experience. The Hindu temple can be conceived as in itself a rite conditioning, if not necessarily determining, the performances that occur within it.

The three following chapters, those of Friedson, Hobart, and Kapferer, develop their arguments through an explicit discussion of the aesthetic dimensions of ritual performance in the contexts of the problematics of everyday life. In numerous ways Friedson's magnificent account of music and trance-dance at an Ewe shrine of a *vodun* order of the Guinea Coast takes us firmly into pragmatic and lived daily realities. Here one finds a powerful break with the linear, relatively fixed, and certain world of a Western aesthetics. Friedson concentrates most of his discussion on music making and possession. His account of possession takes up what phenomenologists such as Merleau-Ponty and Schutz have most fruitfully discussed—that a good deal of human activity involves no firm will, or conscious bodily emplacement: he draws attention to the processes of entering into sleep, daydreaming, driving a car, or listening to a Beethoven symphony in which it could be said that we are away from our selves. Trance is an even more radical way of being away. In the former processes, the "I" or ego is dimly present but in trance appears to be relinquished completely, the entranced becomes totally other or, rather, the space in which the multiple modalities of the god, in the Ewe instance, are revealed. Friedson introduces us to the exciting dance music of the Ewe shrine, in which trance opens to the revelation of the god. The music of the shrines, which Friedson describes as a "barrage of cross-rhythms," forms a reality of shifting centers, breaking beyond the more centered certitudes and linearity of Western musical understanding. In grasping the kind of experience produced within the musical contours of the trance-dance, Friedson presents what he describes as a performance aesthetics, an understanding that is thoroughly and irreducibly created in performance-practice. I believe that Friedson radically extends an understanding of African dance and, too, the dynamics of possession.

Both Hobart and Kapferer concentrate on ritual performances and their aesthetic drive towards establishing ethical and moral unities of community and society, themselves aesthetic formations perhaps only achieved in the dynamics of ritual and festival. Hobart addresses the Balinese Galungan festival and the marvelous processions of Barong and Rangda. The aesthetic wonder of Balinese performances is widely known and too often reduced to European and North American conceptions of the arts and theatrical performance. Hobart shows the radical distance of these from Balinese lived understandings, showing how the dynamics of performance reveal dimensions of everyday life that Balinese in the aesthetic of everyday etiquette hide from themselves.

The aesthetics of Balinese festival and ritual is directed towards the formation of communal balance and harmony—this is the orientation in the dramatic struggles of god, demon, and human being in the performances that Hobart describes. Such striving towards balance is an ultimate aesthetic aim that contains the ethical and moral principles, the virtues, that are the conditionality for communal existence and reproduction. It is out of the repeated performance that the potential for aesthetic union is both generated and placed on reflexive display.

Here Hobart, through the Balinese, returns to universal questions that concerned the European Kant but that are worked out differently in a world like that of the Balinese. Kapferer follows a similar course to that of Hobart. He presents what Sinhalese healers or exorcists regard as their masterwork, a ritual known as the *Suniyama*, which develops as its performance the Buddhist virtues, the ultimate conditionality for the harmonies of body and world. A Sinhalese exorcism is intended to be beautiful; this is the crux of its seductive intensity, which, while it generates the impossible antinomies of existence, leads the way through to the realms of justice and the release from suffering. Beauty in the aesthetics of the ritual practice of the *Suniyama* is the focus of that generative desire or force that is vital to the emergence of the orders of human existence but that simultaneously is the root of their instability and collapse. Through the discourse of the ritual practice, Kapferer argues for a reconsideration of the work of Turner and also of Kant, who in different ways (Kant in his stress on the sublime and Turner in his concern with the liminal) discover in the aesthetic an extension to worlds outside the closure and dictates of conventional reason, a generative creativity, and an opening towards universal questions vital to the human subject.

As we have stressed throughout this introductory essay, the aesthetics of performance is concerned with compositional dynamics wherein human beings come to constitute and reflect upon their realities. Thus, Handelman presents the aesthetics of the Holocaust Martyrs and Heroes Remembrance Day in Israel, as expressing the compositional process of the bureaucratic logic of a modernist state. Such a logic "insists on the exactitude of definitions and categories" building a whole from the fitting together of modular elements. Impatient with traditional philosophies of aesthetics that concentrate on such matters as beauty and truth, Handelman's close analysis of the remembrance day demonstrates how such matters are part of the "aesthetic feel," the sense of intuitive rightness, that is generated through the compositional dynamic of bureaucratic logic; in other words, they are the feelings of rightness or truth integral to the self-legitimation of the unfolding process of the remembrance day and vital to its force. One of the crucial arguments that Handelman develops, which is shared by many of the authors contributing to this volume, is how processes commonly sectioned off into more esoteric discussions of the arts are deeply rooted in everyday life and its ordinary aesthetics.

Carnival in Brazil cannot be understood outside the context of the everyday. If the Martyrs and Heroes Remembrance Day in Israel can be described as an aesthetics of conformity and convention (the crushing power of the state and of the people in compliance with it), Carnival is a bursting through of everyday worlds against the absurdities of restriction and the distortions of reason's power. In DaMatta's excellent turn towards the Brazilian Carnival, one sees an exciting resonance with Friedson's account of the continual decentering of Ewe drumming. Carnival works at decentering and depositioning, and thus it is able to embrace and totalize in nonconformity. It is not so much an inversion of order and reason. This would be to sustain a dialectical stance—one that characterizes many approaches to play and ritual subversions that develop into the endless circularity of chaos and order, play and control, etc. DaMatta points beyond this kind of dialectical closure. The decentering dynamic and the multiple and shifting positioning of Carnival does not turn the centralizing forces of state, reason, and power on their heads so much as overcome them, swamp them, drown them out in the exuberance of the flow and spilling over of the city-possessing crowd of Carnival. For DaMatta, Carnival demonstrates postmodernity's explicit critique and play with the forms and effects of modernist oppression.

Carmeli expands such themes in his discussion of the contemporary circus and the changes that are overcoming it, especially with regard to the treatment of animals, the critical focus of the circus's symbolic work. Here Carmeli effectively addresses the secularism of modernity and its postmodern continuities. He marks the point at which (since Darwin) the traditional play of Nature and Culture, central in one dominant formation of circus acts, has come under increasing attack. Organic to a secularist modernism, this finds continuity in a postmodernist discourse against cruelty and torture. Animals have effectively and metonymically taken the place of humankind. The symbolic play of the traditional circus, of animal-becoming-human, which fascinated audiences with its "culture-fication" of animals, has lost some of its effect in realities where the animal/humankind division is obscured and the rights of one are either synonymous with or metaphoric of the rights of the other. Carmeli shows how another oppositional play, already powerfully present in the circus, humankind-becoming-machine, has perhaps achieved greater emphasis. He notes the anxiety and danger that circus acts encapsulate and the crisis of unity, disunity, and of totalizing distinctions and coherences with which circus performers play and that is the aesthetic wonder of the circus. Conventionally in liminal space, usually outside the regulated order of state/society, the circus works between the marginalized world of the performers and the emplaced world of the audience constantly decentering, destabilizing, and shifting perspective. Carmeli's enjoyment of the circus suggests a sadness. The discourse concerning the cruelty to animals (an audience perception that is integral to the play of performers but by no means empirically the case) indicates the domestication of the circus (the last arena of the "wild" performer) to the governmentality of a popular will, the Foucauldian paradox of postmodernity.

The essays in this volume address the compositional dynamics of aesthetic formation, or the way human realities are constructed before and through the senses. The stress is very much on the practice of construction, and this has demanded an attention to the interface between the artist or the performer-creator (musician, dancer, ritualist) and other participants drawn within the aesthetic formation as this is mediated through the dynamic of the work itself (musical form, dance dynamic, trance-dance, rite of healing, festival, ceremony). These concerns have demanded an attention both to the compositional skills and intentions of the performer-creators and to the effects of their work, which of course frequently transcends the reduction to compositional intention. Indeed, the intentional structure of a created work may be, as Dufrenne, Langer, and other students of aesthetic formation insist, ultimately and irreducibly with the work itself and especially with the work in the practice of its performance, which is constitutive of the aesthetic, its being and life. Performance as an aesthetic formation is very much the emphasis of these essays and therefore their enquiry into the logics and potencies of performance-aesthetic dynamics.

In many ways, the essays mark a return to issues and questions that were at the root of philosophical investigation, in Europe certainly from the Enlightenment and, as the essays here insist, present in the long-term in other religio-philosophical discourse. These questions concern the force that consciously created and manipulated symbolic formations (organizations of the perceptual-conceptual sense field engaging the human organism with its life world) have within and upon the existential realities of human action. If there is a return to such issues, we underline the difference. This is to demonstrate how such questions are raised and approached differently in diverse traditions and, most importantly, how they manifest implicitly in practices that have no philosophical pretensions of an ultimate nature.

These essays depart from issues that have occupied in recent years what might be regarded as aesthetic concerns. We refer to the vast body of materials being published on museums, artistic representations, popular art, etc., especially in the fields of cultural and media studies, the anthropology and sociology of art, and so on. These address matters relating to class and taste, the political role of art forms, museum display, markets and consumption. The importance of such approaches is undoubted, but the direction here suggests the importance of returning to some of the questions that are raised through an attention to the dynamics of aesthetic formation itself. As a few of this collection's essays suggest, such a return may also extend an understanding of the power of aesthetic structures in furthering, resisting, and overcoming the political and social exigencies and problematics of other lived realities of human existence.

Notes

1. A development of a very similar argument in anthropology is that of Sahlins's (1981) analysis of cultural transformation in ancient Hawaii following the death of Cook.
2. In this sense there is a continual aesthetic in all human formations of a social and political character. Domains of human habitation such as villages, neighborhoods, and cities may be conceived as manifesting a particular aesthetic in the constant process of their formation. This is created out of the manifold symbolic forces engaged in their construction. For example, villages in northern Zambia express a particular aesthetic form as a result of the symbolic forces involved in the contradictions of matrilineal kinship that contributes to a particular residence pattern. This contrasts with the much larger and densely populated village formations among populations to the south who are patrilineal and far more hierarchical in the forces conditioning their structuring.
3. Here Cassirer is sharply opposed to those understandings that would reduce human processes to nonhuman processes conceiving the shift from the nonhuman to the human as a single continuous progressive incremental flow: "No matter how the question of the becoming of natural forms is answered, the field of intellectual becoming follows not the law of evolution, but the law of mutation. Here there is not simply wave after wave in uniform flow; rather, here one clear and distinct configuration confronts the next. Even when a new configuration immediately follows upon the earlier ones it is not simply their result, but represents something unique and independent" (Cassirer 1996, 40).
4. Turner (1969) sees ritual as the key domain of human origination and reorigination. In particular he isolates one moment—clearly present in transition rites—that, following Van Gennep, he called the liminal (from which Turner also developed his notion of communitas) within which reoriginating symbolic processes discover a density.
5. Ritualists often insist on the primordial character of their work. Thus, exorcists in Sri Lanka (see Kapferer 1997) insist that their rites are copies of the first performed instance of the rituals they present. However, by insisting that their performances are copies, they are in effect referring to their understanding that their performances have all the originating power of the first rites, *not* that they are the same as the first rites. They are in fact recognizing that their rites, as copies, are always different, always new. The only feature that is continuous is the originating or reoriginating potency.

References

Adorno, Theodor W. 1970. *Ästhetische Theorie. Gesammelte Schriften.* Vol. 7. Ed. Gretel Adorno and Rolf Tiedemann (*Aesthetic Theory,* trans. C. Lenhardt, 1984).

Arnheim, Rudolf. 1974. *Art and Visual Perception: A Psychology of the Creative Eye.* Berkeley: University of California Press.

Austin, J. L. [1954] 2004. *How to Do Things with Words.* Oxford: Oxford University Press.

Bourdieu, Pierre. 1977. *Outline of a Theory of Practice.* Trans. Richard Nice. Cambridge: Cambridge University Press.

———. 1990. *The Logic of Practice.* Cambridge: Polity Press.

Burckhardt, Jacob. 1958. *The Civilization of the Renaissance in Italy.* Trans. S. G. C. Middlemore. 2 vols. New York: Harper and Row.

Cassirer, Ernst. 1957. *The Philosophy of Symbolic Forms.* Vols. 1–3. New Haven: Yale University Press.

———. 1996. *The Metaphysics of Symbolic Forms.* Vol. 4, *The Philosophy of Symbolic Forms.* New Haven: Yale University Press.

Deleuze, Gilles. 1995. *Kant's Critical Philosophy: The Doctrine of the Faculties*. Trans. Hugh Tomlinson and Barbara Habberjam. London: Athlone.

Devisch, René. 2002. "Maleficent Fetishes and the Sensual Order of the Uncanny in South-West Congo." *Social Analysis* 46, no. 3 (Fall): 175–97.

Dufrenne, Mikel. 1973. *The Phenomenology of Aesthetic Experience*. Evanston, Ill.: Northwestern University Press.

Eagleton, Terry. 1990. *The Ideology of the Aesthetic*. Oxford: Blackwell Publishing.

Friedson, Steven. 1997. *Dancing Prophets*. Chicago: University of Chicago Press.

Geertz, Clifford. 1973. *The Interpretation of Cultures*. New York: Basic Books.

Gell, Alfred. 1998. *Art and Agency: An Anthropological Theory*. Oxford: Oxford University Press.

Hegel, G. W. F. [1835] 1975. *Aesthetics: Lectures on Fine Art*. Vol. 2. Trans. T. M. Knox. Oxford: Clarendon Press.

Hubert, Henri, and Marcel Mauss. 1964. *Sacrifice: Its Nature and Functions*. Trans. W. D. Halls. Chicago: University of Chicago Press.

Kant, Immanuel. 1987. *The Critique of Judgement*. Trans. Werner Pluhar. Indianapolis: Hackett.

Kapferer, Bruce. [1983] 1991. *A Celebration of Demons: Exorcism and the Aesthetics of Healing in Sri Lanka*. Washington, D.C.: Smithsonian Institution Press.

———. 1988. *Legends of People, Myths of State*. Washington, DC: Smithsonian Institution Press.

———. 1997. *The Feast of the Sorcerer*. Chicago: Chicago University Press

Kapferer, Bruce, and G. Papigny. 2002. *Tovil: Exorsismes Bouddhistes*. Paris: Editions DesIris.

Langer, Susanne K. 1957. *Philosophy in a New Key: A Study in the Symbolism of Reason, Rite, and Art*. Cambridge, Mass.: Harvard University Press.

———. 1962. *Philosophical Sketches*. Baltimore, Md.: Johns Hopkins University Press.

———. 1994. *Mind: An Essay in Human Feeling*. Baltimore, Md.: Johns Hopkins University Press.

———. 1997. *Feeling and Form: A Theory of Art*. Englewood Cliffs, N.J.: Prentice Hall.

Lévi-Strauss, Claude. 1964. *Mythologiques: Le Cru et le Cuit*. Paris: Librairie Plon.

Lukacs, G. 1979. *Soul and Form*. New York: Merlin.

Panofsky, Erwin. 1955. "The History of Art as a Humanistic Discipline." In *Meaning in the Visual Arts*, ed. Erwin Panofsky, 23–50. Harmondsworth: Penguin.

———. 1991. *Perspective as Symbolic Form*. New York: Zone Books.

Ranciere, Jacques. 2002. "The Aesthetic Revolution and Its Outcomes." *New Left Review* 14: 133–51.

Rappaport, Roy A. 1999. *Ritual and Religion in the Making of Humanity*. Cambridge: Cambridge University Press.

Riegl, Alois. [1900] 2000. "The Place of the Vapheio Cups in the History of Art." In Wood, *The Vienna School Reader*, 105–29.

Rouget, Gilbert. 1986. *Music and Trance*. Chicago: University of Chicago Press.

Sahlins, Marshall. 1981. *Historical Metaphors and Mythical Realities*. Ann Arbor: University of Michigan Press.

Scarry, Elaine. 1999. *On Beauty and Being Just*. Princeton: Princeton University Press.

Turner, Victor W. 1962. *Chihamba, the White Spirit: A Ritual Drama of the Ndembu*. Manchester: Manchester University Press.

———. 1969. *The Ritual Process*. Harmondsworth: Penguin.

Van Gennep, Arnold. 2004. *The Rites of Passage*. London: Routledge.

von Weinberg, Guido Kashnitz. [1933] 2000. "Remarks on the Structure of Egyptian Sculpture." In Wood, *The Vienna School Reader*, 199–241.

Weiner, James F., with Howard Morphy, Joanna Overing, Jeremy Coote, and Peter Gow. 1993. *Debate: Aesthetics Is a Cross-cultural Category*. In *Key Debates in Anthropology*, ed. Tim Ingold, 249–93. London: Routledge.

Williams, Raymond. 1971. *Culture and Society*. Harmondsworth: Penguin.

Wood, Christopher S., ed. 2000. *The Vienna School Reader: Politics and Art Historical Method in the 1930s*. New York: Zone Books.

Zimmer, Heinrich. [1928] 1972. *Myths and Symbols in Indian Art and Civilization*. Princeton: Princeton University Press.

Chapter One

MAKING GROWN MEN WEEP

William O. Beeman

Acoustics and Emotion

I once sang in a production of Puccini's *La Bohème.* In the fourth act, the heroine, Mimi, dies of consumption. The opera's final notes are delivered by her lover, the tenor Rodolfo, who bends over her lifeless body and sobs while singing her name four times on a high G. The effect is universally the same for all audiences. Almost as if a button were pushed, the scene triggers an autonomic response. Grown men and women weep openly. There is rarely a dry eye in the house. During one rehearsal for this production, our director had a problem with the soprano portraying Mimi. "My dear," he said, "you cannot cry when Rodolfo sings your name. You are already dead." "I know!" she wailed, "but I can't help it. It's *so sad!*"

It was this event some years ago that led me to think seriously about the unique ability of performance to affect the cognitive state of its audience, and the reasons why it does so. Added to this was my fascination with the brute fact that human beings in every culture are so extraordinarily engaged with performance. Not only do they enjoy it immensely but they also expend an amazing amount of energy and material resources to arrange for it to happen and to see it. Moreover, they never seem to tire of it. Specific performance experiences are revisited repeatedly—sometimes thousands of times over a lifetime, with no decrease in engagement or enthusiasm. Why this should be so somewhat defies logic and cries out for an explanation.

As I will argue below, singing is a uniquely human behavior. A particular, unusual effect occurs for listeners for particular types of singing that exhibit a special vocal acoustic property known among students of voice

---

Notes for this chapter are located on page 40.

as the "singer (or singer's) formant." The reaction is an autonomic physiological reaction such as occurred for our Mimi above. The singer's formant is a "spike" in the acoustic profile of the voice corresponding roughly to frequencies between 2,800–3,200 hertz (Hz). A more detailed explanation is presented below.

The singer formant is essential for trained voices singing in Western classical traditions. Without the ability to produce it, classical singers cannot have careers on the opera or concert stage. However, this vocal feature is not only a feature of Western vocal music. I hypothesize that it is also a characteristic of most professional singers in music traditions throughout the world. Although some singers produce it naturally, most have to learn to generate it in their vocal production, thus it is a performance achievement.

In addition to its aesthetic properties, the singer formant has the peculiar ability to produce an autonomic reaction from an audience. As I will show below, it appears to be an essential component in the conveyance of emotion in performance. Since expressing emotion is one of the principal functions of singing, this makes the singer formant one of the most interesting of human phenomena.

The singer formant thus presents a human mystery. Why should humans in so many cultural traditions identify a single particular preferred vocal acoustic characteristic and strive to produce it in artistic performance? Why should it produce autonomic reactions that so many identify as emotional? The answers must be hypothetical and speculative at this point, but as I will show in this chapter, the singer formant corresponds to the highest notes composed for the human voice. It also corresponds to the area of greatest sensitivity in the human hearing range. Its ability to produce an autonomic reaction suggests a primordial function. This I suggest exists in its presence in animal and infant cries, and in other human involuntary vocalizations.

Singing as an Evolutionary Act

It is noteworthy that humans especially enjoy seeing performance that emphasizes and underscores the limits of human behavior. Exemplary goodness, badness, and extremes of physical skill are among the most popular themes of performance.[1] It also shows reversal and transformation. In this regard, the mirror of performance is a fun-house mirror. It exaggerates, simplifies, and distorts in the subjunctive mode examined by Turner (1986). It holds the promise and wonder of witnessing things as they might be without the danger of the actual disruption that true change might bring. It is paradoxical that one of the most sophisticated of human cultural activities—singing—may derive its power to move people emotionally from affective expressive urges that predate our emergence as Homo sapiens. Yet our ability to sing and react to singing may be one of the most uniquely human things we are able to do as a species.

Delineating those behavioral capacities that are uniquely human has been a venerable task for students of human biology and culture for most of the twentieth century up to the present time. For a long time, tool making and linguistic communication were presented as the two activities that were the sole purview of humans.

In the last two decades we have learned much more about the behavioral and cognitive capacities of other animal species, particularly our nearest species cousins, the great apes. The research of Jane Goodall (1986), Sue Savage Rumbaugh (1994), and many others working with primate behavior in recent years has shown us that they have the capacity both for tool making and linguistic communication. Although the scientific community continues to split hairs evaluating the details, it is clear that human uniqueness is no longer defined unequivocally by these capacities. If we wish to understand human uniqueness, we may need to look to behavioral capacities that are still more complex than even these two rather complex behaviors.

The search for uniquely human behavior may depend on the exploration of the capacity of humans to engage in expressive communication, which may be defined as the overt and immediate conveyance of affect to others through public symbolic display. One of the primary means by which this is accomplished is through singing.

However, before looking at singing as a unique human activity, we should perhaps answer the more basic question: What value does expressive communication have for humans? One of the principal functions of expressive behavior would seem to be to encourage and facilitate bonding within human groups on a large scale, leading to more effective social organization.

Language itself is good at communicating information, but it is deficient in conveying affective states to others. Humans are able to accomplish a great deal of affective communication with tropic expression, such as metaphor (cf. Lakoff and Johnson 1974; Fernandez 1986), but even these structures lack immediacy. When humans really want to express interpersonal affect, language often breaks down. The deepest emotional expressions between two people, even hostile and violent ones, are usually tactile (perhaps also olfactory and gustatory) rather than linguistic, and this physical contact usually is a central component of bonding between individuals.

How is this bonding through sharing of inner states accomplished for whole groups? Most human societies find orgiastic behavior unpalatable or impractical. Untrammeled tactile intimacy leads also to social disturbance due to another factor in human social behavior: the need to establish hierarchies and the related competition for exclusive sexual partners.

Auditory and visual channels for communication have the advantage of being able to encompass and affect large numbers of individuals without the need to touch, smell, or taste every other person in the group. Normal language is of course primarily conveyed through auditory and visual channels. It is then not surprising that forms of communication conveying affect in an immediate manner have language as a component but provide significant enhancements from other dimensions of communication.

Singing is only one of a number of forms of behavior that qualify as enhanced communication. Two forms that are intermediate between speech and song are useful for understanding the power of singing. These are chant and oratory. Chant can be done by an individual, but it is most often a group behavior that strengthens solidarity among participants through shared vocal activity. It has an affinity in this regard with dance (as shared motor activity), with which it is often combined. The propositional content of chant is secondary to its acoustic properties and the fact that it is a shared activity. Chant is often a way of inducing broader shared experience in the form of trance or a deep meditative state as seen in the practices of religious orders. It often constitutes a profound experience for those engaging in it.

Oratory enhances communication through performative and poetic overdetermination of linguistic features (cf. Bauman 1977). The acoustic properties of speech (volume levels, pitch contours, pauses) and the structural properties of language (word choice, sentence structure, and logical interrelationship of expressions) are enhanced and exaggerated.[2] At the same time, there is a purposeful underdetermination of the "noise" found in ordinary face-to-face communication (errors, repetitions, interruptions). Oratory creates shared experience for a group by creating a common activity for audience members receiving the message of the orator. The underdetermination in noise in communication allows the audience to appreciate the overdetermination in the acoustic and structural properties of speech. These overdetermined features in oratory are the factors that communicate the affective messages of the speaker and allow the audience to share them as a group.

When it is understood that it is the nondiscursive and shared elements of vocal performance that bring about the transmission of affective content, it is a short leap to understand the power of singing—and singing is very powerful indeed.

Our most elementary vocalizations as a species both ontogenetically and phylogenetically relate to our affective states. Fear, pleasure, and discomfort rank as the most elementary of these expressions. Our nearest animal relatives possess call systems that articulate these affects. These calls are extended to express concern not just for the individual issuing the call but also for the group (cf. Fitch and Hauser 1995; Owren, Seyfarth, and Cheney 1997; Owren and Rendall 1999).

Humans also express themselves through powerful elementary vocalizations. Both the ability to produce these vocalizations and the ability to understand them may be genetically encoded, as may be seen from the first instant of birth with a baby's lusty crying on emerging from the womb. Babies are wonderful vocalizers. Their cries are penetrating, and they are able to continue for hours without getting hoarse or damaging their vocal apparatus. Their breath support system is perfect and natural. Sounds of pain or distress are deeply disturbing to adults; vocalizations of pleasure from babies are likewise directly communicative of joy to adults who are in contact with them (Drummond et al. 1999; Huffman et al. 1994; Lester 1978; Lester and Boukydis 1992).

Adults, too, have a remarkable repertoire of elementary vocalization forms, all tied to affect. Involuntary shouts of surprise, anger, or fear are as penetrating and physically efficiently produced as a baby's cries. Sounds of pleasure are equally involuntary on the part of the producers and recognizable on the part of hearers. A relaxing massage, a hot bath, eating a favorite food, or sexual activity all have characteristic, virtually involuntary vocalizations associated with them.

I hypothesize that singing is built on this human system of vocalizations. Singing produces an emotional response in listeners precisely because listeners are genetically programmed to respond to the acoustic properties of song, as they respond to other prelinguistic vocalizations, but in a more directed and differentiated fashion. Whereas response to elemental cries and vocalizations may be limited and diffuse, response to singing is directed and nuanced. The specific response is controlled through a delicate set of interactions between singer and audience that aims for fine, specific communication of affect. This additional power of singing comes from the ability to combine these powerful elemental vocal contours with other symbolic, discursive, poetic elements through text and visual means, including metaphor and narrative. This provides for a "double enhancement" of language that is effective and powerful as communication (Sundberg 1993, 1998; Sundberg, Iwarsson, and Hagegärd 1995; see also Feld 1982 and Feld 1988 for work in a non-Western context).

Singing in a way that produces an affective response in others is by no means an easy matter. Sadly, our inborn abilities as vocal artists are trained out of us early in our socialization. Children's exuberant cries are toned down by parents who exhort their offspring to use their "indoor" voices. Children with loud voices are often placed at a disadvantage in society. Added to the modulation of the voice in childhood training is the narrowing of accepted emotional expression during socialization. Display of affect is confined within narrow boundaries in most cultures, and only allowed full, untrammeled public expression on limited occasions.[3]

The Singer Formant

Singers in virtually every music tradition must learn to produce a culturally meaningful acoustic envelope for their vocalizations. This means finding a means of regulating their vocal apparatus to produce an acoustically pleasing sound. For some societies this sound will involve more resonance in the nasal cavities, for some it will involve more throat constriction. In modern times singers may get help from electronic enhancement to achieve the aesthetic ideal of their culture.

For singers in the Western classical tradition, this aesthetic involves three essential elements aside from the musical requirements that one sing on pitch and with rhythmic accuracy. The first, which I will deal with in this section, is the production of the so-called singer formant, a consistent high-frequency sound wave component to the voice that allows the voice to "carry" in a large hall over a symphony orchestra. This is the vocal feature that allows singers to perform at the Metropolitan Opera and other large houses without amplification.

Second, the singer must execute "line." This is the ability to sing long overarching musical phrases without perceptible interruption due to the consonants within words. Third, the singer must sound as if he or she is singing with the same vocal quality on every pitch and on every vowel. This final ability is one of the most difficult goals to achieve, because different muscle groups control pitch and resonance in different parts of the voice, and their coordination to make the voice sound uniform is challenging.

The first of these three elements—the production of the singer formant—is the most basic of the three. It must be mastered first. Line and uniformity of production depend on the muscle control needed to produce the singer formant, which carries, I hypothesize, the basis for essential affective expression in song and allows singing to communicate to the largest number of people. This is also the one element of singing that seems to be common to the vocal traditions of the world. It seems to be the aspect of vocal art that unites the adult singer with the crying infant, the person screaming in grief or fear, the individual doubled over in involuntary laughter, and the child squealing in delight at a pleasant surprise.

The "singer formant"[4] gives the trained voice its acoustic "ping," or *squillo* in the Italian term used in singing instruction. It has been ably described in an extensive literature, spearheaded by the pioneering research of Johan Sundberg (Sundberg 1972, 1977, 1987, 1998; see also Sataloff 1992; Hong 1995; Titze, Mapes, and Story 1994). This acoustical property, as mentioned above, is a "spike," or high decibel feature, in the acoustic profile of a singer occurring at between 2,800 and 3,200 Hz. As some researchers have pointed out, and as I will cite below, the spike may be produced at higher frequencies, up to 4,000 Hz. In lay terms, the singer formant may be thought of as a consciously reinforced cluster of overtones.[5]

Sundberg (1972, 1977) studied recordings of the famous operatic tenor Jussi Björling, who was particularly admired for the brilliant "ring" in his voice. Sundberg discovered the singer formant in Björling's voice at 3,000 Hz and determined that it was especially strong when he was singing over a loud orchestra. The graph in figure 1.1 represents Sundberg's findings. The solid line is the average frequency spectrum of the

Figure 1.1 Average frequency spectrum of tenor Jussi Björling plotted against the average frequency spectrum of the orchestra accompanying him

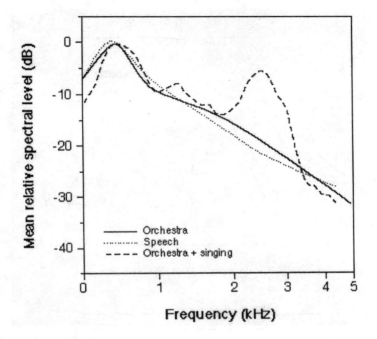

Source: After Sundberg (1972, 1974).

symphony orchestra, and the dotted line, the average frequency spectrum of Björling's voice.

Because of this increased energy clustering at 3,000 Hz, the singer can easily be heard above the orchestra. The singer's voice is said to "cut through" the orchestra. It is noteworthy that the ability of the singer to be heard above the orchestra can be seen as independent of the volume of the fundamental frequency. A trained singer can be heard above an orchestra even when singing softly, because the energy at the point of the singer formant can be made higher than that of the orchestra. As I will show below, the singer formant gets an additional boost, because the human ear hears better at 3,000 Hz than at lower frequencies.

Sundberg discovered that the origin of the singer formant is the presence of a second resonator in the vocal tract, in addition to the vocal folds. The singer generates this second resonator through muscle control of the vocal tract. To generate the singer formant, this second resonator must be about one-sixth as long as the entire vocal tract and also have about one-sixth of the cross-sectional area of the vocal tract. Figure 1.2 shows Sundberg's model for the operation of this mechanism.

Figure 1.2 Model of primary and secondary resonators in vocal tract producing the "singer formant"

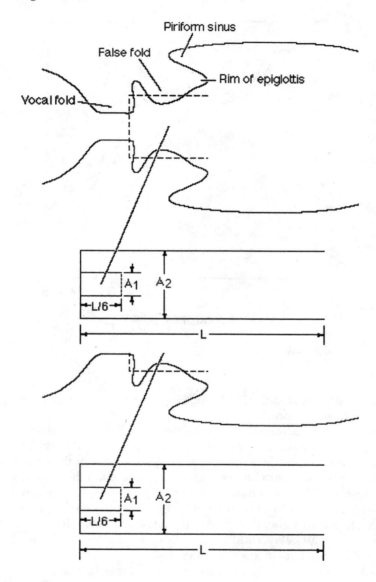

Source: Sundberg (1972).

As can be seen from figure 1.2, the "false folds" are used to create the secondary resonator. These are controlled by involuntary muscles. This secondary resonator is naturally activated when humans scream in fright or fear, and as I hypothesize, they are also naturally brought into play in infant cries. Learning to control them voluntarily to create performative artistic expression is part of the aim of vocal training.

Singer Training

Singers must train long and hard to develop control over this secondary resonator and to produce the even, uniform vocal line and vocal registration required for aesthetically pleasing singing. Normal training takes a number of years[6] and is extremely demanding for most singers with professional aspirations in most classical traditions, including Western classical music.

Instruction is athletic in nature—akin to Olympic training in its demands for perfection. It involves the training of muscles throughout the body. The primary muscles are those of the mouth, throat, and breathing apparatus, but in effect every part of the body must be involved in the singing process. In order to produce smooth and even tones, the singer must deliver a steady stream of air at precisely the right pressure to both the vocal folds and the secondary resonators. The muscles that control the resonators themselves must be trained to engage them with exactly the right tonus. Too strenuous an application can create vocal injury; too light, and the proper acoustic profile will not emerge.

As with an oboe reed or trumpet mouthpiece, the singer cannot over- or underblow or the vocal tone will lose its essential quality. In order to achieve even more resonance and color, the singer must activate other parts of the vocal tract, including the nasal cavities. In some vocal traditions, such as those of Tuva (Levin and Edgerton 1999), even more complex formant structures can be produced with proper manipulation of the tongue and throat.

Singers must also learn to overcome inhibitions that prevent control of the delicate vocal musculature and that keep them from producing full and expressive sounds in public. The singer is exposed and defenseless before the public. Thus, there may be involuntary reflexes such as "fright or flight" adrenaline production that need to be brought under control through the training process lest they hinder the free and relaxed working of the voice. Meditative techniques that involve mental focus and bodily flexibility such as ta'i chi and yoga are used by many to aid in overcoming these difficulties (cf. Helfgot and Beeman 1993).

Vocal line and uniform vocal registration make singing seem speech-like. We talk in unbroken phrases, and when speaking our voices have the same characteristics throughout our speech range. The difference for the singer is that the need for articulation is greater than that of the orator, and the pitch ranges that are used in singing are three or four times more extensive than those of the normal speaking voice. Achieving conversational smoothness while operating in these nonconversational acoustic parameters is a great artistic challenge.

The length of training for a singer is extreme because, paradoxically, singers cannot hear themselves. The singing voice is filtered through the bones of the head and is misleading to the singer. From the singer's own perspective, a seemingly big sound may in fact lack the essential singer formant; an apparent legato line or acoustically equalized vowels may sound jerky or uneven to an audience. Eventually singers learn to work not by hearing themselves but by being trained by expert teachers to monitor the physical sensations of their bodies to produce the best sounds. They in fact learn to feel their voice rather than to hear it.

The effects of singing for the singer are far more visceral than for the audience. When singing correctly, the singer achieves a physical release that might best be compared to the rush of an Olympic athlete executing a winning floor routine in gymnastics or achieving a record-setting high jump. Moreover, as with Olympic athletes, these peak experiences may be rare, but when they occur they are powerful enough to motivate the singer to try to achieve them again and again, even at great personal sacrifice.

When the singer reaches these goals, adding to them the emphatic nuances of the orator and the facial and bodily expressions of the best actor, the experience is overwhelming for an audience. The communication of affect is complete, and the audience is united in a reaction of empathy and common understanding. So all in attendance cry at Rodolfo's grief, audience and singers alike (even the recently deceased Mimi). Everyone leaves the theater with the certain knowledge that for a brief moment they have shared something remarkable—something both elementary and primitive and yet at the same time sophisticated and uniquely human.

Thus, for singers the training is severe and difficult. The chances for success are extremely slim. The personal rewards for achieving vocal skill are great, but perhaps not in proportion to the effort. Nevertheless, as I have already noted several times, both singers and audiences find the activity itself physically as well as mentally fulfilling to the point that both expend enormous effort to experience it. So, the question remains, Why should humans so highly privilege vocal production that emphasizes the singer formant? I will try to answer this question in the next sections of this discussion.

The Singer Formant and Emotion

There is some evidence that the singer formant plays an important role in the registering of emotion on the part of an audience. Although most researchers have associated the conveyance of emotion in singing with prosody, phrasing, and tempo variation (Sundberg 1998; Sundberg, Iwarsson, and Hagegärd 1995; Flanagan 1981), a few studies have shown the singer formant to be essential in emotional expression (Johnstone and Scherer 1995; Siegwart and Scherer 1995; Scherer 1986; Berndtsson and Sundberg 1995).

Johnstone and Scherer compared recordings of the cadenza in the aria "Ardi gli insensi" from Donizetti's *Lucia di Lammermoor*. Working from earlier work by Siegwart and Scherer, they wanted to find out why, of five famous sopranos sampled, listeners preferred the rendition by soprano Editha Gruberova, finding that her rendition expressed more "tender passion" and "sadness" than the other singers. To the surprise of the researchers, they found that Gruberova did not exhibit high energy in the area of the singer formant. Rather, she exhibited energy at a higher frequency—namely, at approximately 3,600 Hz. A comparison of Gruberova's sound spectrum and that of Joan Sutherland is contained in figure 1.3.

Figure 1.3 Vocal spectrum of Editha Gruberova (*solid line*) and Joan Sutherland (*broken line*) rendering the cadenza in the aria "Ardi gli incenti" from Donizetti's *Lucia di Lammermoor*

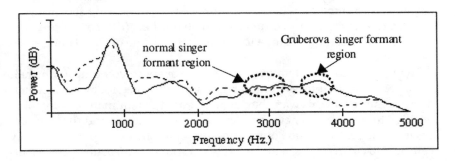

Source: After Johnstone and Scherer (1995).

As Johnstone and Scherer (1995) concluded, "the singer's formant is not a single formant as such, but rather a clustering of formants around a predicted frequency of about 3,000 Hz (in sopranos). When clustered sufficiently closely, individual formants tend to reinforce each other, leading to a spectral region with increased overall resonance." Gruberova, in effect, had "relocated" her singer formant region to a higher frequency, and this was read by the judges as conveying greater emotion.[7]

Johnstone and Scherer have exhibited two important principles. The first is that the singer formant has a complex interaction with harmonics (overtones) and that it can be created at frequencies higher than the canonical 2,800–3,200 Hz and convey even more emotional content.

We will see these two principles at work when analyzing the cries of infants below, but first we need to ask why humans react to frequencies in this range with particular attention. For this we need to look at classic research into human hearing.

The Fletcher-Munson Curves

One part of the answer to the above question involves the properties of human hearing. Humans do not hear all frequencies of sound at the same level. The measurement of loudness of sound is a highly subjective phenomenon, but it was first described in a spectacularly successful manner by Fletcher and Munson (1933). The Equal Loudness Contours reveal the average human hearing sensitivity at frequencies in the human hearing range over various listening volumes. They were determined something like this: Fletcher and Munson played a reference tone at, for example, 1,000 Hz, at a designated sound volume. They would then play a different frequency, adjust the volume, and ask the listener to indicate when the new frequency sounded like it was at the same volume as the original frequency. They continued this process through several frequencies to come up with a "contour" of human hearing sensitivity at that one reference sound volume, say at 80 decibels (dB) sound pressure level. Next they would change to a reference volume of 85 dB and repeat the process.

They averaged this data over several listeners to come up with their published Equal Loudness Contours—commonly called today the Fletcher-Munson Curves. In this way, they demonstrated that human ears are more sensitive to some frequencies and less sensitive to others and that the sensitivity changes with the sound pressure level. More importantly, they were able to calibrate the actual energy in a sound as measured in decibels with the perceived loudness of the same sound. Figure 1.4 shows the changes in the sensitivity level of the ear over a range of frequency levels; energy is expressed here in decibel intensity along the vertical access and frequency on the horizontal axis shown as a logarithmic scale.

Each curve in figure 1.4 represents a gradient of ten *phons*, a subjective measure of loudness corresponding to decibel levels when measured by physical measurement equipment. From about 500 Hz to roughly 1,500 Hz, the 10 phon line roughly corresponds to 10 dB. This means that for humans to perceive the sound being a loudness level of 10 phons, frequencies from 500 Hz to 1,500 Hz must have an energy level of 10 dB. However, at 5,000 Hz the 10 phon line dips. This shows that the human ear perceives 4,000 Hz to be 10 phons when the source is actually only approximately 5 dB. One gets twice the effect for the energy expended. At 4,000 Hz, the phon curves turn up. To perceive 10,000 Hz at the same level of 10 phons, the energy level needs to be approximately 20 dB.

Figure 1.4 Fletcher-Munson equal loudness contours

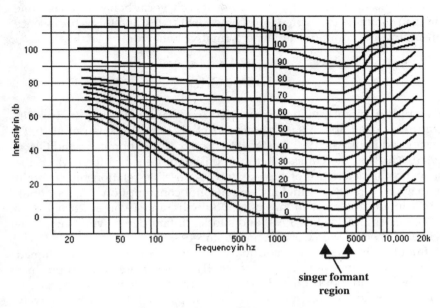

singer formant
region

Each curved line on the chart represents a gradient of ten *phons*, a subjective measure of loudness.

Source: Fletcher and Munson (1933).

Fletcher and Munson's research shows that the ear is less sensitive for low frequencies and at frequencies above 5,000 Hz. For this reason manufactures of sound equipment put "bass boosters" on their amplifiers to compensate for the lower sensitivity of human hearing. Subwoofers and tweeters (to boost the extreme high frequencies) as specialized loudspeaker equipment accomplish the same end.

For the purposes of this discussion, however, the most interesting fact revealed by the curves is that human hearing is more sensitive in the 2,800 kHz to 4,000 kHz range. This range of intense sensitivity in hearing corresponds to the region of the singer formant. Thus we can conclude that, at least in terms of hearing sensitivity, humans are uniquely attuned to hearing the singer formant.

This cannot be mere happenstance. The coincidence of the primary acoustic feature of the primary form of human music making and the dominant characteristic of human auditory sensitivity suggests an evolutionary adaptation. Any conclusions I might draw, like all statements about the evolution of human behavior, must be hypothetical and speculative. Nevertheless, I believe a compelling case can be made, as I suggested at the beginning of this discussion, for the origin of the singer formant, if not singing itself, in infant cries, primate calls, and involuntary human vocalizations. All of these nonspeech vocal behaviors have one thing in common: the expression of emotional states, and this is the essence of singing as a communicative performative behavior.

Infant Cries

The study of infant crying has produced an exceptionally large body of literature as cited above (cf. Drummond et al. 1999; Huffman et al. 1994; Lester and Boukydis 1992; Lester 1987; Lester 1978; Thompson and Olson 1996). Much of the clinical literature on infant cries has focused on the acoustic characteristics of the cry and its possible relationship to brain damage as a result of smoking and alcohol consumption (Nugent et al. 1996), infant drug addiction (Lester, Boukydis, and Twomey 2000; Lester 1999; Lester and Tronick 1994) and sudden infant death syndrome (Corwin et al. 1995, Lester, Corwin, and Golub 1988).

Infant crying causes extraordinary reactions in adults. As mentioned above, infants are astonishing vocalists. They never tire and can produce piercing cries for hours on end. Few adults can tolerate these vocalizations for a long period of time, and this can lead to parental distress. In relatively benign cases it causes parents to lose sleep as they repeatedly rise in the middle of the night to comfort and calm their baby. However, the adult reaction can have effects that are more deleterious. As parents' nerves become frayed, their reactions to their child's crying can lead to infant battering and even infanticide. For this reason, a number of researchers have focused on the structure of bouts of crying and adult reactions to them (Lester 1984; Bisping et al. 1990; Lester, Garcia-Coll, and Valcarcel 1989; Huffman et al. 1994; Thompson and Olson 1996; Green, Gustafson, and McGhie 1998).

In nearly all studies of infant crying to date, the fundamental frequency of the cry, that is, the basic pitch (F0), is taken as its primary acoustic characteristic. Researchers have generally tried to categorize cry types (fright, hunger, illness, etc.) and gauge parent reactions according to variations in F0 (Gustafson and Green 1989; Bisping et al. 1990; Protopapas and Eimas 1997; Lenti-Boero et al. 1998). I wish here to suggest that the salient element in infants' cries eliciting reaction from adults is not (or is not exclusively) F0 but rather the presence of prominent energy in the area of the singer formant.

Lester provides a spectral analysis of an infant cry that shows clearly the spike of energy characteristic of the singer formant. This is shown in figure 1.5.

Lester's spectrum of the infant cry in question shows the characteristic clustering of mutually reinforcing frequencies in the singer formant region noted by Johnstone and Scherer, resulting in the formant "spike" or "hump" in the smooth Fourier transform of the overall spectrum.

Figure 1.5 Smooth Fourier analysis of infant cry

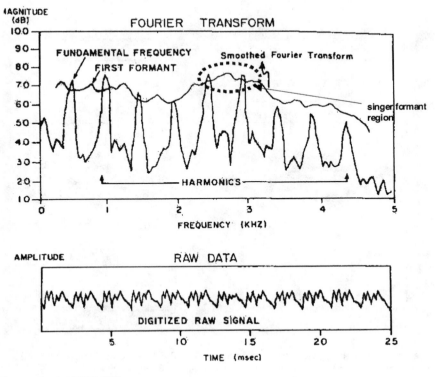

Source: Lester (1987: 531).

To test this phenomenon further, I ran four examples of infant cries (very kindly supplied by J. A. Green of the University of Connecticut, whose work on the acoustics of infant cries has already been noted in this discussion). These were provided as digital computer files and analyzed through a Fourier transform program, The BLISS program developed at Brown University.[8] Figures 1.6-1 through 1.6-4 show the results of this analysis.

In the four analyses of infant cries, we see a clustering of energy at the area of the singer formant in all four examples, thus replicating Lester's results with independent data. Additionally, in examples 1.6-3, and particularly 1.6-4, we see an additional area of intense energy corresponding to the "Gruberova" formant noted by Johnstone and Scherer. An additional, intriguing body of research on primate cries reveals that these too exhibit strong energy in the singer formant region (Owren, Seyfarth, and Cheney 1997; Owren and Linker 1995). Figure 1.7 shows this clearly. Owren, Seyfarth, and Cheney go on to point out that the frequencies in the singer formant region are even higher and exhibit stronger energy when the cry is associated with an infant (1997, 2956, 2960).

Figures 1.6-1, 1.6-2, 1.6-3, 1.6-4 Fourier transforms of four infant cries recorded by J. A. Green as analyzed by the BLISS speech analysis programs

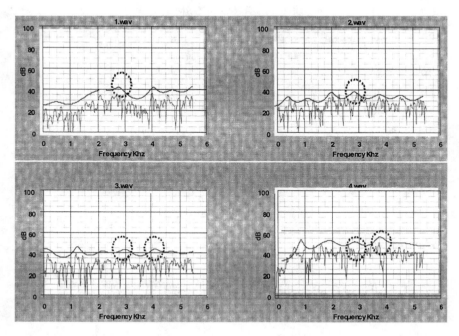

Singer formant region is indicated by a dotted oval. In the case of cries 3 and 4, a second "Gruberova" formant region is indicated at approximately 3800–4100 Hz.

Source: Sound files provided by James A. Green, University of Connecticut.

Hearing, Emotion, and Performance

Joseph Ledoux has associated autonomous emotional response with particularly strong auditory stimulus (1996, 162–65). The hearing channel seems particularly hardwired to the thalamus and the amygdalar regions, particularly for reactions associated with fear. As I have shown above, the areas of hearing that are most sensitive in human beings also correspond to the singer formant region of vocal energy.

In considering babies' cries and baboon articulations, it seems that both contain strong concentrations of energy in the singer formant area. This suggests that evolutionarily, selectivity favored creatures who could both generate and hear accurately sound energy at this particular high frequency. What is especially interesting about the singer formant region is that it does not interfere with the comprehension of normal speech, the formants for which are at a much lower frequency level.

Figure 1.7 Adult female chacma baboon cry

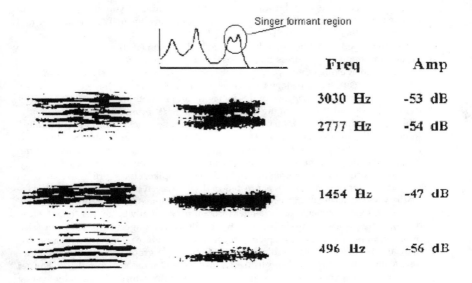

		Freq	Amp
		3030 Hz	-53 dB
		2777 Hz	-54 dB
		1454 Hz	-47 dB
		496 Hz	-56 dB

Source: Owren, Seyfarth, and Cheney (1997, 2954).

This suggests that humans evolved to be able to both comprehend the speech of others and comprehend the emotional tone of speech, particularly when it consisted of strong affective dimensions such as fear.

At least one research team has suggested that there is even more going on. Babies may be actually performing when they cry. Moreover, they may be manipulating or fooling their parents, who are often powerless to resist them when they produce high-pitched wailing (Thompson and Olson 1996). Thus as students of performance we are tempted to the conclusion that crying may be the first real human performance. Moreover, it may be one of the most effective forms of performance in which humans ever engage. A crying baby nearly always gets a strong emotional reaction from its audience—perhaps not as pleasurable a reaction as that effected by the high notes of a romantic operatic tenor, but a rousing response nevertheless.[9]

Notes

1. Wise theatrical producers who want to attract the attention of young people put children in their productions. If they are used well, the children virtually guarantee the rapt attention of other children in their audience.
2. This is the "poetic function" so ably analyzed by Jakobson (1960).
3. Performers frequently express their pleasure at performing for children's audiences because of their exuberant response. My suspicion is that children scream and shout at all-children's concerts and stage performances precisely because this is one of the few occasions where adults approve of this behavior, and do nothing to control it.
4. Also variously called the "singing formant" or "singer's formant"
5. This is a simplification. Every basic tone has an overtone series that occurs "naturally." In general the overtone sequence for a particular fundamental frequency consists of energy peaks at regular higher intervals—generally multiples of the fundamental frequency, usually with the same, or decreasing energy as the fundamental frequency. The singer formant, as I have suggested by the term "spike," is a shorthand term for an unusual cluster of high energy, expressed in decibels, seen in a particular set of wave frequencies clustering at 2800–3200 Hz (and, as noted, sometimes ranging to 4100 Hz). As will be seen, the energy of the singer formant may actually be greater than the fundamental frequency that underlies it (cf. Sound 1999). The singer "formant" is revealed by determining the average frequency spectrum of the voice. For those with a mathematical bent, this formant is indicated by a "hump" in a graph of a smoothed Fourier transform of the entire vocal spectrum of a given sound sample. Naturally the Fourier transform will change with the size and selection of the sample. What is interesting about the singer formant is its constant presence in the voice of trained singers even over very large samplings of sound. Those who know the term "formant" from the study of speech may find this terminology confusing. In principle, however, although the singer formant is not a component of speech sounds, it is analytically identified in the same way as the formants of speech.
6. In my own case, training at a major conservatory and with private teachers, it took about seven years to develop consistent control.
7. Johnstone and Scherer report that "long term spectra of all Gruberova recordings displayed a high energy region between 2900 and 4100 Hz" (1995).
8. This program is available free of charge to researchers in acoustics through the Department of Cognitive and Linguistic Sciences, Brown University.
9. Since this essay was originally formulated, research by Bachorowski, Smoski, and Owren (2001) has demonstrated that the "singer formant" also dominates in spontaneous human laughter.

References

Bachorowski, Jo-anne, Moria J. Smoski, and Michael J. Owren. 2001. "The Acoustic Features of Human Laughter." *The Journal of the Acoustic Society of America* 110, no. 3: 1581–97.
Bauman, R. 1977. *Verbal Art as Performance*. Rowley, Mass.: Newbury House.
Berndtsson, G., and J. Sundberg. 1995. "Perceptual Significance of the Centre Frequency of Singer's Formant." *STL-QPSR* (KTH) (Stockholm) 4: 95–105.
Bisping, R., H. J. Steingrueber, M. Oltmann, and C. Wenk. 1990. "Adults' Tolerance of Cries: An Experimental Investigation of Acoustic Features." *Child Development* 61, no. 4 (August): 1218–29.
Corwin M. J., B. M. Lester, C. Sepkoski, M. Peucker, H. Kayne, and H. L. Golub. 1995. "Newborn Acoustic Cry Characteristics of Infants Subsequently Dying of Sudden Infant Death Syndrome." *Pediatrics* 96, no. 1, pt. 1 (July): 73–77.

Drummond, Jane, Nicole LeTourneau, Susan Neufeld, Harriet Harvey, M. Ruth Elliott, and Sandra Reilly. 1999. "Infant Crying and Parent-Infant Interaction: Theory and Measurement." *Infant Mental Health Journal* 20, no. 4: 452–65.

Feld, Steven. 1982. *Sound and Sentiment: Birds, Weeping, Poetics and Song in Kaluli Expression*. Philadelphia: University of Pennsylvania Press.

———. 1988. "Aesthetics as Iconicity of Style, or 'Lift-Up-Over Sounding': Getting into the Kaluli Grove." *Yearbook for Traditional Music* 20: 74–113.

Fernandez, James. 1986. *Persuasions and Performances: The Play of Tropes in Culture*. Bloomington, Ind.: Indiana University Press.

Fitch, W., and M. Hauser. 1995. "Vocal Production in Nonhuman Primates: Acoustics, Physiology, and Functional Constraints on 'Honest' Advertisement." *American Journal of Primatology* 37: 191–219.

Flanagan, J. L. 1981. "Emotions, Voice, and Music." In *Research Aspects of Singing*, 51–79. Stockholm: Royal Swedish Academy of Music.

Fletcher, H., and W. A. Munson. 1933. "Loudness, Its Definition, Measurement and Calculation." *Journal of the Acoustical Society of America* 5: 82–108.

Goodall, Jane. 1986. *The Chimpanzees of Gombe: Patterns of Behavior*. Cambridge, Mass.: Harvard University Press.

Green, J. A., G. E. Gustafson, and A. C. McGhie. 1998. "Changes in Infants' Cries as a Function of Time in a Cry Bout." *Child Development* 69, no. 2 (April): 271–79.

Gustafson, G. E., and J. A. Green. 1989. "On the Importance of Fundamental Frequency and Other Acoustic Features in Cry Perception and Infant Development." *Child Development* 60, no. 4 (August): 772–80.

Huffman, Lynne C., Yvonne E. Bryan, Frank A. Pedersen, Barry M. Lester et al. 1994. "Infant Cry Acoustics and Maternal Ratings of Temperament." *Infant Behavior and Development* 17, no. 1: 45–53.

Jakobson, Roman. 1960. "Closing Statement: Linguistics and Poetics." In *Style in Language*, ed. Thomas Sebeok, 350–77. Cambridge, Mass.: MIT Press.

Johnstone, T., and K. Scherer. 1995. "Spectral Measurement of Voice Quality in Opera Singers: The Case of Gruberova." In *Proceedings of the XIIIth International Congress of Phonetic Sciences*, vol. 1, ed. K. Elenius and P. Branderud. Stockholm.

Lakoff, George, and Mark Johnson. 1974. *Metaphors We Live By*. Chicago: University of Chicago Press.

Ledoux, Joseph E. 1996. *The Emotional Brain*. New York: Simon and Schuster.

Lenti-Boero, D., C. Volpe, A. Marcello, C. Bianchi, and C. Lenti. 1998. "Newborns Crying in Different Contexts: Discrete or Graded Signals?" *Perceptual and Motor Skills* 86, no. 3, pt. 2 (June): 1123–40.

Lester, Barry M. 1978. "The Organization of Crying in the Neonate." *Journal of Pediatric Psychology* 3, no. 3: 122–30.

———. 1984. "A Biosocial Model of Infant Crying." *Advances in Infancy Research* 3: 167–212.

———. 1987. "Developmental Outcome Prediction from Acoustic Cry Analysis in Term and Preterm Infants." *Pediatrics* 80, no. 4 (October): 529–34.

———. 1999. "To Covary or Not to Covary: What Is the Question?" *Journal of Drug Issues* 29, no. 2: 263–68.

Lester, Barry M., Michael Corwin, and Howard Golub. 1988. "Early Detection of the Infant at Risk through Cry Analysis." In *The Physiological Control of Mammalian Vocalization*, ed. John D. Newman, 395–411. New York: Plenum Press.

Lester, Barry M., Cynthia T. Garcia-Coll, and Marta Valcarcel. 1989. "Perception of Infant Cries in Adolescent and Adult Mothers." *Journal of Youth and Adolescence* 18, no. 3: 231–43.

Lester, Barry M., and C. F. Zachariah Boukydis. 1992. "No Language but a Cry." In *Nonverbal Vocal Communication: Comparative and Developmental Approaches*, ed. Hanus Papousek and Uwe Juergens, 145–73. Studies in Emotion and Social Interaction. New York: Cambridge University Press.

Lester, Barry M., and Edward Z. Tronick. 1994. "The Effects of Prenatal Cocaine Exposure and Child Outcome." *Infant Mental Health Journal* 15, no. 2: 107–20.

Lester, Barry M., C. F. Zachariah Boukydis, and Jean E. Twomey. 2000. "Maternal Substance Abuse and Child Outcome." In *Handbook of Infant Mental Health*, 2nd ed., ed. Charles H. Zeanah, Jr., 161–75. New York: The Guilford Press.

Levin, Theodore C., and Michael E. Edgerton. 1999. "The Throat Singers of Tuva." *Scientific American* 281, no. 3 (September): 80–82.

Nugent, J. K., B. M. Lester, S. M. Greene, D. Wieczorek-Deering, and P. O'Mahony. 1996. "The Effects of Maternal Alcohol Consumption and Cigarette Smoking during Pregnancy on Acoustic Cry Analysis." *Child Development* 67, no. 4: 1806–15.

Owren, Michael J., Robert M. Seyfarth, and Dorothy L. Cheney. 1997. "The Acoustic Features of Vowel-like Grunt Calls in Chacma Baboons (Papio cyncephalus ursinus): Implications for Production Processes and Functions." *Journal of the Acoustic Society of America* 101, no. 5, pt. 1 (May): 2951–63.

Owren, Michael J., and D. Rendall. 1999. "An Effect-Conditioning Model of Nonhuman Primate Vocal Signaling." In *Perspectives in Ethology*, ed. D. H. Owings, M. D. Beecher, and N. S. Thompson. Vol. 12. New York: Plenum Press.

Protopapas, A., and Peter D. Eimas. 1997. "Perceptual Differences in Infant Cries Revealed by Modifications of Acoustic Features." *Journal of the Acoustic Society of America* 102, no. 6 (December): 3723–34.

Sataloff, Robert T. 1992. "The Human Voice." *Scientific American* 267, no. 6 (December): 108–115.

Savage-Rumbaugh, Sue. 1994. *Kanzi: The Ape at the Brink of the Human Mind*. New York: John Wiley & Sons.

Scherer, K. R. 1986. "Vocal Affect Expression: A Review and a Model for Future Research." *Psychological Bulletin* 99, no. 2 (March): 143–65.

Siegwart, H., and K. R. Scherer. 1995. "Acoustic concomitants of emotional expression in operatic singing: The case of Lucia in Ardi gli incensi." *Journal of Voice*.

Sound. 1999. Encyclopedia Britannica Online. http://www.eb.com:180/bol/topic?eu =117555&sctn=38: Encyclopedia Britannica.

Sundberg, Johan. 1972. "Production and Function of the Singing Formant." In *Report of the 11th Congress of the International Musicological Society*, vol. 2, ed. H. Glahn, S. Sorenson, and P. Ryom, 679–88. Copenhagen: Edition Wilhelm Hansen.

———. 1977. "The Acoustics of the Singing Voice." *Scientific American* 236, no. 3 (March): 82–91.

———. 1987. *The Science of the Singing Voice*. Dekalb, Ill.: Northern Illinois University Press.

———. 1993. "How Can Music Be Expressive?" *Speech Communication* 13, no. 1/2: 239–53.

———. 1998. "Expressivity in Singing: A Review of Some Recent Investigations." *Log Phon Vocol*. 23: 121–27. Paper presented originally at the PEVOC-II conference, August 29–31, 1997 in Regensburg, Germany.

Sundberg, Johan, J. Iwarsson, and H. Hagegärd. 1995. "A Singer's Expression of Emotions in Sung Performance." In *Vocal Fold Physiology: Voice Quality and Control*, ed. O. Fujimura and M. Hirano, 217–32. San Diego: Singular Publishing Group.

Thompson, Nicholas S., and Carolyn Olson. 1996. "Babies' Cries: Who's Listening? Who's Being Fooled." *Social Research* 63, no. 3: 763–85.

Titze, Ingo R. 1994. *Principles of Voice Production*. Englewood Cliffs, N.J.: Prentice-Hall.

Titze, Ingo R., and Sharyn Mapes. 1992. "Acoustics of the Tenor High Voice." *Journal of the Acoustical Society of America* 91, no. 4: 24–33.

Titze, Ingo R., Sharyn Mapes, and Brad Story. 1994. "Acoustics of the Tenor High Voice." *Journal of the Acoustical Society of America* 95, no. 2: 1133–42.

Turner, V. 1986. *The Anthropology of Performance*. New York: PAJ Publications.

Chapter Two

THE BUZZ OF GOD AND THE
CLICK OF DELIGHT

David Shulman

1.

What is it that we hear when we listen to a *dhrupad* singer in performance? In what ways does this aural experience differ from that of listening to the recitation of a Sanskrit verse? In both cases, the texts and teachers insist that, assuming excellence in performance, a psycho-physical change takes place within the listener. Can we define and describe this process analytically? Do the texts at our disposal help us to do so?

In a sense, there is a simple, negative answer to the latter question. The musicological texts, at least, like their refractions in modern discourse, are saturated with categorical and morphological discussions of a normative tone that distract from the kind of issue outlined here. Moreover, a certain recalcitrant opacity adheres to the language and terms. The more ancient musical traditions have been effectively lost, and the medieval textbooks, such as *Sangita-ratnakara* (from the thirteenth century), which concerns us here, stand on the other side of a significant break.

On the other hand, in the closely allied realm of poetics, *alankāra-śāstra*, we do find exhaustive discussions of precisely these questions. What is the nature of the transformation that poetry (or drama or dance) achieves, and how does it work? What triggers it, and how can we understand the psychological and processual components of its success? But just here, surprisingly, we come up against a no-less formidable obstacle—the set of explanatory theories crystallized around the notions of *rasa* and *dhvani*, particularly as formulated by the great Kashmiri theoretician Abhinavagupta in the eleventh century. So powerful and attractive was Abhinavagupta's magisterial synthesis that, in the course of its assimilation and elaboration in the normative literature on poetics over the following centuries, it more or less blinded the tradition to the kinds of tensions and questions that had originally shaped the discussion. It also tended to blind even highly perceptive critics and listeners to many kinds of beauty that lay at the heart of individual masterpieces, poetic as well as musical.

Nonetheless, there is perhaps a way forward—as usual, by somewhat circuitous routes. There are questions we can ask of our texts that may spark unconventional answers. These questions relate to the axiomatic concerns that inform the musicological literature and to the relations between terms and elements within this axiological mode. Moreover, we have another source that is all too rarely utilized—the continuing oral teaching that the *ustads* of our own generation impart, in what is presumably a strong relationship of faithfulness to the concepts of earlier teachers. Here it is a question of listening carefully and extrapolating, in systematic ways, from what we are being taught.

2.

Music and poetry coincide at the most basic level. Both deal in sounds— their production, their internal organization, their patterns of repetition and other formal or figural features, and their relation to a domain of meaning. As far as figuration goes, there is, in fact, an astonishing similarity in the two disciplines, although the analysis of musical "figures" (including *śleṣa* superimposition, exaggerated elaboration, simile, and a striking series of rhetorical devices involving anaphora of various types) is not an explicit subject for the classical musicologists, in marked contrast with the poeticians. Moreover, the interest in the physical production of sounds in and by the human body is shared by both fields; more specifically, musicology appears to borrow directly from the classical grammarians when it comes to descriptions of the processes of articulation. But perhaps even more striking is the common fascination with the metaphysical side of sonic production. For both traditions, God is a kind of subtle and pervasive hum emerging into audibility in complex forms and ways that also determine the structure and development of the created universe. One aspect of the listener's experience is a reconnection to this level of true sonic existence, usually felt to be internal to every consciousness but also, in everyday states, blocked off from that consciousness. Poetry and music, in other words, have not a little to do with overcoming a resistance or obstacle. In this sense, a strong link also exists to the medieval Yogic traditions such as those we find in the *Hatha-yoga-pradipika*, which culminates in a lyrical chapter on *nāda*, sound, as ultimacy. We need to pay attention to this linkage and this identification, even as we attempt to understand just what the authors meant when they spoke in terms of "resistance" as part of the artistic enterprise.

On another level—still, however, closely related to these Yogic concerns—we can ask somewhat more technical questions about sound and its production. Even in normal, everyday speech, what we hear is not what we understand. Our ears and minds register sequences of articulated sounds—what the grammarians call *vaikṛta-dhvani*, the "crude" or "external" resonance—and somehow translate these phonetic materials into something else, that is, into utterances (taking the sentence as the primary unit for such a process, as Bhartṛhari discovered). Bhartṛhari offers more than one description of this obviously rather complicated business; but, simplifying somewhat, we can say that the crude phonetic vibrations trigger or reveal what is called the *sphoṭa*—the integral meaning-bearing word unit that cannot be heard as such but that enables comprehension.[1] *Sphoṭa* is literally a "bursting open," a flowering or unfolding. The *sphoṭa* contains within itself the miraculous relation of meaning, *artha*, to sound, *śabda*, a relation actualized by the unrolling, in linear sequence, of the compacted *sphoṭa* reality. This process takes place both within the mind of the speaker and within that of the listener or decoder, who effectively puts back these unrolled or unfolded sonic materials into a once-again unified and sequence-less whole. Some modern scholars, such as Brough, have insisted that the *sphoṭa* is devoid of any "mystical" or, for that matter, metaphysical traits—that it is simply the "word" in its symbolic aspect as bearing meaning. Yet Bhartṛhari tells us that the *sphoṭa*, insofar as it is unitary, is integrally related to the divine whole that is language, or god, *tout court*. I must confess, at this stage, to being suspicious of any use of a word like "symbolic" in Indian contexts such as these.

Is there an analogous conceptual structure in the musical discourse? Even before addressing this question, we should note that poetics itself defines a profound tension between semantic and nonsemantic operations; in a certain sense, semanticity itself is something of a problem, almost a diversion from the path of the more powerful effects that poetry makes possible. But it will, perhaps, be easier if we start with the analysis of levels of sound, and their interaction, which the musicological literature itself puts forward.

3.

What we hear is not a datum. There are objective sonar energies at work in the world (the world itself is, in fact, a dense crisscrossing net of such energies, as we have said), and the poet or musician uses these forces to produce artistic forms. But this does not mean that we hear the primary aural events themselves. Perhaps advanced Yogins can do so, but our experience is far more limited than theirs. Nonetheless, the musicologists

offer a highly sophisticated and nuanced analysis of the process that produces the sounds that we do hear.

We follow that masterpiece of musicological synthesis, Sarngadeva's
Sangita-ratnakara, composed in the western Deccan in the mid-thirteenth
century. An elaborate and indispensable commentary on this work, by
Kallinatha, was produced at the imperial center of Vijayanagara in the
second half of the fifteenth century. Although both Sarngadeva and Kallinatha innovate radically in terms of the internal evolution of the discipline
of music, we will take their relatively standard descriptions of sonic emergence as useful points of departure. The very act of integrating diverse
strands of the tradition—musicology proper, Ayurvedic physiology, phonetics, linguistic metaphysics, and poetics in its mature (post-Abhinav-
agupta) phase—in this work allows us to extrapolate from Sarngadeva in
a more general mode. We begin, then, with his distinctions among the
three primary levels of sound. Historical observations on musicology and
poetics are deferred to our final section.

What we call sound, in a musical context, evolves through three stages
or terms: *nāda*, *śruti*, and *svara*. Let us take them one by one.

Nāda

Sarngadeva begins his book with a simple identification: music consists of
a subtle buzz or drone called *nāda* (*gītaṃ nādâtmakam*, 2.1). In fact, this
equation is but a condensation of a much wider claim. *Nāda* is the reservoir out of which phonemes (*varṇa*) emerge (*vyajyate*);[2] and since words
(*pada*) emerge from phonemes and complete utterances (*vacas*) from words,
and since all of everyday life (*vyavahāra*) comes out of language, the world
itself (*jagat*) is entirely dependent upon *nāda* (2.2.).

But just what is this all-pervasive, fundamental force of *nāda*? It exists
in two forms or modes, "struck" (*āhata*) and "unstruck" (*anāhata*, 2.3)—
perhaps in the sense that a string, or the vocal chords, can be "struck" to
produce audible sound. *Nāda* is thus both audible and inaudible,[3] and its
inaudible mode may well be thought to retain a certain primacy. This *anāhata* or inaudible level of *nāda* is, in fact, active in performance, as we
shall see. Nonetheless, since *nāda* does manifest itself luminously (*pra-
kāśate*) in the body (*piṇḍa*), our author first turns his attention to anatomy
and physiology, offering in effect a synopsis of Ayurvedic thinking—
including a concise description of the well-known series of Yogic *cakras* in
the subtle body, in their relation to the self (*ātman*), and to the production
of sound.[4]

All of this is, of course, subordinate to the main goal of describing the
business of producing sounds that can be used to make music. At the start
of his third chapter, Sarngadeva tells us how this process happens, borrowing from the ancient Sanskrit handbooks on phonetics (*śikṣā*):

ātmā vivakṣamāṇo 'yaṃ manaḥ prerayate manaḥ/
dehasthaṃ vahnim āhanti sa prerayati mārutam//
brahma-granthi-sthitaḥ so 'tha kramād ūrdhva-pathe caran/
nābhi-hṛt-kaṇṭha-mūrdhasyeṣv āvirbhāvayati dhvanim//3–4

This inner being (ātman) wishes to speak: so it puts the mind (manas) into motion. The mind ignites the fire that exists within the body, and the fire propels air [breath] which, rising upwards from the knot of Brahma [at the navel] makes sound manifest in the navel, heart, throat, head, and mouth.

There are two salient features in this description, which at first follows the *Paniniya-siksa* almost verbatim:[5] first, the originary impulse is an autonomous wish to speak (*vivakṣā*) rooted in the inner self; secondly, this self-propelled, self-defining act of desire moves through the various inner organs, gaining force and concreteness, to emerge as the revelation (*āvirbhāva*) of audible sound. *Vivakṣā*, the urge to utter sound, leads to *āvirbhāva*, a graspable, intelligible manifestation. This progression is standard and repetitive, indeed continuous. *Nāda*, that is, as the initially "unstruck" and subtle wholeness that comprises reality itself, is subject to an incorrigible impulse towards expression. The self, alive somewhere within this subtle domain of godly sound, is driven to speak. This is a fact of existence, applicable to God no less than to human beings. Creation—the unfolding of a cosmos—is no more (and no less) than this need to find a voice.[6] Music, we can assume, is one eventual manifestation of this urge, crafted, molded, and regulated in ways that we will discuss. What we are hearing, then, in a concert is first of all (and perhaps above all) this self-driven movement of *nāda* towards a perceptible surface or domain. We hear *nāda*, a divine power in its audible mode, in the process of its emergence. The same description, incidentally, applies to poetry, which is never silent but rather consistently breaks out onto or into audible surface, but which also normally contains within it the potential tensions of specific semantic burdens. I will return to this point.

Nāda, we now know, is twofold, audible and inaudible. But once we have made the transition from the former to the latter, a more complex classification comes into play:

nādo 'tisūkṣmaḥ sūkṣmaś ca puṣṭo 'puṣṭaś ca kṛtrimaḥ/
iti pañcâbhidhā dhatte pañca-sthāna-sthitaḥ kramāt//5
nakāraṃ prāṇa-nāmānaṃ da-kāram analaṃ viduḥ/
jātaḥ prāṇâgni-saṃyogāt tena nādo 'bhidhīyate//6

Nāda is fivefold: extremely subtle, subtle, full, not-so-full, and molded, according to the five above-mentioned bodily points of origin [navel = extremely subtle, heart = subtle, throat = full, head = not-so-full, mouth = molded, if we follow the logical order of the verses].[7] *Na* means breath, *da* indicates fire—hence, being born from the conjunction of breath and fire, it is called *nāda*.

The etymological identifications are Tantric, reinforcing the central image of emergent sound as a fiery process fanned by the breath. As usual, still further categorical divisions are possible and must be mentioned. Thus, *nāda* is also threefold: low, medium, and high (pitches), according to whether it is produced from the heart, throat, or head, respectively (*mandra, madhya, tāra*, 3.7).

Śruti and Svara

At this point Sarngadeva is ready to deal with the true building blocks of musical sound, which, following his predecessors, he calls *śruti*:

> tasya dvāviṃśatir bhedāḥ śravaṇāc chrutayo matāḥ/
> hṛdy-ūrdhva-nāḍī-saṃlagnā nāḍyo dvāviṃśatir matāḥ//8
> tiraścyas tāsu tāvatyaḥ śrutayo mārutâhateḥ/
> uccoccataratā-yuktāḥ prabhavanty uttarottaram//9
> evaṃ kaṇṭhe tathā śīrṣe śruti-dvāviṃśatir matāḥ/ 10a

> *Nāda* has 22 differentiated "grades" called *śrutis*, because you can hear them (*śravaṇāt*); they sit upon the [two?—*iḍā* and *piṅgalā*,[8] Kallinatha] upward-moving channels of the heart. There are 22 such channels (*nāḍī*), obliquely placed [within the body], equal to the number of *śrutis* produced when struck by the breath, according to pitch; and there are also, correspondingly, 22 in the throat and 22 in the head.

We are still clearly in the realm of Yogic or Ayurvedic physiology; our author posits a relation between the subtle, invisible channels (*nāḍī*) in the body and the twenty-two *śrutis* that are the stuff of music—"the shades of minute tonal distinctions that are audible to the human ear."[9] These are deep waters; we cannot begin to do justice to the concept of *śruti* in this essay, which is focused on more general themes. But if we are to understand the process that takes us from inaudible *nāda* to musical performance, we have to tarry a moment longer with this passage. We are used to being told that classical Indian music uses microintervals, half-tones or quarter-tones in terms of our system; and indeed, the authorities insist that actual musical notes (*svara*) are to be defined in terms of the twenty-two basic *śruti* intervals, understood not in purely mathematical terms (as in Greece) but in somewhat looser, relational terms vis-à-vis one another and the system as a whole.[10] There is also discussion about the exact number, with some claiming that sixty-six *śrutis*—or even, theoretically, an infinity of *śrutis*[11]—exist, thus clearly straining the human faculty of hearing far beyond its limits. And, as we shall see, it is always possible to recategorize the universally accepted twenty-two in terms of various parameters (the three registers mentioned earlier; a fourfold system reflecting the dominance of wind (*vāta*), bile (*pitta*), or phlegm (*kapha*) respectively, or of excess in all three humors; and so on). Indeed, a vast set of potential correlations and homologies is evolved by the theoreticians out of the initial premise of twenty-two dependable tones.

But the central problem is always the relation of *śruti*, the raw material, and *svara*, the fully audible, expressive, systemically meaningful musical sound. As the great Carnatic composer Tyagaraja (1767–1847) said, "To be able to distinguish the seven *svara* notes out of the background of everyday cacophony is to achieve liberation."[12] The *svaras* are referred to by the following seven terms: *sadja, rsabha, gandhara, madhyama, pancama, dhaivata,* and *nisadha,* or, in short, *sa-ri-ga-ma-pa-dha-ni-*[*sa*]. The *śrutis* are distributed among the *svaras,* to begin with, in twos, threes, or fours, each such group defining the possible range of the *svara* (including its rise to *tīvra*, "sharp," or *komal*, "flat"). In addition, each *svara* is related to a social category (*varṇa*), a color, a bird or other animal that naturally utters it, a mythical source, a place of origin within the body, and so on, as the following chart (following Sarngadeva) makes clear:

note	śrutis	varṇa	color	animal	origin
sa	1–4	brahmin	red	peacock	divine
ri	5–7	Ksatriya	pale yellow	cātaka bird	sages
ga	8–9	Vaisya	gold	goat	divine
ma	10–13	brahmin	white	krauñca bird	divine
pa	14–17	brahmin	black	cuckoo	ancestors
dha	18–20	Ksatriya	yellow	frog	sages
ni	21–22	Vaisya	karbura	elephant	asuras

As is well known, the medieval *rāga*-system makes a further, practical selection, fixing the *svaras* of any given *rāga* in particular *śruti* intervals and determining which *svaras*, and which turns of musical phrase, are allowed in ascending and descending order.

But none of this actually explains the way *śrutis* emerge in performance as *svaras*, or makes full sense of the relation of one set to the other. The older system operated in terms of relatively fixed equations of *svaras* with given *śrutis*, with equally distinct intervals *between* svaras—so that *śrutis* were either attached to a certain *svara* or placed between two *svaras*. The commentator Kallinatha, in a historical mood, shows us this older view in contrast with his own, more modern perspective:

> *Śruti* is either one or manifold. In fact, it is one. In the beginning, the sound (*dhvani*) that comes from the interaction of space and breath within the body, set in motion by human effort, proceeds upwards from the navel into space (*ākāśa-deśam*) like smoke, along the rungs of the ladder,[13] through the desire of the breath. Climbing in manifold ways, it appears as if divided into parts such as [any] "four *śrutis*" because of the process of filling up from within (*antarbhūta-pūraṇa-pratyayârthatayā*). Such, at any rate, is our view. Others, however, believe *śruti* is two-fold, because of the *śruti*-intervals between *svara* notes.[14]

The *śāstra* was actually moving in the direction of recognizing any *śruti* as a potential *svara*, depending on contextual (*rāga*-dependent) factors and needs, as Mukund Lath has shown.[15] It is perhaps this later development, which we hear in practice today, that makes it somewhat difficult for us to see what lies behind the classical discussions of the *śruti-svara* relation, though the implications of those discussions are crucial for the questions with which we began.

Take, first, Sarngadeva's definition of *svara*:

śrutyanantara-bhāvī yaḥ snigdho 'nuraṇanâtmakaḥ/
svato rañjayati śrotṛ-cittam sa svara ucyate//3.24–25//

Svara is what comes into being immediately upon *śruti*. It is smooth [dense, creamy—*snigdha*] and is, in essence, a sympathetic vibration that brings joy, of itself, to the mind of the listener. (Lath, 1998)

The etymological play at the end (*SVAto RAñjayati= svara*) has its own importance as an affirmation of notions of autonomy and sheer, purpose-less delight as built into the very foundations of musical praxis; but for our purposes it is the opening that counts. *Śruti* is there first, immediately fol-lowed by *svara*, which is defined as a kind of resonance, *anuraṇana*, thick or creamy to the ear. *Śruti*, that is, is (barely) audible and is rapidly converted, as it were, into the active resonance that we actually hear. As Kallinatha explains: "Although audibility exists [primarily] for that sound that is, in essence, an enduring sympathetic vibration (*anuraṇana*) in the form of *svaras* and *tānas* and so on, when we speak of *śrutis* we mean that barely audible sound (*dhvani*) that is produced only at the very first moment that the breath strikes [the vocal chords] and does not resonate."[16]

Just as with other forms of language, then, music as we know it is really a sort of sustained echo of something we cannot truly hear, some-thing hushed and subtle, almost at the edge of silence. Recall the *sphoṭa* mentioned earlier in connection with everyday words. What is more, it is precisely this almost inaudible level, whether of speech or song, that gov-erns, determines, sustains, and informs the manifest phenomena of music or poetry, for example. It may be this level that we need to listen for above all else.

Statements such as that contained in the previous sentence have an unfortunate mystical ring. Musicological texts like the *Sangita-ratnakara* do, of course, make metaphysical statements, as we have seen. Nonethe-less, they are overwhelmingly empirical and systematic in their approach. The notion of resonance, with its implication of an almost silent prototype or substratum, is no less empirical than discussions of *śruti* intervals, tun-ing, or scales.[17] Modern *ustads* will also say, in the most practical way, that when you begin to intone a note you have to listen for the preexisting, per-sistent *svara* that is just beyond ordinary hearing and that *your* note will join and ride upon. Or, when singing *ni*, you are meant to hear the silent *sa* that is the next note above it and that, in fact, already participates in *ni* by lending it the lowest of the four *śrutis* that comprise *sa*. *Ni* and *sa*, like *sa* and *ri*, like *ma* and *ga* or *ma* and *pa*, are potentially intertwined. This overlapping has a technical name and is very precisely described in our texts. Thus, when *sa* loses its fourth *śruti* to *ri* and its lowest *śruti* to *ni*, this is [*cyuta-ṣaḍja*]-*sādhāraṇa*. When *sa* gives its two lower *śrutis* to lower *ni*, this is *kākali*.[18] And even apart from this rather prominent matter of overlapping, we can be confident that, in concert, actualized *svaras* both graduate delicately and deliberately into neighboring *śrutis*—the microtones we can hear if we are attuned to them—and also contain within them, in the perception of the singer and of an informed listener—the "silent" notes that surround them and are felt to give them meaning.

What, then, can we say of the relation of *svara* and *śruti*? Kallinatha offers the following lucid survey of the possibilities:

1. They are, in fact, the same, both being audible. No categorical distinction applies except for that between the general (*jāti*) and the particular (*vyakti*). This view cannot, however, be correct, since one (*svara*) depends upon the other (*śruti—āśrayâśrayitva*). Non-distinction in perception is not the same as being the same (*nirviśeṣaṃ na sāmānyam*).
2. It is like a mirror reflecting a face: the *svaras* reflect the *śrutis* as an illusory image reflects reality. This explanation is also wrong: the *svaras* are no less real than the *śrutis*.
3. It is like the relation of material cause (*upâdāna*) to effect, like mud to the earthen pot. But no—although the *svara* follows upon the *śruti* in time, the *śruti* is not the cause of the *svara*. The mud disappears into the pot, but the *śrutis* *do not disappear into the svaras*. Moreover, logically you cannot have the sympathetic vibration of the *svara* without the continuing vibration (*raṇana*) of the *śruti*.
4. Let us then speak of transformation (*pariṇāma*), as when milk is transformed into curd. The *śrutis* turn into *svaras* (in performance).
5. Or we can use the language of revelation (*abhivyakti*), as when a lamp manifests by its light already existing objects (previously in darkness). Thus, the *śrutis* manifest the *svaras* (not vice versa).

Both 4 and 5 are acceptable to Kallinatha.[19]

We should pay attention to the insistence that *svara* is not caused by *śruti*. The *śruti* continues to exist in the *svara*, but this is more like a process of actualization, externalization, and selective (systemic) reorganization than like the physical generation of something new. The *svaras* are new in only two senses: they assume a place within a relational system that gives them meaning and existence, and they are conceived of as an additional resonance or vibration that follows necessarily upon the initial striking of the string. In both cases, we hear only part of what is there—quite possibly the less important part, as already stated. It follows, though the textbooks of music do not say this as explicitly as the poeticians do, that the task of the performer may well be that of helping us to hear what is not, in fact, audible in the material presented to us.

Later theoreticians sometimes formulate the issue in slightly different terms that sustain this direction of interpretation. Pundarika Vitthala, in the sixteenth century, says that "*śruti* is [that sound] which is heard *before* [a pitch-position] is actually struck; *svara* is the after-sound that it produces."[20] As Mukund Lath correctly notes, we have now returned to the distinction between "struck" and "unstruck" *nāda*; *śruti* is unstruck (*anāhata*) sound, that is, the *potentiality* of a sound rather than an actual one, the latter now equated with *svara*.[21] Although this statement extends and, in a sense, radicalizes the earlier debates on the relation between the two terms, it remains faithful to the primary intuition. Music, like poetry, is the breaking through to audible surface of a subtler, or deeper, more intense, more continuous, or more complex reality. A century after Pundarika, another innovating musicologist, Ahobala, writes that "*śrutis* are no different from *svaras*, since both are audible. The *śāstras* tell us that the (only) difference is like that between a snake coiled or uncoiled (*ahi-kuṇḍalavat*)."[22] The *svaras* uncoil the latent reality of the snake, turning a spiraling simultaneity into linear sequence.[23] Such is music (or, for that matter, language), which, as Bhartrhari says, is always "infested with sequentiality."[24] Music and language unfold in time, and this temporal dimension entails an unavoidable loss, a flattening out or even falsification of the unmanifest utterance (in the case of language, semanticity itself is said to contribute to this process of self-impoverishment).

If this conclusion sounds a little pessimistic, we can revert to the perspective of the Tantric Yogins. The *Hatha-yoga-pradipika* assures us that, with practice, the Yogi ceases to hear the many external (*bāhya*) noises of everyday consciousness; little by little he hears the *nāda* that is ever more subtle (*sūkṣma-sūkṣmaka*).[25] This *nāda*, the true object of meditation, is the net that snares the inner deer—no doubt, the mind (*manas*); or, better still, it serves as the hunter that slays the inner deer (4.94). Clearly, there is music and there is music. The choice is ours.

By now we are, I believe, in a position to give a tentative answer to our first question. What we hear in a *dhrupad* concert, for example, is precisely this process of emergence, however we wish to describe it—as unwinding a snake, unrolling a mat, stretching out a space, catching a ride on a preexistent current, opening a window to a vast (unimagined) reality, weaving a net, fishing the depths, echoing and vibrating harmonically, rising up through invisible bodily centers, igniting and blazing with the aid of breath or wind, or breaking through a crust. All of these images crop up in our texts, and all contain the tension that is inherent in emergence—the tension of what is lost as depth generates a surface. There are always profound issues of continuity, as we will see. What is more, a dimension of resistance is normally built into this process. The latent *śruti* does not so easily metamorphose into *svara*. Indeed, it is this very struggle that comprises a great part of what is audible. We listen not to the thing itself—not to an object, in any sense of the word—but to the tension and drama that precede and accompany breakthrough. In this sense, music, again like poetry, is something of a release. Both regularly reproduce the tension that drives towards utterance—*vivakṣā*, as we saw in relation to *nāda*. Both incorporate the struggle between the unresonant and the resonant. If one intensifies this struggle to a certain point, the result is what the poeticians call *camatkāra*, the "click" of amazement or "delight" that is art.

4.

Naturally, we have seen only the beginning of the story. Music is, in the most general sense, the making of the inaudible audible, as sculpture (for example) seeks to make the invisible visible in the process of its emergence.[26] But if the to-and-fro of emergence and disemergence continues throughout any concert, or any poem, our attention nevertheless goes elsewhere—to the patterned grid of performance that is energized by these countervailing vectors. Here we can point to certain consistent and recurrent features that offer a field for serious analysis.

The heart of the matter has to do with the notion of repetition itself—perhaps the basic tool we have to study aesthetic forms anywhere. Without repetition, there are no patterns, and little or nothing can be said.[27] Repetition rarely repeats as one moves from one cultural matrix to another—for that matter, repetition internal to a culture, even to a single genre or a single performance, rarely repeats exactly. Rhythms, sequencing, and the internal organization of repeating elements have their own context-dependent integrity, usually unique to a given moment, and their own metaphysical rationale.

Anyone who listens to *dhrupad*, or who reads widely in Sanskrit poetry, becomes aware of repetition as a fact of life. Repetitive variation is evident at practically every moment. Even the "first" instance—of impulse or theme, of creative utterance or act—is classed as repetition.[28] There is, however, always the question of what, precisely, repeats, to say nothing of "how" or "why." Much interesting work has been done in this area, for South Asian aesthetic domains, in recent years.[29] As a preliminary statement of possible direction, and in light of the aesthetics of emergence that I have sought to define in this essay, I want to suggest three major patterns of coherent and systematic variation that we see in classical musical and poetic praxis as sound unfolds into form. These have to do with attempts to establish or reestablish continuity in the face of perceived gaps or incongruities (*samnidhāna*); with attempts to intensify presence or to bring something into existence through what is called "ornamentation," *alankāra*; and with the production of matching or coincident complexes that systematically re-create or restate the premises of figurative emergence (*pratibimbana*).

The first is, perhaps, the most prevalent pattern, incorporating a consistent, very powerful drive towards reconnection or reintegration. As we have seen, there is a tension implicit in any musical or linguistic emergence; resistance has to be overcome; what is latent or potential reduces to the apparent, the naturally audible or otherwise perceptible. Very often this process entails taking apart and distributing an originary whole, as the ancient creator-god Prajāpati is said to fragment and disperse in the process of creating the world. What we hear on the apparent surface is always somewhat discontinuous with the generative realm of the potential. Hence the tremendous drive to recompose what has been sundered. We have seen several rather innocent instances of this drive in our discussion of *śruti* and *svara*. Recall that a *svara* note is never only itself; it exists only within the relational system of all other actualized *svaras* (at any given moment of performance), and it is integrated vertically and horizontally with its contiguous or otherwise resonant (or dissonant) *svaras*—through overlapping, through sympathetic vibration,[30] and through "riding upon" the inaudible and continuous "unstruck," or very subtle, level of sound. Recall, also, that the resonance or reverberation, *anuraṇana*, used to define audible *svara* to begin with is described, strikingly, as *snigdha*, "smooth," "creamy," "dense." Audible sound is "creamy" in the sense of providing or maintaining a viscous, continuous linkage to the unheard or barely heard first vibration (*raṇana*). Music, that is, as the *śāstra* authors repeatedly tell us, rhythmically reconnects (*laya*).

Many of the most common "figures of sound" that make up actual musical performance serve this same purpose or conduce to this effect. The *mīṇḍ* "glides" so prevalent in *dhrupad* literally connect the disparate *svara* notes in an unbroken flow of sound, as do, in other ways, the many varieties of *gamaka* grace-notes and the dramatic "swinging" between notes, *andolan*.[31] Ahobala, whom I quoted earlier, goes to the extent of describing music itself as being like the swinging motion that calms a crying child.[32] Notice that here the sense of reconnecting what is severed shades off into a sense of music (or poetry) as potentially healing, in its very nature. Sarngadeva, as we have seen, sets his musicological treatise within a framework borrowed from medicine, Ayurveda.

There is another common way to describe this same process. The idea of continuous connection is also a matter of opening up a space, perhaps more than one kind of space. This is one function of emergence. Thus, our teachers sometimes tell us that "everything depends on the *mīṇḍ* (glide)" that stretches out a space for the musical reality and at the same time produces depth.[33] Here continuity and smooth transition are critical; the voice must not break or hesitate, must not become uneven, as it traverses the deepening space between one *svara* and another. The sound is actually the life-breath, *prāṇa*, itself (or, again, it "rides upon" the *prāṇa*). Hand movements accompanying the singing, a standard feature of *dhrupad*, weave this ongoing breath in a ceaseless, curvaceous image, following the *prāṇa*. If one performs Rag Yaman well, the space that opens between *ri* and *pa* stretches out to the very end of the cosmos, reverberating expansively and providing a vista nearly infinite in scope—but only if there is no rent or tear in the musical weaving, no loss of even a single *śruti*.[34] Such an opening is, once again, very close to healing. Expansiveness, *vistāra*, is also a key concept in Abhinavagupta's understanding of what constitutes aesthetic (especially poetic) experience.[35]

Unfolding space, in this musical cosmogony, is usually rich in affect. In Bhairav, for example, the upper *ni* generates longing, a consuming homesickness that can only be eased by reaching the next note, *sa*. Performers always linger on this ardent *ni*, deliberately denying release and intensifying the feeling. The space of longing has its own integrity, and the energy that infuses it has something to do with the fact that *sa* is already present, through overlapping and in the subtle, unheard or "unstruck" note that we now recognize in principle, in the audible *ni*. This presence, at once potential and real, is actually inimical to discontinuity. Absence, that is, the tantalizing absence of the as-yet-unsung *sa*, is only the absence of audible surface, thus not truly a matter of a gap or break. One can, we are told, "smell" the as-if-absent *sa* as one listens to or sings the yearning note of *ni*. Such a space is an arena for the erotic, or for what modern musicians call *rasa*, borrowing the term from the by now conventional lexicon of poetics.

Poetics runs parallel to musicology in the prominence given to our second pattern, ornamentation (*alankāra*)—the notion that actually gives poetics its name, *alankāra-śāstra*, the science of ornament. In the early centuries of scientific poetics, this term implies the categorical analysis of all the standard figures or ornaments, *alankāra*. This fascination with the logical status and cognitive mechanisms internal to the figures, seen systemically, never died in the discipline of poetics, even when the emphasis shifted (in Kashmir) to the psychology of the listener as the key to understanding aesthetic experience. In music, ornamentation remains basic to the theory of performance and includes such figures of sound as were mentioned above, among many others.[36] But in both disciplines *alankāra*, which requires repeated acts of decoration, ritually regulated and familiar, is never a purely external business. The Sanskrit *ālankārikas* discuss at some length the very meaning of the term: decoration is not the inner essence (*ātma*) or even the actual body (*śarīra*) of poetry, yet it is in some ways like applying turmeric and saffron (*kunkuma-pītika*) to a woman's body.[37] Thus Abhinavagupta; others, such as Bhoja, distinguish external (*bāhya*, i.e., purely sound-based) ornaments from internal (*ābhyantara*, meaning-based) ones and from those that are at once external and internal (*bāhyābhyantara*—a category of some importance for the best poetry, *kāvya*).[38] The first category is like putting on clothes, bracelets, and so on. The second, entirely internal, is like brushing one's teeth or combing one's hair. The third is like bathing or, again, applying turmeric and sandal.

One can all too easily miss the significance of this last theme. Smearing turmeric paste on the body is no adventitious affair, and hardly external except in the sense of bringing someone—a goddess, for instance—into being. In South India, applying *kunkum* is clearly aimed at intensifying a deity's presence (*pasupp'ekkincaḍam* in Telugu) or deepening (or waking) the deity's self-awareness.[39] Turmeric soaks or seeps into the surface and—rather like the *mīṇḍ* glide—creates depth. Indeed, though applied externally, it ultimately belongs deep inside. The goddess, in fact, can be said *to be* this thick layer of *kunkum*. In this sense, adorning—*alankāra*—is really "making" or "making present." Literally, etymologically, the word means "making enough," and this ancient understanding of what we call "decoration" survives in both musical and poetic performance. The *alankāra* makes the emergent sonar force "enough" in the sense of causing it to become fully manifest. From here there is but a short step to the use of both poetry and song to "force" a god into being.[40]

Both recomposing (*samnidhāna*) and adorning (*alankāra*) belong to a much wider category that we could call marking, *lakṣaṇā*. When a space is opened up by a poem or a musical cadence, it needs to be marked if it is to continue to exist.[41] Marking fills the available space with coordinates that give it orientation, direction, velocity, and depth (these coordinates are, however, rarely fixed; they may shift continuously).[42] A theory of poetry or music in performance requires a nuanced theory of marking, which I cannot attempt here. (Such a theory might allow us to dispense with the symbolic once and for all.) But one major set of markings can be briefly outlined as our third pattern of repetition, which I have called *prati-bimbana*—literally, "reflecting." Such reflection can take many forms, none of which have much to do with the usual notion of mirroring as the reproduction of external surface. Think, rather, of the mirror as a generative space with attributes of depth, out of which complex reflections or, perhaps, self-replicating models can arise.

We see such reflections almost everywhere we look in South Asia, in all artistic media and, perhaps above all, in ritual forms.[43] They are sometimes relatively simple. In other cases they approximate the "coherence of overlaid cycles" of which A. L. Becker and Judith Becker have written (with reference to Javanese musical performance).[44] One level—verbal, rhythmic, sonar, or semantic—may be superimposed, with varying degrees of completeness and precision, on another. In effect, two relatively independent relational systems may thus coincide. In poetry, this type of coincidence or superimposition is usually called *śleṣa*, literally an embrace; we subsume it under paronomasia, but in fact *śleṣa* is widespread not only in verbal media[45] but also in music (the superimposition of two or more *rāgas*) and in visual art.[46] Correspondence and coincidence of this sort share part of the impulse to reconnect and recompose that we saw in our first pattern of repetition. Here, too, *śleṣa* could be set to open up a space that has attributes of complexity, extreme internal movement, surprising amalgams and combinations, and depth. Think, again, of the sympathetic vibration (*anuraṇana*) that replicates and corresponds to the initial striking of the string (*raṇana*).

Perhaps more common still, yet motivated by similar impulses, are those complex sets of musical or verbal images or constructions that reflect or model one another as complete, self-contained wholes, each element internal to one such complex corresponding more or less exactly to an element in the other. Musical repetition is replete with such patterns, as careful listening will reveal (in the elaboration of melodic lines, in the resonance of rhythm and melodic form, and so on). In poetry they are conspicuous, transparent, and explicitly thematized by the poeticians. Sanskrit poets have a marked fondness for these effects. In Vedic, for example, there is the complex syntactical repetition of an entire construction, which we call "responsion." "The most characteristic feature of responsions is that they typically possess a vertical dimension. That is, their internal linear (=horizontal) constituents may generally be placed in vertical alignment and match up, to a greater or lesser extent, on a word-for-word basis. When the alignment is exact, we may speak of a perfect (vertical) responsion."[47] Note that responsions may easily combine purely verbal (*śabda*) repetition with semantic (*artha*) repetitions.

Certain classical figures, *alaṅkāras*, have a preference for such constructions. Thus, Ruyyaka defines a class of similes in which one set of features, comprising a single entity, is "mirrored" by another, autonomous but corresponding set (*bimba-pratibimba-bhava*).[48] His example is taken from Kalidasa:

This Pandya king,
his shoulders draped with necklaces,
his body red with sandal paste,
is radiant as a regal mountain,
its peak on fire from the rising sun,
its slopes bursting with cascades.[49]

One set of images reveals the king, the second his reflection in the mountain; the necklaces correspond to the waterfalls, the red sandal-paste to the rubescent peak. Notice that the order of these images is reversed, mirror-like, in the reflection. But it is the nature of the link between the two sets that interests us; each is complex and theoretically self-contained, yet both, by definition, share common features that are present in the paired elements and that create a certain "sameness" (*sādharmya*), even, in this case, identity (*abheda*)[50] between the sets. This is repetition of a specific, fairly elaborate kind, modular in essence, extraordinarily coherent, and active on several levels (visual, linguistic-phonetic, logical, and semantic) simultaneously. Again, both horizontal and vertical vectors are present if we think of this simile as a single complex figure, like responsion.

Rūpaka, the "metaphoric" superimposition of one form upon another, similarly tends to the coincidence or far-reaching overlapping of complex sets, each with many elements that can be shown to correspond—although frequently such complex *rūpakas* leave a residue of at least one key element that has no pair.[51] One could easily continue along these lines, probing the major figures, but I believe the point is clear. On a different level entirely, we find complex modular repetition in such narrative structures as ring composition and embedded frames.[52] Indeed, the universal problem of framing can be shown to assume such reflective devices in classical India with astonishing regularity. What is more—and at this point we will have to leave marking and repetition for a more detailed study—such patterns are pregnant with metaphysical implication. They speak to a notion of reality, in varying intensities and degrees of integrity, as resonance, reflection, or modular repetition understood as eruption or manifestation (*āvir-bhāva*) from a deeper reservoir of existence, a restless domain driven by the undying urge to speak (*vivakṣā*).

5.

Following the musicologists, we have moved from *vivakṣā*, the wish to give voice, to *anuraṇana*, the resonance that marks appearance (*āvir-bhāva*) and that opens a space rich in specific patterns of repetition. We focused on three of the latter, all matters of marking (*lakṣaṇā*): the reintegration of what is dispersed in the course of becoming accessible to perception and cognition (*samnidhāna*); the intensification of being or presence that comes from adornment (*alankāra*); and the reflective range of modular coincidence, matching, or correspondence. Although these features by no means exhaust the arena of performance, they are all regularly present and make sense of some, at least, of what we hear. If we follow the logic of these systems, something always remains to be heard, something that resists audibility or visibility and that is, in a certain perspective, the true object of the performance.

Such an elusive object creates a special problem for indigenous theoreticians. Some, such as Sarngadeva, attempt to confront it head-on, only to shift rapidly into a grammar of what is audible after all. We can hardly complain about this, since our own investigation made the same, perhaps inescapable choice. A syntax of the apparent is what is allowed us and is no doubt enough to keep us busy for years. Still, we should bear in mind that we are standing on a somewhat brittle, attenuated surface. When musicians do speak of the more serious goal—*laya*, reabsorption, rhythmic reconnection—it is far more than a façon de parler.

Historically, poetics also took a somewhat devious path. If we follow the *rasa* theorists, we will surely be cut off from the deeper processes that Sanskrit poetry has undergone in the last thousand years. This is not to deny that *rasa* theory, as articulated by Abhinavagupta, has its own compelling vision of ultimacy, that is, of the transformative potential and true meaning of poetry. But most Sanskrit poetry is not, in fact, about *rasa* (and of course the same can be said about music). It is about the kind of effects that I have hinted at throughout this essay, and that normally assume an objective character. A poetry that enacts the move from the inaudible to the audible, and that then acts upon the audible by allowing for its disemergence, by reattaching discrete domains or unfolding space or bringing a god into being—such a poetry does impact upon what passes for reality, and not merely in a psychological sense. Such a poetry requires a new analytical framework if we are even to begin to understand its workings. In this sense, it is, once again, not so different from music.

Both the accomplished poet and the gifted singer are magically potent. They bring something seemingly remote to the surface, mark it in such a way that it comes fully alive on that surface, and allow for the further career of what has been thus marked. They cannot do this alone; an active listener is always necessary. Neither poetry nor music is a matter of silent participation. Neither of them is "expressive" in the common, Romantic use of the word. This point is worth repeating: these are disciplines that deal in objective process, empirically noted or experienced. A strong empiricist tendency survives in Sanskrit musicology; less so in poetics.

Once we begin to think along these lines, new, urgent questions arise. In southern India, at least, poetic praxis bifurcated in the late-medieval period (fifteenth and sixteenth centuries). On the one hand, a new, almost prosaic discursivity was discovered; Telugu poets began writing what are effectively modern novels, in metrical verse. At the same time, in both Tamil and Telugu, we see poetry that has cut loose from nearly everything discursive, almost from semanticity per se: poets begin to experiment with pure acoustic techniques, probing deep into the depths of language to create amazing symphonic works, rich in *śleṣa* and the modular imaging or coincidence of domains (visual and sonar) that we have mentioned. The objective, quasi-mathematical, often dissonant quality of these texts anticipates Schönberg by several centuries. No one—certainly none of the southern Indian poeticians—tried to produce a grammar of such radical enterprises. Equally striking, Sanskrit poetic theory also turned away from the *śabda*-based realm of pure musicality—at the very moment in which this realm was dramatically extending its range.[53] Why did this strange divide open up between praxis and theory at a moment of true creative innovation? Why were the theoreticians deaf to the new music the poets were inventing?

Fortunately, at least for music, we are not entirely dependent on the theoretical texts. We can still trust the sensitivity we bring to bear on living performance; and the living tradition of oral teaching is accessible and unusually rich in unrecorded insights, in both the north and south of India. For poetry, we need to reconstruct historical contexts of performance—and here the normative texts, though oblique to praxis, do have enormous value. But perhaps we should follow through more systematically the implications of a notion such as "resonance," at the same time relying, with our authors, on the reality of *camatkāra*—that involuntary "click of delight" that remains today, for both poeticians and connoisseurs, the dependable signal that performance works.[54]

Notes

I wish to thank my two music teachers, Pantula Rama of Visakhapatnam and Osnat El-Kebir of Varanasi and Tel Aviv, who made it real.

1. Bhartrhari envisages an intermediate stage of *prākṛta-dhvani*, "the phonological structure, the sound-pattern of the norm," triggered by the *vaikṛta-dhvani*. See Kunjunni Raja 1963, 120.
2. This verb, *vy-anj*, plays a critical role in all classical Indian aesthetic theory. It links two basic notions: "revealing, bringing into being, manifesting" (hence, "suggesting") and "decorating, adorning, beautifying." See section 4.
3. See Simhabhupala's commentary on this verse: "yo 'yaṃ varṇa-viśeṣam apratipadyamānasya dūrāt karṇa-patham avatarati mandatva-tīvratvâdi-bhedaṃ ca varṇeṣvāsañjayati sa dhvanir ity ucyate." "*Dhvani*—audible sound—is what reaches the ears from afar, from that which is not yet phonematic, and attaches various differentiated tonal qualities to phonemes." Cf. *Hatha-yoga-pradipika* 4.100.
4. Sarngadeva's psycho-physiological map has been studied by Mukund Lath (1998, 247–63). *Nirukta* of Yaska 1.18.
5. See discussion in Lath 1998, ibid. Sounds are produced by a process of internal combustion beginning in the depths of the body.
6. See Shulman 2001, 204–8.
7. Simhabhupala, citing Matanga (*Brhaddesi* 2.22), reverses the first two locations, thus locating the "extremely subtle" *nāda* in the heart—perhaps because of the Yogic identification of *anāhata-cakra* with the heart (*Sangita-ratnakara* 2.126). In *Brhaddesi*, *tālu* (palate) replaces *mūrdhan* (head).
8. The two major conduits of energy in the Tantric Yogic (subtle) body.
9. Lath 1998, 262.
10. This sentence condenses what is, in effect, a long historical development leading away from the notion of strictly fixed tones. See the brilliant, path-breaking discussion by Mukund Lath (1998, 307–35).
11. *Brhaddesi* 3.11.
12. Jackson 1991, 126.
13. Cf. *Brhaddesi* 3.1.
14. Kallinatha, 70.
15. Lath 1998, 324–30.
16. Kallinatha, 67.
17. Note that we are not speaking here of overtones.
18. *Sangita-ratnakara* 3.40–41. Similarly, if *ma* gives a lower *śruti* to *ga* and an upper *śruti* to *pa*, we have *madhyama-sadharana*; if *ma* gives two lower *śrutis* to *ga*, we have *antara-gandhara*. *Dha* can absorb the upper *śruti* of *pa*, thus attaining four *śrutis*. In sum, this will

give us 19 "clear" (*śuddha*) notes (7 "usual" *svaras* + 12 *vikāras*). See *Raghuvaṃśa* of Kalidasa 1.39, with the commentary of Mallinatha, on *cyuta-* and *acyuta-ṣaḍja*. The notion of overlapping is clearly very ancient.

19. Cf. *Brhaddesi* 3.28–43, apparently preferring the final answer.
20. *Ṣaḍ-rāga-candrodaya*, cited by Lath 1998, 329 (my emphasis).
21. Ibid.
22. *Sāngīta-pārijāta* 38. See Lath 1998, 331.
23. See Handelman and Shulman 2004.
24. *kramopasṛṣṭarūpā vāk*: *Vakya-padiya* 1.88; I adopt the apt translation of Jan Houben (1995, 278).
25. *Hatha-yoga-pradipika* 4.83–84.
26. As Carmel Berkson has argued forcefully, classical sculptors are not "representing" visible realities but are rather attempting to capture the moments and dynamics of emergence. See Berkson 2000.
27. See Rimon-Kenan 2002.
28. See Narayana Rao and Shulman 2002, 193–95.
29. For example, Klein, n.d., on stylistic variation in RgVeda; Brereton 1997; Handelman, n.d.
30. Including the specified relations of *vādi*, *samvādi*, *vivādi*, etc.
31. Similarly with *kampit* repetitions and *muran* "turns."
32. *Sangita-parijata* 1.12. On swinging more generally, see Shulman, n.d., *Nala Unhinged*.
33. Osnat El-Kebir, citing Ritvik Sanyal, in conversation with the author.
34. Reported from Mohineddin Dagar, private conversation.
35. *Locana* on *Dhvanyaloka* 2.4. Abhinavagupta seems to have borrowed this term from Bhattanayaka.
36. See *Sangita-ratnakara* 6 for a detailed list.
37. Abhinavagupta ad *Dhvanyaloka* 2.29.
38. This passage is discussed in a well-known essay by Raghavan 1973, 60.
39. See Flueckiger, n.d.
40. As in various ritual and liturgical texts; see Shulman 2001, 370–71 (on Annamayya).
41. See Narayana Rao and Shulman 2002, 190–96.
42. I wish to thank Don Handelman for discussion of this theme.
43. Very conspicuously in Vedic ritual, for example. Here it seems we can go beyond Brian Smith's (1989) somewhat limited principle of "resemblance" as constituting Vedic thought. Not resemblance but repetition, of this modular variety, is the underlying principle of creating reality. See also Malamoud 2002.
44. Becker 1995, 360. The Beckers speak of iconicity, the "nonarbitrariness of any metaphor" (350), as providing a logic to these overlays.
45. Sometimes on a staggering scale, as when a poetic text simultaneously tells the stories of the *Mahabharata* and the *Ramayana* by allowing for alternative segmentation and resegmentation of the words (e.g., the *Raghava-pandaviya* of Kaviraja).
46. See the pioneering study of Bronner 1999. For visual *śleṣa*, see Rabe 1997.
47. Klein, n.d., 10. He cites as an example of parisyllabic responsion RV 10.106ab: "asmabhyam gatuvittamo/devebhyo madhumattamah/."
48. *Alankara-sarvasva* 37–39 (under *upamā*).
49. *Raghuvaṃśa* 6.60: "pāṇḍyo 'yam aṃsârpita-lamba-hāraḥ klptânga-rāgaḥ haricandanena/ābhāti bālâtapa-rakta-sānuḥ sanirjharodgâra ivâdri-rājaḥ//."
50. As Appaya Diksita claims for *bimba-pratibimba-bhāva*.
51. The poeticians refer to this pattern as "samasta-vastu-viṣaya-(sâvayava)-rūpaka."
52. See the lucid exposition by Brereton 1997.
53. I thank Yigal Bronner for discussion of this point. We hope to pursue this question in a joint study.
54. See discussion in Shulman, n.d., "Notes on *Camatkāra*."

References

Alankāra-sarvasva of Ruyyaka. 1965. Ed. S. S. Janaki. Delhi: Meharchand Lachhmandas.

Becker, A.L. 1995. *Beyond Translation: Essays toward a Modern Philology*. Ann Arbor: University of Michigan Press.

Berkson, Carmel. 2000. *The Life of Form in Indian Sculpture*. New Delhi: Abhinava Publications.

Brereton, Joel. 1997. "'Why Is a Sleeping Dog Like the Vedic Sacrifice?' The Structure of an Upanisadic *Brahmodya.*" In *Inside the Texts, Beyond the Texts: New Approaches to the Study of the Vedas*, ed. M. Witzel, 1–14. Vol. 2, Harvard Oriental Series, Opera Minora. Cambridge, Mass.: Harvard University Press.

Bṛhaddeśī of Matanga. 1992. Ed. and trans. Prem Lata Sarma. Delhi: Indira Gandhi National Centre for the Arts.

Bronner, Yigal. 1999. "Poetry at Its Extreme: The Theory and Practice of Bitextual Poetry (*Śleṣa*) in South Asia." Ph.D. diss., University of Chicago.

Citra-mīmāṃsā of Appaya Dīkṣita. Varanasi: Chawkhamba, 1971.

Dhvanyāloka of Ānandavardhana. With the *Locana* of Abhinavagupta. 1935. Ed. Pandit Durgaprasad and Kasinath Pandurang Parab. Bombay: Nirnaya Sagar Press.

Dīkṣita, Appaya. See *Citra-mīmāṃsā.*

Flueckiger, Joyce B. n.d. "Guises, Turmeric, and Recognition in the Gangamma Tradition of Tirupati." In *Incompatible Visions: South Asian Religions in History and Culture*, ed. James Blumenthal. In press.

Handelman, Don. n.d. "Towards a Braiding of Frame." In *Behind the Mask*, ed. D. Shulman and D. Thiagarajan. Ann Arbor: Department of South and Southeast Studies. In press.

Handelman, Don, and D. Shulman. 2004. *Śiva in the Forest of Pines: An Essay on Sorcery and Self-Knowledge*. Delhi: Oxford University Press.

Haṭha-yoga-pradīpikā of Śāntārāma. Madras: Adyar Library.

Houben, Jan E.M. 1995. *The Sambandha-samuddeśa (Chapter on Relation) and Bhartṛhari's Philosophy of Language*. Groningen: Egbert Forsten.

Jackson, William J. 1991. *Tyagaraja, Life and Lyrics*. Delhi: Oxford University Press.

Klein, Jared. n.d. "Categories and Types of Stylistic Repetition in the Rig Veda." Forthcoming in the journal *Indo-Iranica*, Israel Academy of Sciences and Humanities.

Kunjunni Raja, K. 1963. *Indian Theories of Meaning*. Madras: Adyar Library.

Lath, Mukund. 1998. *Transformation as Creation: Essays in the History, Theory and Aesthetics of Indian Music, Dance and Theatre*. Delhi: Aditya Prakashan.

Malamoud, Charles. 2002. "A Body Made of Words and Poetic Meters." In *Self and Self-Transformation in the History of Religions*, ed. D. Shulman and G. Stroumsa, 19–28. New York: Oxford University Press.

Narayana Rao, Velcheru, and D. Shulman, trans. 2002. *The Sound of the Kiss, or The Story That Must Never Be Told: Piṅgali Sūranna's* Kaḷāpūrṇodayamu. New York: Columbia University Press.

Nirukta of Yāska. 1967. In *The Nighaṇṭu and the Nirukta*, ed. L. Sarup. Delhi: Motilal Banarsidass.

Powers, Harold. 1980. "India, Subcontinent of." In *The New Grove Dictionary of Music and Musicians*, ed. S. Sadie. Vol. IX. London: Macmillan.

Rabe, Michael. 1997. "The Mamallapuram Praśasti: A Panegyric in Figures." *Artibus Asiae* 57: 189–241.

Raghavan, V. 1973. *Studies on Some Concepts of the Alankara Sastra*. Madras: Adyar Library.

Raghuvaṃśa of Kalidasa. 1982. Delhi: Motilal Banarsidass.

Rimon-Kenan, Shlomit. 2002. *Narrative Fiction: Contemporary Poetics (New Accents)*. London: Routledge.

Saṅgīta-pārijāta of Ahobala. 1879. Ed. Kalivara Vedantabagisa and Sarada Prasada Ghosha. Calcutta: The New Sanskrit Press.

Saṅgīta-ratnâkara of Śārṅgadeva. With *Kalānidhi* of Kallinātha and *Sudhâkara* of Siṃhabhūpāla. 1943. Ed. S. Subrahmanya Sastri. 2 vols. Madras: Adyar Library.

Saṅgīta-ratnâkara of Śārṅgadeva. 1991. Ed. and trans. R. K. Shringy and Prem Lata Sharma. Delhi: Munshiram Manoharlal.

Shulman, David. 2001. *The Wisdom of Poets: Studies in Tamil, Telugu and Sanskrit*. Delhi: Oxford University Press.

——. n.d. "Nala Unhinged: Pukalentippulavar's *Naḷaveṇpā*." Ed. Susan Wadley. In press.

——. n.d. "Notes on *Camatkāra*." Forthcoming in a volume of *Indo-Iranica*, Israel Academy of Sciences and Humanities.

Smith, Brian. 1989. *Reflections on Resemblance, Ritual, and Religion*. New York: Oxford University Press.

Chapter Three

SONGS OF LOVE, IMAGES OF MEMORY

Saskia Kersenboom

I.1. Alapana One: Mood and Melody

Sa Ri MaGaMaGaMaaa Pa Dha SaNiSaNiSaa
SaNiSaNi DhaNiDhaNiDha Paa Ma MaGaRi Sa

These musical notes form the ascending and descending scales of the raga
Bhairavi. However, they do not move from one fixed position to the next.
Instead, some passages elaborate the trajectory between the notes and create an effect that is characteristic of the raga. For example, in Bhairavi the
ascent from Ri to Ma envelops the position of Ga, while Dha investigates
the possibilities of Ni as it moves to Sa. These embellishments create the
exhilarating optimism, resolve, and grandeur of this raga. The descending
scale evokes an entirely different world of emotions: the path from Ni to Pa
deepens the Dha in anxiety; it pierces the senses with intense longing and
gasps for breath in the passage from Ma to Ri via a sad Ga.

The song "Kamakshi anudinamu" is a Telugu composition by Shyama
Shastri (1762–1827) in the classical tradition of southern India. Its structure
sets off with improvisatory explorations into the melodic scope of the raga
Bhairavi. This research, called "alapana," intones the vast contrast between faith, love, vulnerability, and trust on the one hand, and doubt,
indignation, melancholy, or affliction on the other. In terms of "Kamakshi
anudinamu," this means both deep devotion and utter helplessness, as
well as the ardent plea for generous compassion. Shyama Shastri was a
true devotee of the goddess Kamakshi; his father served her as priest. Like
his father he performed her ritual worship in the same temple. Tradition
holds that he composed most of his songs during the moments that he

spent in its inner shrine.[1] His devotional inspiration was deeply rooted in the Cosmology of the Shri Vidya cult, a topic to which I shall return later. Paccimiriyam Adiyappa, who played the southern Indian lute, the vina at the royal court of Tanjore, groomed him into a subtle musician in whom the creative artist, inspired devotee, and erudite scholar combine. In each of his compositions the emotional richness of the raga couples mood to rhythmical structure (Seetha 1981, 208–9).

In the first melodic improvisations K. G. Vijayakrishnan (born 1952) opens up these emotional realms and guides us via rich elaborations into the landscape of raga Bhairavi. His art is in a direct line of inheritance for over two hundred years, right down to the composer. K. G. Vijayakrishnan studied vina from childhood with his mother Karpagavalli, a student of R. Rangaramanuja Ayyangar who learned southern Indian music through the phenomenal example set by T. Vina Dhanammal (1867–1938). She in turn is considered the grand dame of southern Indian music for the vina, as a direct descendant from the professional musicians and dancers at the Tanjore court. The compositions of Shyama Shastri and his son Subbaraya Shastri were felt to be property of her family as the student and devotee of goddess Shri Kamakshi. Her grandmother carried the name of their family deity, Kamakshiyamma; it is well known that during Navaratri, the festival of nine nights dedicated to the goddess, Dhanammal would arrange a bough of fragrant jasmine and rose flowers, sit under it, and play the vina after applying sandal paste mixed with pure rose water to her body. At that moment she would be an incarnation of goddess Sarasvati herself. During ordinary weeks she offered a vina concert on Fridays in worship of Shri Sarasvati, the goddess of learning who holds the vina in her hands. The instrument is often referred to as Sarasvati Vina, in contrast to the northern Indian variant, the Rudra Vina. K. G. Vijayakrishnan keeps up this tradition of Friday concerts. He played the svarajati "Kamakshi anudinamu" during a Friday concert on June 11, 1999 in Leiden, Holland.

In our example, the svarajati "Kamakshi anudinamu," he establishes the emotional intensity in the very first notes. The alapana builds up a depth of feeling by its purely instrumental treatment of the melodic scope of the raga Bhairavi. Once the mood has been established, a clear rhythmical structure emerges in which melody, rhythm, and poetry find their way into the compositional structure of the svarajati; sometimes their synergy prompts the performer to sing the underlying poetic song along with the vina. Shyama Shastri was famous for his treatment of this compositional form. A svarajati follows the traditional three-part structure of the southern Indian basic form, the kriti, and consists of a pallavi, an anupallavi, and several charanams (te Nijenhuis 1974, 100–115). Indian musical theory plays freely with the metaphor of growth: the introductory alapana prepares the feeding ground from which the stem of the tree, the pallavi, can sprout. The stem generates its branch, the anupallavi that grows its rich foliage, called charanam. In the case of this svarajati, K. G. Vijayakrishnan stresses that his mother's teacher, R. Rangaramanuja Ayyangar, did not separate the first lines into a separate pallavi and anupallavi. However, as a metaphor of organic growth, the standard musical progression will frame and develop our central argument in gradual movements of the following parts: (1) alapana, exploration through improvisations and elaborations; (2) pallavi and anupallavi, articulation; and (3) charanam, incorporation. As in a musical concert, a short mangalam, or fruition, will conclude this essay as the fourth movement. The first movement, the alapana, will be approached in three different ways: musically, theoretically, and visually. The second and third movements, the pallavi and anupallavi, and eight charanams, will interrelate the song text, the recording of the vina, the audiovisual, and hint at the theoretical first movements. The mangalam summarizes this musical essay in the light of the aesthetics of performance.[2]

I.2. Alapana Two: Performance and Aesthetics

The Sanskrit term alapana literally means conversation, exchange, discussion; in music it is an exploration of feelings, moods, motifs, a getting acquainted with the performers, their skills, their tastes; it tests the rapport with the audience and sets out a scope for an artistic experience. Who are the players in our alapana of thoughts on performance and its aesthetics? What arguments do they bring to the discussion? First of all, there is Bharata, the legendary authority on Indian performing arts; he hosts our reflection, "Songs of Love, Images of Memory." Our conversation includes Victor Turner, who foregrounds the dramatic mode of human culture, and Johan Huizinga, who understands the same in terms of "the ludic." William Dilthey and Michael Csikszentmihalyi[3] reflect upon its experiential dimensions. How does this alapana evolve? Which ideas meander freely through our improvisatory introduction?

The leitmotif is set by Bharata; he proposes that performance apportions "good luck as well as the lack of it."[4] Its relevance and validity are rooted in the interaction between gods and humankind. Performance as a mode of metaphysical communication, called Natya, was created by Brahma, the Creator, himself:

A performance of Natya reveals the state-of-being of the three worlds, it serves as a method of instruction, it supports this world and it maintains "the coherence of eternity." Brahma advises all gods to engage themselves in Natya; they will enjoy worship that brings them good luck when they descend through Natya in the world of mortals. (...) Not only the gods who descend in Natya enjoy good-luck, the organizer and the performer of the ritual will enjoy good luck, happiness and wealth as well; finally, they will even reach heaven.

The pragmatic nature of Natya earns its qualifications as an applied science. Any Natya performance should be clear about its aim, method, and precision of procedures. Therefore, Brahma taught this science to Bharata in the form of a performance manual: the Natyashastra. He has in turn introduced colleague-sages in the theoretical part of the manual, first dealing with crucial questions concerning the origin, purpose, and operating principles:

> From the onset of the silver age people became characterized by the codes of village life; passions like lust, greed, power, joy, anger, etc., created experiences of well-being as well as unhappiness. The gods kind of "lost contact" because people following the sensuous village ways were not allowed to either recite or hear the four original Vedas, and therefore they felt lonely and neglected. So, the gods, too, wanted to sway with emotion and sensuous experience. They asked Brahma to create some form of play that would engage both the eye and the ear. Only in this way communication could be restored. Brahma went into deep concentration, distilled the sensory essence from the four existing Vedas, and processed it into a fifth Veda: the Veda of Natya.

Side by side, Bharata trained his one hundred sons in the practical part of the manual and ordered them to apply this expertise in the form of powerful performances (NSh.I-7ff).

I.2.i. Melodic Explorations

A number of central features emerge from Bharata's opening statements: first, the essence of performance is sensory. Brahma's crucial innovation was to distill the aural, visual, olfactory, tactile, and gustatory energies from the earlier four Vedic ritual texts, to process them into the performance of Natya and thereby to restore communication between the gods and humankind. This new science was first and foremost experiential. Second, performance should be free and authoritative. Both the villagers and the gods were eager to enter the Natya and involve themselves fully in this interaction. Third, performance "works" on a physical as well as on a metaphysical level. Bharata is quite clear about its force: Natya bears fruit, it generates well-being for the king, the country, and the people; even the gods renew their strength and return to their realms with fresh energy.

I.2.i.a.-1. Improvisation: Experience

Victor Turner pleads for an anthropology that understands other people and their expressions on the basis of experience. He is convinced that "we can learn from experience—from the enactment and performance of culturally transmitted experiences of others." But how? In his plea for an anthropology and theatre of experience, he feels deeply indebted to William Dilthey, whose understanding of experience in terms of *Erlebnis* opens up a very promising road for reflection on experience and its realization through performative expression. Dilthey himself argued with Kant about the data of experience. According to Kant, the data out of which experience emerges are basically empty; according to Dilthey, they certainly are not. First, all forms of thought including experience can be analyzed in terms of formal relationships that make up structures of experience. Second, within these structural relationships Erlebnis unfolds in five moments. In the course of this process, the last moment completes Erlebnis in real time and real space through performative expression (Turner 1982, 13ff).

I would propose that the data out of which experience emerges reside in memory and become accessible through imagination; it is through dramatic performance that experience is made explicit and activated. Csikszentmihalyi contributes a third characteristic of experience to the discussion. He diagnoses the processes of experience as "flow." While Dilthey speaks of the processual development of experience in five moments, and Huizinga attributes five characteristics of the "sacred play," Csikszentmihalyi analyzes six "elements," "qualities," or "distinctive features" in the "flow experience." These voices are in unison with Bharata's analysis of the development of experience. He distinguishes five movements of "bhava," that is, "phases of 'being' into a resultant stage of 'rasa,' which means 'juice,' 'taste' and at the same time the 'process of tasting.'" These moments, characteristics, elements, and phases will form rich variations of themes in the reflection on performance and recur throughout the course of this essay.[5]

I.2.i.a.-2. Improvisation: Freedom
All discussants agree on the second point that experience has to be free and authoritative in order to affect both the performer and the spectator. Bharata's villagers forced Brahma to create a ritual performance that would suit their temperament, expertise, and authority. Even the gods desired that worship should take the form of Natya; they were eager to descend into the world of humans and enter the performance. Huizinga joins the discussion and points out that freedom is the basic condition for play, in particular for "serious, sacred play." The ludic is voluntary activity; this is true for those who freely believe in its sacred status, its beauty, and wholesome efficacy. Therefore, the serious, sacred play or *sacer ludus* is "off-ordinary," it transcends the fragmentation of daily life, it has a homogenizing effect on the players and their world. Huizinga points out that the players' sense of freedom, belief, and truth should not be disrupted: during its performance "unbelievers" should rather "play false" and "pretend to believe" than that they would openly question the magic circle that the performance establishes. The cynic is ousted and advised to find his own playground (Huizinga 1955, 7–13).

Performers of a *sacer ludus* form a select group that develops into an intimate and internally free community. Csikszentmihalyi distinguishes the existence of a community that flows together by its noncontradictory demand for action and unambiguous feedback. Similarly Bharata's villagers had their own way in seeing their Natya established as the fifth Veda. Neither a forceful access to the other four Vedas nor a forced conversion to these ritual traditions, or a forced policy the other way round, would have worked. Even the gods understood this, and for the sake of effective communication they followed Brahma's advice to engage themselves in Natya.

Both Turner and Huizinga underline the importance of the limen, of borders that demarcate sacred space and sacred time. Internal freedom can exist by the grace of borders and border control. Freedom takes shape not in spontaneous, impulsive action but rather within careful and methodically regulated behavior. Adherence to rules that are taught, internalized, and lovingly executed generates the sense of freedom that we could call serious, off-ordinary, and beatific. Rules do not figure here as limitations but rather as trigger, as the cradle of freedom.

I.2.i.a.-3. Improvisation: Force

Apart from the characteristics of experience and freedom, the element of force is evident in Bharata's leitmotif: the Natya performance apportions good luck, shubha, as well as its absence, ashubha. Good luck can take many shapes: material fruits like prosperity, vitality, and fertility will be generated for the king, the country, and the people; even the gods who have entered the performance will leave the event strengthened and with fresh energy.

Performance creates strong affects that generate powerful effects on the performers and their audience (figure 3.1). The major effect that comes true in performance is "mangalam," "auspiciousness," or "beatitude," "beatitudo" according to Huizinga. He holds that even after the performance has ended, a beatific holiness lingers, affecting every detail of the performance. Dilthey detects a special "clarity" of awareness due to a special strength or energy in the evocation of past experience. Csikszentmihalyi sees flow as "autotelic," or as a force that yields goods and rewards but only within its own realm of experience. In the chain of cause, affect, and effect we see that affects come about only by careful engineering of the performance. Within the demarcation in time and space, says Huizinga, performers create a field that is very tense: every detail counts; the performance is the sacred order and at the same time creates that order. Csikszentmihalyi observes an intense centering of attention. While in flow, awareness and action are fully focused on the "now" of the event; this in its own turn creates a powerful feeling of control over one's own actions and the environment. Dilthey explains the clarity in the evocation of past experience by a very intense energy or *Kraft*. Again he locates that force not in an empty realm of data but in a very tightly knit tissue of three "strands of thought." These strands are thought, feeling, and will; together they connect memory, value, and decision in the moment of performance.

Figure 3.1 Darshanam: Seeing and being seen

Video still from *Darshanam* by Thomas Voorter.

I.2.ii.a.-1. Elaboration: Experience as Rite and Myth

The alapana now moves into deeper elaborations of the themes of experience, freedom, and force. We will investigate how the three strands of thought are actually knit into the formal relationships that Dilthey hinted at earlier. He called these formal categories: unity and multiplicity, likeness and difference, whole and part, degree, and similar elementary concepts. They form a network within which all thought about any subject matter can be enclosed (Turner 1982, 12–13). Such structures of experience are not bloodless, static cognitive structures. Cognition as such forms an important dimension of any structure of experience. Behind Dilthey's worldview is the basic idea of "a total human being," at grips with his environment, perceiving, thinking, feeling, desiring: here "life embraces life" in the interactions between man and his world. This total human being embraces life time and again to experience himself as total, or he does so in order to become total in different stages in his life. The processes of change and transformation rank as the foremost theme of coming to grips with oneself, one's environment, and one's interaction with the world. How should we imagine such structures that accommodate these formal relationships and categories of thought in a lasting yet flexible manner? In search of an answer to this question we turn to Van Gennep. Originally Van Gennep intended to use the phrase "rite of passage" for rituals accompanying an individual's or a cohort of individuals' changes. He distinguishes the following three phases in any rite of passage: separation, transition, and reaggregation, or incorporation (in Turner 1982, 24). These rites are by their very nature a fluid integration of structures and processes, and we will examine them later as "performing" and "becoming." Through symbolic behavior the performers of the rite transform from one phase of being into another. The first phase, separation, clearly demarcates sacred space and time from profane or secular space and time; it operates through sub-rites that change their qualities, so that the performer enters a realm out of space and out of time.

Moreover, it includes symbolic behavior that reverses or inverses objects, relationships, and processes that are considered ordinary into new situations that seem acutely different or detached. During the second phase, transition, the subject passes through a period and area of ambiguity, a kind of vexing limbo that has to be transgressed and left behind. The third phase of either reaggregation or incorporation opens a new perspective to the ritual performer: now, the subject enters into a new state-of-being, an experiential rebirth that was longed for at the outset of the rite of passage. The images that initially evoked this longing are images stored in memory. They form the data out of which experience emerges. Imagination unlocks these data and directs their articulation in dramatic performance. It is in this sacred play that rite and myth come true.

I.2.ii.a.-1.i.Rite: Performing and Becoming
Inspired by the performative experiments of Richard Schechner, Victor Turner explored the dialectic movement between flow (Csikszentmihalyi) and reflexivity that characterizes performative genres. When rites of passage are understood as performances that bring about a lasting change, we might infer that to perform means to reflect in a pragmatic, experiential way; it also means to learn in the process of flow and even to transform gradually during that process into a new state of being. Turner's dialectic between performing and learning is extended to a dialectic playground where performing and learning gradually turn into a new becoming.

In chapter 6 of his Natyashastra, Bharata traces the birth of rasa, the experiential "tasting" from beginning to end via various stages-of-becoming called bhava. From a germinal cause (vi-bhava), an effect automatically follows (anu-bhava). This state-of-being sets out to interact with the world (vi-abhi-cari-bhava), reaching out to the world and being affected by it. In today's practice of mimetic dance, a further stage in investigation is termed "concurrent stages-of-being" (sam-cari-bhavas). These can be best understood as associative chain-reactions triggered off in communication. At this point we are reminded of Dilthey; he saw how meaning emerges from "feelingly thinking" about the interconnections in past and present, and from the "evocation of past experience." When this cumulative and associative process has been going on for some time, a dominant state-of-being is generated in the flow of the process. This dominant state (sthayi-bhava) prepares the spontaneous surge of rasa. The taste of devotion, of Bhakti as "melting into belonging" and as "surrender" to an all-encompassing love, herald an ultimate becoming, a return to the unambiguous, holistic unity of life; this taste craves an incorporation, an "ultimate transformation" that was the cause of all longing expressed in Bhairavi alapana.

I.2.ii.a.-1.ii. Myth: World and Genre

Dilthey argued that the data out of which experience emerges are rooted in the structures of experience. I suggest that these data are drawn from memory and organized strategically in the course of performance. I propose that these strategies resemble the formal relationships that underlie the structures of experience, and that they organize the various moments of Erlebnis or of the experience of flow in an optimal way. Memory itself is the key to the cognitive dimension of experience and operates through sensory activation.

Turner sets out to search for semantic dimensions in the working of symbols. He gropes for a comparative symbology, for various types of meaning in language and context to pause at the concept of what he calls "dynamic semantic systems." These systems manifest themselves not only in traditional "tribal" cultures but also in the "cultural refreshment" genres such as poetry, drama, and painting (Turner 1982, 22). They produce simultaneously the structures and processes of meaning in performance. Their semantic potential contextualizes symbols in the concrete, historical fields of their use by "men alive" as they act, react, transact, and interact socially. Even when the symbolic is the inverse of the pragmatic reality, it remains intimately in touch with it, affects it, and is affected by it. Symbolic presence provides the positive figure within its negative ground, thereby delimitating each.

At last we have arrived at a crucial step in the reflection upon the experience of meaning in performance. Whether we speak about the ludic, the *sacer ludus*, about ritual performance, social drama, or theatrical drama, these performances are not only about worlds, they constitute worlds and their underlying cosmologies in the very process of their being performed, communicated, and shared. Performances do not tell stories, they generate them. Here the term "Cosmos" rings true; the world that is being created and shared is truly beautiful. (I will consider in more detail later the relationship between Cosmos, Myth, and Rite in performance.) Turner's search for a comparative symbology couples the notion of "dynamic semantic systems" to "genres of social drama." In our terms of performance we may restate this quest as the search for the strategic intelligence of rite, coupled to an evocative, compelling myth to establish a Cosmos that generates a sense of flow within and among its performers. Bharata would gladly join this discussion and suggest that the experience of flow has close affinity to rasa as juice, taste, tasting in experiencing the resultant of a performance. In the development of rasa structure, process and contextual data flow together and transcend both verbal and nonverbal communication. This cognitive approach frees us from the sociohistorical demarcation of genres, or that of literary genres. Bharata's approach to genre is remarkable in its broad, conceptual scope and at the same time in its capacity for minute detail. He distinguishes eight rasas: the erotic (shringara), the heroic (vira), the compassionate (karuna), wonder (adbhuta), laughter (hasya), fear (bhayanaka), disgust (bibhatsa), fury (raudra); a ninth rasa of transcendence (shanta) was added later to the original eight. I would like to suggest that these final emanations of rasa are rooted in eight different worlds, each producing their own genre, forces, and experiences. They form a cognitive base that might well be the structures of experience that Dilthey was hinting at, organizing memory in an easily recognizable and accessible form.

I.2.ii.b. Elaboration: Freedom as Memory and Scope

The etymology of the Sanskrit term "smara" covers memory, love, and worship, as well as the god of eros, Kama, whose five arrows pierce the five senses. Once again this cluster of possible meanings, objects, and physical realities points in the direction of memory as a key to experience that unlocks by sensory activation. It attributes the storage of memory not to the brain but to the senses. It also broadens the content of memory far beyond information into the realm of imagination. One step further allows imagination the status of fantasy and brings us to the striking statement by Frank Smith (1985): "Reality is fantasy that works." In trying to break away from the model that perceives language as synonymous with communication, communication with the transmission of information and the brain as the repository of that information, Smith suggests another metaphor. According to him the brain contains nothing less than a "theory of the world." The world in all its dynamic complexity never ceases to impress our senses with a vast array of signals. All these signals would constitute information according to the information theory, but this turns out not to be so. Only those signals that can be interpreted can yield a sense of direction; the rest is "noise." In this sense, information can only exist in the world, not in the brain. What the brain must contain is the understanding that can interpret signals, that can transform noise into clarity—therefore, the brain should contain a "theory of the world" (Smith 1985, 195–213).

How does the brain learn to form such theory? As an alternative to data storage, information model. Smith sees the brain as "artist": the brain learns the way an artist learns, not by accumulating facts but by exploring possibilities, by testing its own creations. In fact, the brain learns best when it is most creative. This creativeness brings out the brain's talent to create experiences for itself and for others. Here we are reminded of Dilthey's "feelingly thinking" and "evocation of past experiences" and Bharata's "double interaction" (vy-abhi-cari-bhava) and "concurrent associations" (sam-cari-bhava). These experiences are the experiences of worlds that the brain creates on the basis of its own theory of the world. The data for its creative theory are all past experiences interpreted in a sense that makes sense. It contains all our knowledge, beliefs, and expectations about the objective world in which we find ourselves. This scope of imagination is called "manodharma," a term freely translated as the "realm of the mind" but most often understood in Western translations as "improvisation" in music and mime, although in fact it constitutes the artistic research of the brain, making sense of the world. Manodharma explores the worlds of feeling, or the coherence of feeling, that grid of empathy that generates a "theory of the world." This theory creates symbolic presence as a positive figure, as a Cosmos within its negative ground, that is, Chaos full of "noise." In the process of that creation it delimitates Cosmos and Chaos in a crystal-clear fashion. It does so by means of performance, by interactive performances that bring worlds into contact with each other, merge or separate them, testing their theories of the world, and that ultimately make imagination work.

Freedom is the inner dynamic of memory as "smara": memory, love, and worship. A free selection of memory forms the basis for the theory of the world that is acted out in performance.

I.2.ii.c. Elaboration: Force as Prism in Action

In his pivotal essay, "The Anthropology of Performance," Victor Turner underlines his epistemological position in the tradition that stresses "lived experience" (Turner, 1987 72–99). He sharply distinguishes between static models for thought and action, such as cosmologies, philosophical systems, ethical systems, and ideologies and what Dilthey calls Weltanschauung. The former are static, the latter is dynamic. He shares his fascination with the "riddle of life" that presents itself in humankind's unending struggle amidst the forces and necessities of nonhuman nature, the never-ending task of satisfying with limited means unlimited appetites, the paradoxes of social control in which a person's or a group's loyalty to a legitimate cause, or a moral principle, automatically renders the individual disloyal to other causes that are possibly equally valid—in summary, the "whole mystery of humanity in the world" (Turner 1987, 85). Dilthey insists that experience is equally woven from three strands: one of thought, one of feeling, and one of will, thus experience has a three-sided structure, like a prism. He further analyzes the nature of these strands as the cognitive force that formulates a body of knowledge and belief about what is understood to be the "real world," the connative force of value judgements that relates adherents to the world and its meaning, and the third strand as the affective force of the "action of the will," in which at the moment of praxis, social interaction, the individual develops himself and in doing so society at large (in Turner 1987, 85).

This powerful constant correlation of knowledge-structures, processes of application and environments of acceptance, is found in a striking way in the cosmologies that underlie and frame the devotion to the goddess Kamakshi. Her worship is deeply rooted in the epistemology of Shri Vidya "Auspicious Wisdom," a pan-Indian goddess-centered whose roots are traceable to the sixth century. Shri Vidya centers on the beneficent mother goddess as Amba, "mother," or as Shakti, the dynamic principle of the force of life. As a form of Tantric Shaktism it flourishes today in both north and South India among women and men of many castes (Brooks 1992, xiii). In the Tantric Shaktism of Shri Vidya the goddess is the focus of ritual worship because she is the source of the individual Self's own, self-cognitive reflection as an "I." She thus provides the initial access to the source of cognitive reflection, a concrete framework of abstraction as well as the possibility of ultimate realization. The "Auspicious Wisdom," or Shri Vidya, is an expression of primordial sound (Skt. "vac" or "shabda"). However, it is not merely "one" of the phonic emanations that parallel the material world but "the" form from which the whole of creation has evolved. Her presence is understood as the living presence of "Vakshakti," the Force of Speech. Within this Weltanschauung each stage of speech is associated with the goddess in a particular aspect and each of these corresponds to her creative forces of desire (Skt. "iccha"), knowledge (Skt. "jnana"), and action (Skt. "kriya"). Each of these divine aspects of the Shakti is identified with a corresponding male deity and his respective powers. In her supreme form, the goddess emerges as "Mother," that is, as Amba, Ambika (Skt.), Ammal/Ambal or Amman (Ta.). In this form she is wholly identical to the eternal Shiva and at the same time involved in the process of transforming herself into the universe (cf. Brooks 1992, 91–92).

As proof of the confluence of static knowledge structures, models of thought, and processes of application, we find the prismic pyramid of the Shri Yantra on the outer temple grounds, while the procession of the triple form of the goddess moves in a fast pace with intense energy and exertion around the focal point of power: the sanctum sanctorum hidden in another two layers of temple walls. Here, in the inner shrine, resides the tranquil, central, pitch-black image of Shri Kamakshi. The three-dimensional pyramid structure of the Shri Yantra outside is represented inside by its two-dimensional diagrammatic version, installed in front of the central goddess. Both express the dialectics of structure and process in a strikingly concrete way: a complex of intertwining triangles pointing upward and downward. The triangles pointing upward represent the forces of structuring, abstraction, and transcendence, while the triangles pointing downward deal with processes of concretization and creation. It is interesting to note that five triangles point downwards against four upwards. In anthropomorphic form it explains the appearance of the male figure who precedes the procession of Shri Kamakshi: he is Shri (Adi) Shankaracharya, the primordial ascetic, sage, teacher, and "super-Brahmin" who took his abode in Kanchipuram to "counterbalance" the powerful presence of goddess Kamakshi as Parashakti, the "supreme power." Local stories tell of Shri Kamakshi's uncontrollable temper as she was moving out of her temple during the nights creating havoc in the city in the form of goddess Kali. Shri (Adi) Shankaracarya prayed with intense devotion to Kamakshi and appeased her wrath. He made her promise that she would not leave her abode without his permission.[6] However, considering both the audiovisual *Darshanam* and the song text "Kamakshi Anudinamu" reveals the division of labor, attention, and power between the two.[7] It is evident that the sight of Amba Kamakshi as a triple icon, with her aspects of Parvati and Sarasvati on her sides, answers and nourishes the deep desires and hopes of the vast majority of the devotees present.

The prism of her Shakti, her power as Vakshakti, the Goddess of Speech, articulates itself through the forces of knowledge, action, and desire; as such it finds a shared ground in metaphysical speculations on the Tamil language. The saint Tirumular (from the sixth century C.E.) describes himself as "one who has been ruminating the rare food 'Muttamil' that forms the essence of the eternal form of Shiva" (Kersenboom 1995, 7). The term Muttamil, the threefold Tamil, is central here. It indicates that the Tamil language is not considered to be just one, that is, a language of words alone. Tamil is a language that expresses itself through three limbs: one of words (iyal), one of sounds (icai), and one of images (natakam). These three media of word, sound, and image can be identified as the triadic power of the goddess as knowledge, action, and desire. In stanza 15 of his "Tirumantiram" (Holy Mantra) Tirumular prides himself on the fact that "the Lord has made me well in order that (I) make him well in Tamil." This performative aspect connects the Tamil language as threefold Mutamil with the triadic prism in Sanskrit-Tantric-Shaktism and the three strands of experience of Dilthey that weave performance into a powerful and effective event.[8]

I.3. Alapana Three: Appearance and Sight

I.3.i. Appearance

In our first alapana of sound we hinted at the investigations in mood and melody of the tonal scale of the raga Bhairavi. These investigations do not express themselves well on paper but can be followed in an actual performance of raga Bhairavi, available in the audio recording of K. G. Vijayakrishnan's rendering on the vina. The second "alapana of word" tries to trace the motivations that underlie human performance. These orientations to the world, or Weltanschaungen, in the words of Dilthey, must be performed to gain "critical mass" like all else that motivates humankind in order to become "real," that is, to interact with and ultimately affect life in a concrete way. Where does the third alapana take place, the alapana of image, of the living metaphor, that foregrounds life that embraces life? These musings, preludes, pragmatic reflections, and procedures of performance take place deep in the soil, in the dark humidity of the earth, during the night and in the no-man's-land of social utility.

In Indian terms, a festival, an utsava[9] marks mainly a procession. The Friday evening procession in Kanchipuram shown in the Voorter's audiovisual file is a succinct example of an utsava. Hindu temples organize their rituals of worship, basically, along three parameters of time and three parameters of space. Time cycles return in concentric ways: the daily worship finds its place in the regular festival calendar or in the rituals that have been offered as private initiatives by patron-devotees (Kersenboom 1987, 87ff.). In the case of this Friday evening procession we encounter a weekly festival. At the same time, a similar procession is performed every day in the form of a small-scale indoor circumambulation of the sanctum sanctorum. Private initiatives do not follow the logic of the day, the week, the half month, month, or season but take place in a moment that is considered "auspicious " according to astrological calculations. The dimension space makes a basic division between indoor and outdoor shrines, altars, or platforms, indoor and outdoor icons and rituals. A third space of ritual worship is the human body itself and its internal and external processes. The ritual idiom expresses in infinite variations degrees of the process of "incorporation" of devotees into the central icon of the shrine, the so-called root-icon (mula-vigraha). This central icon is fixed in the "womb-chamber" (garbha-griha). Devotees can come to see the god or goddess on a daily basis (Skt. "darshana," Ta. "taricanam," anglicized as "darshanam") and thus secure their close ties to the divine. On the other hand, the god or goddess him or herself sets out to incorporate the territory in and outside the temple in the course of a procession.[10] For this purpose an anthropomorphic, ambulant icon, or utsava murti, is ritually prepared for an outdoor circumambulation. Such ritual circumambulation can traverse smaller or larger concentric circles. The icon may stay within the protection of walls of the inner shrine, but it may also move out into the outer courtyard, or it may enter into the streets that surround the temple. Sometimes the icon travels even further into the town or the village. All images of gods sprout from a seed that is planted with great ritual care under the pedestal of the icon. This vegetative logic shapes the alapana of image, its emergence, and visual accessibility of the god or goddess. This emergence transforms the "life quality" of the image from the status of an "icon" to that of an "index," as a marker, an emergent presence, a living sign for all to behold and to interact with (Kersenboom 1995, 49ff.). Without the necessary and correct rites, the image remains but an icon and does not come to life as an index-ical presence. By implication, a god or goddess may decide to leave the image and withdraw the indexical quality from the material form of the statue, if he or she feels neglected or improperly served.

The procession of Shri Kamakshi on her golden chariot takes places every Friday evening around 7:30 p.m. and draws large crowds of devo-tees (figure 3.2). Hindu temple manuals attribute the concrete generation of material enjoyment (bhukti) and transcendent liberation from rebirth (mukti) to a procession; it is considered divine and yields pleasure for all in the three worlds of gods, of mankind and of the dark, chthonic forces; it is auspicious and causes victory, success in everything, beauty and the desired fruits of all wishes; it destroys all enemies, makes the demons (bhutas and raksasas) perish, and shields all mortals. In the words of vil-lagers, the force of a procession is simple: "it brings prosperity to the peo-ple, and, it instills some kind of knowledge" (Reiniche 1979, 110). The

Figure 3.2 Shri Kamakshi in procession

Video still from *Darshanam* by Thomas Voorter.

Kumaratantra, a Sanskrit manual for Hindu worship, distinguishes sixteen steps in the performance of an utsava. These in their turn can be grouped into eight "movements" of performance (Kersenboom 1987, 107ff.). The first three movements are as follows:

I. Preparation of the site: step 1, sowing of the seed (ankura); and step 2, the fire offering (shikhi yaga);
II. Starting signal: step 3, beating of the ritual drum (bheritadana), and step 4, hoisting of the banner of the gods (dhvajarohana);
III. Preparation of the god to be taken outside the temple: step 5, preparation of the outdoor seat of the god (yagakarma); step 6, bestowal of weapons and protective threads on the god (astrayaga); and step 7, propitiation of gods residing along the processional route, accompanied by weapons; and circumambulation of the clothes that the god is to wear during the procession (balidana).

I.3.ii.Sight

Our alapana in image has to go through these initial movements in secret, away from the public gaze. After completion of these rites of planting the appearance of the divine idol, we leave the alapana proper and enter into the equivalent of what will be the pallavi, the stem of the tree, its braches in the anupallavi, and its rich foliage unfolding in the charanams. These first seven steps mark the possibility of "sight" (darshana) that prompts large crowds of devotees to flock to the shrine and try to catch a glimpse of the idol, to see her face-to-face, eye-to-eye, to be able to pull her golden chariot by their own hands around the temple courtyard. The movement into the temple, the ritual circumambulation, and the devotional urge to see the goddess and to express one's innermost desires to her glance were captured in an audiovisual recording by Thomas Voorter on Friday evening, January 31, 2003. The recording, *Darshanam*, follows roughly steps eight to fourteen of the processional ritual; our description continues here with movement four:

IV. Procession of the god or goddess, surrounded by all pomp: step 8, circumambulation (pradakshina);
V. The display of divine splendor for the benefit of the crowd of devotees: step 9, dressing (parivesha), step 10, offering light (nirajana), step 11, protection by means of tying a protective thread (kautuka);
VI. Purification of evil influences that have attached themselves to the god: step 12, bath in holy water (tirthasamgraha), step 13, rinsing with protective powders (curnakara), and step 14, further ablutions (tirtha).

The next movements will again be hidden from our view; the audiovisual document ends with the sharing of the protective powders, that is, the red powder kumkumam and the cleansing touch of the ritual lamp by the devotees.

VII. Withdrawal of the procession into its source: step 15, lowering the gods banner (dhvajavarohana).

Devotees usually bow or prostrate themselves once more before the flagpole displaying the banner of the god or goddess; here they physically connect from their position in the outer courtyard to the central idol in the inner shrine. Her seat and glance are aligned with the flagpole. The action of circling their hands over the ever-burning flames of sacrificial fire establishes the physical contact.

VIII. Peaceful auspiciousness established: step 16, final washing (snapana).

A serious devotee sits down for a moment on the temple ground before leaving the shrine through its huge temple towers, in order to make the auspicious power that was accumulated in worship "firm."

These eight movements reside in the cultural memory of the devotees. A deep yearning to renew these experiences, to repeat them, to articulate every procedure with loving precision and marvel afresh at the cherished and familiar scenarios, preludes an actual visit. The wish to refresh the bond between gods and humankind, to reinforce their mutual incorporation, to anchor the known into the mysteries of the unknown form the alapana of image.

The following dialogue between the song text and the audiovisual record described above attempts to deploy lived experience of Hindu worship as "images of memory." As a result the text, the music, and the imagery build up an improvisatory, emotional field that we discussed earlier in terms of rasa. This field resides in the realm of the mind, of memory and imagination; in this field, reality may prove to be (to return to Frank Smith's idea) the "fantasy that works." In Indian terms we investigate the sounds and images of the manodharma that nourish the text of the svarajati "Kamakshi anudinamu." This attempt at such a dialogue is emphatically not a description, a definition, or a proven fact nor is it meant to be prescriptive for future performances. We leave the cognitive and conative logic to their own territories. In this field of improvisatory imagery, the affective resultant is the taste of love. In the rasa of Shringara Bhakti, devotional love reveals itself here as Vatsalya, the love between a mother and her child. And indeed Kamakshi is often addressed as Amba, mother, who is moved by deep compassion for her devotees; she envelops them in her love and protects them from the hardships of life. This bond is voiced very clearly in the last charanam: "I am your son. Have you no affection for me, Devi? Why this indifference? Protect me ... now, Shri Bhairavi." K. G. Vijayakrishnan considers this charanam "as the best example of a line of music combining expression of emotion, rhythmic intelligence (especially the Ranga Ramanuja Ayyangar's resolution of the eights and sixes within the tala beats coming in between the pauses) and breathtaking melody. It is unparalleled."

II. Pallavi/Anupallavi: Articulation

II.a. Pallavi

Song of Love:[11]

"Kamakshi amba, amba Kamakshi!... anudinamu maravakane...."
[Kamakshi mother, mother Kamakshi!... daily not forgetting....]

Images of Memory:

We see the procession of the idol of (Adi) Shankaracarya, the primal Brahmin preceptor, approaching the temple tower on his return from his outdoor procession. The temple elephant (whose name is Kamakshi) and the musicians make their way through the crowd. Many devotees hurry through the temple gate to be in time for the procession of Shri Kamakshiyammal on her golden chariot. They purify themselves by taking the blessings of the fire that burns in the circumambulatory of the temple. The chariot is adorned, ablaze with neon lights, and awaits the arrival of the goddess in her triple aspect. She follows shortly after the idol of (Adi) Shankaracarya. In the generative logic of rasa, the repetitive images of more and more people, musicians, the elephant's auspicious presence, and her blessings, the golden chariot and officiating priests, can all be understood as the immediate reaction (anubhava) of devotees to their urgent feeling of love for the goddess (vibhava). The enclosure of the temple grounds by huge towers and firm walls forms the limen that marks the holy, positive figure from its ordinary, negative surroundings.

II.b. Anupallavi

Song of Love:

"Ni padamule dekkanucu nammiti ni Shri Kanchi Kamakshi amba...."
[That your lotus-feet are my refuge, I believe in you, Shri Kanchi Kamakshi mother....]

Images of Memory:

The expectations that urge the devotees to be in time at the chariot, their attempts to catch a glimpse of the goddess as the priests lift her onto her chariot, mark the stage of double-sided interaction (vyabhicaribhava). Suddenly, events unfold very quickly: the chariot is pulled by men and women around the outer circumambulatory route, the sight and sound of fireworks and gunshots demand attention and scare off evil forces. Upon her return to the entrance of the central shrine, devotees can observe the goddess closely and direct their faith to her. Especially moving are a mother and daughter who stand face-to-face with the goddess.

The clockwise circumambulation of the inner shrine, and again its sanctum sanctorum within these walls, encloses the beatific power of the central idol, the pitch-black image of the supreme Shakti, Shri Kamakshi.

III. Charanam: Incorporation

Song of Love:

1. "Kunda-radana kuvakaya-nayana talli raksincu"
   [Jasmin-teethed! Lotus-eyed! Mother, protect me.]
2. "Kambugala norada cikura vidu-vadaba mayamma"
   [Conch-necked! Dark-cloud braided! Moon-faced!, my mother.]
3. "Kumbha-kuca mada-matta; gaja-gama padmabhava- hari-shambhu-nutapada Shankari nivu cittalu vevega dorcamma vinamma"
   [Round-breasted! Elephant-gaited! One whose feet are honored by Brahma, Vishnu and Shiva! Shankari! Drive away my anxieties speedily; please hear me ... mother.]

Images of Memory:

Here we arrive at the many concurrent associations that the sight of the goddess (darshana) triggers. The first associations (samcharibhava) concentrate on her looks, which reveal her qualities as a benign goddess. The devotees approach her in the hope that she is willing to interact with them and for a moment end their separation; this would alleviate their existential plight.

Song of Love:

4. "Bhaktajana kalpalatika karunalaya sadaya giritanaya/Kavave sharanagatudda gada tanasamu seyaka varamosagu"
   [To the devotees, the keeper of paradise! Temple of grace, merciful daughter of the mountain! Protect me please; am I not a refugee, without delay grant me a boon.]

Images of Memory:

Waiting is an important part of worship and can be understood here in terms of Van Gennep as the phase of "transition." Devotees cue up, wait till their moment of eye contact with the goddess has come. Many of them bring offerings that the temple priests present to the deity: red kumkumam powder, flowers, incense sticks, camphor and fruits, and especially bananas are considered auspicious gifts. As the priest offers them to the goddess, reciting their names, birth star, and sign of the zodiac, devotees concentrate on sharing her presence or on the boon that they would like to receive from the goddess. After this personal offering, the priest returns part of the gifts that have now been blessed by the touch of the goddess. Meanwhile, until that moment comes, they wait and rest, assured by the images on the walls, telling the stories of the goddess, her myths, legends, and local anecdotes, the sound of the musical instruments, or the presence of the auspicious elephant.

Song of Love:

5. "Patakamulanu dirci nopadabhakti santata moyave/pavani gada mora vinava parakelanamma vinamma"
   [Removing sins, give me piety to worship ever your lotus feet.Are you not a purifier? Can't you hear my plaints? Why this indifference mother, hear (me) mother!]

Images of Memory:

The priests purify the goddess from the pollution that she might have incurred during her journey before she reenters the inner shrine. They rest her on a special temporary pedestal. The priest enjoys the music while performing his ritual task: with his right hand he marks the same rhythm cycle that the musician (a small boy) beats on his cymbals. This priest could very well be today's Shyama Shastri or his father.

Song of Love:

6. "Durita harini sada nata phala dayakiya/ni birudu bhuvi lo galigina vedamulu moralinganu"
   [Dispeller of sins! That you have the reputation of ever granting the desires of those who bow to you and bestowing grace in the world, the Vedas do proclaim.]

Images of Memory:

The priests recite Sanskrit verses to protect the goddess from evil influences and prepare her for the next stage in the Friday service: an evening meal. One servant brings in a huge plate with food, and the curtain is drawn to enable the deity to enjoy its "essence" in private; she returns the gross material form as "grace" (prasada) to her devotees. In the meantime the devotees spend their time waiting or visiting the various auspicious places on the temple territory, such as the tree that yields fertility and childbirth or the huge form of the Shri Yantra, the Prism of Auspicious Wisdom referred to earlier.

Song of Love:

7. "Nipavana nilaya sura samuday kara vidrata kuvalaya sada/
danuja varana mrgendra 'shrita kalusha dahana dhana/aparimita
vaibhavamugala ni smarana madilo dalicana janadulaku/bahu
sampadala nice vipudda makabhaya miyave"
[Dweller in the Neepa forest! One in the assemblage of the gods!
One who holds a lotus in her hand! One who is to the demon as a
lion to the intoxicated tusker! One who burns the sins of (her)
devotees! On people who meditate on your boundless excellence
you shower immense wealth. Now, please grant me fearlessness.]

Images of Memory:

As the curtain reopens, a horn blows loudly to announce the goddess in
her transcendent state. In the development of experience we have reached
the dominant mood (sthayibhava) of devotion and surrender. Her epi-
thets show her strength and supremacy that melt all fear. One notes the
prostrations and the little boy who enthusiastically beats his cheeks as a
sign of submission and penance. When the lamps are waved in front of
the goddess, her mystery lights up for a moment and triggers off rasa, the
tasting of deep devotional love.

Song of Love:

8. "Shyamakrishna sahodari Shiva Shankari Parameshvari/Hari-
haradulaku ni mahimalu ganimpa taramasutu/Immay abhi-
manamu leda napai Devi/Parakelate brovave ippudu Shri
Bhairavi...."
[Sister of Shymakrishna, Shivashankari, Parameshvari. Can Vishnu,
Siva and others fathom your greatness? I am your son. Have you
no affection for me? Devi! Why this indifference? Protect me now.
Shri Bhairavi....]

Images of Memory:

In the flow of the ritual it is clear that the image of (Adi) Shankaracarya
receives relatively little attention compared to the crowds that flock to
receive the protective red powder from the goddess. The sensory experiences of the ritual—the touch of fire and gift of red powder as the living
sign of her protection—complete the devotee's longing: reciprocal love like
the child for its mother, or the mother cow for her calf. Shri Kamakshi sur-
passes all the gods. She is the one who can protect her devotees now and in
the future. Loving devotion, Vatsalya Bhakti, reaches a breaking point into
"almost incorporation" and intensifies here beyond endurance: "brovave
ippudu Kamakshi" (protect me now, Kamakshi).

Mangalam: Fruition

The aesthetics of performance is in the tasting of experience. Such fruition is realized in full only in the course of active participation in performance. Here, life grasps life with an intensity and directness that allows the performers to live through and think back, as well as to will or wish forward. Culture reveals itself as an ensemble of dynamic, interactive expressions that foreground experiences of individuals and makes them available to society and accessible to the penetration of other "minds" (Turner 1982, 13ff.). Dilthey contrasts the fixity of cosmologies, philosophical systems, ethic systems and ideologies, to the flexible character of Weltanschauungen as dynamic events; I would like to add that Weltanschauungen gain critical mass only in performance. At that moment, complex cosmologies achieve concrete fruition in embodied cosmo-praxes. Whereas ideologies are mostly linear and homogenizing, performance is fuelled by a logic that is emphatically cyclical and thrives on heterogeneity. Bharata offers two metaphors to grasp its aesthetics: on the one hand, performance builds up like the process of cooking. The process of tasting its result, rasa, necessarily involves great heterogeneity of ingredients, a balancing and contrasting of their potential, various careful procedures of processing, and timing to achieve the final experience of definite taste. Performance is a matter of expert cooking and expert tasting. The participants and spectators of a performance are excellent tasters, or rasikas. Here the Western metaphor of the science of alchemy is not out of place. On the other hand, Bharata also offers the image of painting as a mode of reflecting on performance. The painting, however, is done with real-space and real-time ingredients and results in a "canvas of the world," to borrow this fortunate phrase from Foucault. In his "Les mots et les choses," he speaks about three relationships between the "word" and the "world": as an ancient, classical, and modern sign. These three exist in time like archaeological layers. We will see that this notion of layered time does not exclude their simultaneous presence and enactment. The "canvas of the world" belongs to the "ancient sign," where the word and the world are tightly intertwined in a relationship of double-sided "incorporation": the spoken word operates like a live sign, interacting with the "grand sign" that is the world. This grand sign was there before our human articulation and maintains an ontogenetic relation with its spoken offspring: to utter the word meant to enter the thing, and to meditate on the thing was to find the word. This circular relationship between the "word and the world" is sustained by repeated performance of generative speech. This cyclical logic connects "La prose du monde," the prose of the world (Foucault 1966, 32ff.), with the metaphysical speculation on the power of speech (Vakshakti) that we discussed earlier in the context of Shri Vidya and the threefold Tamil.

The reflection of the phenomenon of performance confronts us with an episteme that belongs to a layer in the archaeology of sciences with which the modern academic world is no longer familiar or at ease. Performance as a paradigm of the human sciences is vastly represented by humankind even today, outside the arena of academia. However, its logic escapes our notice because of its "ancient" character and because of its different modes of representation. Whereas cosmologies, philosophical and ethical systems, or ideologies lend themselves easily to the printed word and can be disseminated in the circles of the modern sign, performance fully settles in the ancient sign. It thrives on seemingly endless series of resemblances and maintains intricate networks of physical and metaphysical reference, transformation, and regeneration. This paradigm is indeed cyclical, thoroughly sensory, experiential, and fully applied in concrete expressions. Today's reflection on performance as a paradigm of the humanities, coupled with the use of interactive multimedia in representation, may cast a new light on the work of Claude Lévi-Strauss. Here, we are indeed entering "*La pensée sauvage*," in which theory is subservient to its application in praxis (Lévi-Strauss 1962). We meet the flexible bricoleur whose touchstone is the efficacy of performance, its force, its Shakti, or fruition. Energized by an agricultural logic, performance gives the human argument critical mass and brings about transformation again and again, as life continues to change and transform, performance changes with it.

Aesthetics of performance enters the core of performance studies as an ancient science, a cross-cultural science, as a challenge in the representation of human knowledge, as an interdisciplinary meeting ground where science and the performing arts meet, and as an ultramodern, contemporary experiment in which the various media interact with the various modalities of cognition.

Its Fruition is in the Tasting.

Notes

The following abbreviations have been used throughout this chapter: NSh. (Natyashastra), Skt. (Sanskrit), Ta. (Tamil).

1. Shyama Shastri was born in Tiruvarur, where his paternal house is maintained as a shrine to his musical genius. His father Visvanatha migrated to Tanjore and served in the temple of Bangaru Kamakshi, a southern version of the same goddess at Kanchipuram.
2. This essay tries to address a broad audience, not necessarily Indologists only. In the interest of readability, I have chosen to transcribe Sanskrit, Tamil, and Telugu terms as closely to the originals as possible and to set them in roman script without diacritic marks.
3. This essay is largely based on an experimental course on "tradition" that I taught several times since 1998 at the Department of Cultural Anthropology at the University of Amsterdam. The course investigated creative tension between "fixables" and "flexables" that enables ancient traditions to adapt to ever-changing circumstances and emerging traditions to organize themselves in a relatively short span of time. The

course addressed three themes: (1) Rite, the "form element" of tradition, (2) Myth, its "content or fascination," and (3) Commentary, the mechanism of "contemporary relevance" to the community of believers. Especially in the context of "Commentary," I thank my students for their contributions, creativity, and enthusiasm; they forced me to develop the central themes treated here in the alapanas.

4. For full references of the Sanskrit original, see "Natya—the Desi Yajna" (Kersenboom 1991), in which I develop the theme of Natya as a mode and model for worship in Hindu temples. This essay was part of a panel entitled "The Syntax of Ritual," hosted by Frits Staal in the International Sanskrit Conference, Leiden, Holland, 1987.

5. These analyses of performance use building blocks from the following four sources: I. Dilthey's five moments of Erlebnis: (1) Feelings revived ({a} originally felt and {b} if willingly opened); (2) Rapture (perceptual intensity); (3) Meaningful occurrence arising from (a) feelingly thinking about the interconnections in past/present, and (b) evocation of past experiences; (4) Clarity by strength/energy in evocation of past experiences; (5) Expression by self-action completes experience. II. Huizinga's five characteristics of "sacred play": (1) Free (voluntary activity); (2) Serious (off-ordinary); (3) Liminal (framed in space and time); (4) Tense (is order and creates order); (5) True (homogenesis, rules); (6) Select (intimate, formation of play-community). III. Csikszentmihalyi on Flow: (1) Union (merging action and awareness; loss of individualism); (2) Surrender (loss of ego); (3) Focus (centering attention in Now); (4) Control (over own actions and environment); (5) Autotelic (no goods/rewards outside itself); (6) Communitas (non-contradictory demand for action and unambiguous feedback). IV. Bharata on Natya: (1) cause, (2) effect, (3) interaction, (4) association, (5) dominant impression, and (6) rasa, tasting. The correlation of these "building blocks" in a gradual process of five or six phases form the basic insight that emerged from the course "Tradition" and that underlies the second alapana.

6. Even this local legend, found in R. K. Das (1964, 224–25), reveals the different layers and inclusions in Hindu orthodoxies and orthopraxes. Douglas Renfrew Brooks (1992, xiii) introduces this field of tension as follows: "Few contemporary Hindus associate the word 'Tantra' with themselves, their beliefs, practices, or traditions. For Brahman caste 'Vaidikas' this is especially true. These 'high-caste' devotees imagine themselves the custodians of the so-called Vedic tradition. For them, 'Tantra' suggests all that they are not: disdain for the brahmanic legacy, a corruption of age-old morality and ritual custom, and a preoccupation with sex and black magic. To be a Vaidika and a Tantric seems to some of them incommensurate." Adi Shankaracarya is the guardian saint of Vaidika "Smarta" Brahmans.

7. An audiovisual recording of the Darshanam and the Friday evening procession of Shri Kamakshiyamman in Kanchipuram is available on CD-ROM; film and montage by Dr. Thomas Voorter, University of Amsterdam; the procession was taped on January 31, 2003. A performance of "Kamakshi anudinamu" by Shri K. G. Vijayakrishnan, vina and vocals, is available on CD.

8. The confluence of these three forces has provided this essay with its triple organization of improvisatory introductions: one on sound, one on words, and one on image. The DVD *Eye to Eye with Goddess Kamakshi* (Voorter and Kersenboom 2005) offers a threefold representation, with the text, the vina audio, and the audiovisual recording *Darshanam* as interrelated files.

9. The term "utsava" translates in Sankrit as "enterprise, beginning; opening, blossoming; a festival" and is derived from the verb root "ut-suu-" (to cause to go upwards, to stir, to agitate).

10. It is interesting to note that Bernard S. Cohn (in Hobsbawm and Ranger, 1996, 165ff.) diagnoses the "act of incorporation" as the "central ritual" in the Mughal court. It formed the major cultural contradiction in the construction of ritual idiom in representing authority in Victorian India. Its "theory of authority" faced an unbending paradox: "[T]he English could not be incorporated through symbolic acts to a foreign ruler,

and perhaps more importantly they could not incorporate Indians into their rulership through symbolic means."

11. The Telugu text and English translation are taken from Vidya Shankar's (1979) "Shyama Sastry's compositions," vol. 1, 2nd ed., 16–17. The transliteration of the original is mine in line with this essay as a whole.

References

Brooks, Douglas Renfrew. 1992. *Auspicious Wisdom: The Texts and Traditions of Srividya Sakta Tantrism in South India*. New York: State University of New York Press.

Das, R. K. 1964. *Temples of Tamilnad*. Bombay: Bharatiya Vidya Bhavan.

Foucault, M. 1966. *Les mots et les choses*. Paris: Gallimard.

Hobsbawm, E., and T. Ranger. 1983–1996. *The Invention of Tradition*. Cambridge: University of Cambridge.

Huizinga, Johan. 1955. *Homo Ludens: A Study of the Play Element in Culture*. Boston: Beacon Press.

Kersenboom, S. C. [1984], 1987, 1998, 2003. *Nityasumangali: Devadasi Tradition in South India*. Delhi: Motilal Banarsidass.

———. 1991. "Natya—the Desi Yagna." *Indologica Taurinensia*. Vol. 15–16 (1989–90), 187–205.

———. 1995. *Word, Sound, Image: The Life of the Tamil Text*. With interactive CD "Bhairavi Varnam." Eindhoven, Philips Media/Codim. Oxford, Washington, and New York: Berg Publishers.

Lévi-Strauss, C. 1962. *La Pensée Sauvage*. Paris: Librairie Plon.

Natyashastra. 1967. Ed. and trans. by M. Ghosh. Vol. 1. Calcutta: Granthalaya.

Nijenhuis, E. te. 1974. *Indian Music: History and Structure*. Leiden, Holland: Brill.

Reiniche, M. L. 1979. *Les dieux et les homes: Etude des cultes d'un village du Tirunelveli*. Paris: Mouton.

Seetha, S. 1981. *Tanjore as a Seat of Music*. Madras: University of Madras.

Shankar, Vidya. 1947–79. *Shyama Sastry's Compositions*. Vol. 1 (with text, translation, transliteration, and notation with gamaka-signs). Madras: Gitalaya.

Smith, F. 1985. "Literacy: Inventing Worlds or Shunting Information?" in *Literacy, Language, and Learning: Learning: The Nature and Consequences of Reading and Writing*, ed. David R. Olson, Nancy Torrance, and Angela Hildyard, 195–216. Cambridge: Cambridge University Press.

Turner, V. 1982. *From Ritual to Theatre: The Human Seriousness of Play*. New York: Performing Arts Journal Publications.

———. 1987. *The Anthropology of Performance*. New York: Performing Arts Journal Publications.

Voorter, T. J. H., and S. C. Kersenboom. 2005. *Eye to Eye with Goddess Kamakshi*. Interactive DVD. Utrecht, www.parampara.nl.

Chapter Four

THE HINDU TEMPLE AND THE AESTHETICS OF THE IMAGINARY

Rohan Bastin

Imaginary numbers are not just puzzling because we cannot understand them, but because they solve problems in mathematics and physics.

– Frits Staal, "Artificial Languages: Asian Backgrounds or Influences?"

There could be no developing consciousness without an imaginative consciousness, and vice versa.

– Jean Paul Sartre, *The Psychology of the Imagination*

When the intellect is in its own pasture it beholds all things at once as if in a mirror.

– *Lankavatara Sutra*

This chapter explores aspects of temple aesthetics in order to examine the relationship between humanity and divinity in contemporary Hinduism. Its focus is the Munneśvaram temple in northwest Sri Lanka (a site explored in an extended form in my 2002 book, *The Domain of Constant Excess*). This temple largely follows the general principles of design and rite of the contemporary southern Indian Śaiva (Śiva-worshipping) temple, and, in that regard, my analysis draws from ethnographic description framed by more general statements about both the Hindu temple and Śaiva Siddhanta cosmology by numerous scholars.

The Hindu cosmos consists of a holistic and hierarchical arrangement of entities whose existence derives from a unitary source of potentiality

Notes for this chapter are located on page 106.

that encompasses and ontologically precedes matter. While it precedes through being the source of creation, it also succeeds creation through being its teleology of eternal return. This double movement of creation and return, which lies at the heart of Hindu temple aesthetics, reveals the Hindu cosmos to be a hierarchically arranged whole whose parts are not simply defined by the whole, but through an oscillation of identity and difference or uniformity and multiplicity expressive at different levels of macrocosmic and microcosmic relation. These relations are evident in different aspects of the design and ritual of the Hindu temple. In this essay, I argue that the study of these aspects of temple aesthetics is important for the development of an anthropological understanding of the Hindu social imagination, which bears upon certain long-standing debates in the anthropology of India.

My analysis of temple aesthetics is informed by Mikel Dufrenne's comments on the aesthetic experience of monumental architecture (Dufrenne 1973, 95, 360–65) and his delineation of the relation between image, the imagination, and the imaginary (1987, 39–67). I will explain this delineation first, as I wish to use it to develop an idea of the Hindu imaginary. The image is not imagination, but what "provokes the play of imagination" (1987, 39). Imagination is that power of opening consciousness, and the imaginary is that quality of the image that allows the opening to take place. Image, imagination and the imaginary thus open distinct lines of philosophical inquiry concerning (1) the nature of human being and its capacity to create images, (2) the nature of knowledge as a dimension of human experience (imagination), and (3) the nature of being in general and as an idea—the ontology of the imaginary. Critical and fundamental, therefore, is the imaginary as the quality of the image opened in the act of the imagination. The image is not, then, simply the object and the imagination the subject, because they are ontologically entwined by the imaginary as both "the look and the thing seen" (1987, 4).

Dufrenne continues that one might loosely say that the inquiry into the human capacity to create images is psychological, the issue of the imagination is epistemological and the question of the ontology of the imaginary is metaphysical. However, he emphasizes that not all images (and hence imaginings) are imaginary; rather, he highlights those areas of imagination associated with language and desire. I illustrate this through my opening quotation from Frits Staal concerning imaginary numbers such as the square root of minus one ($i = \sqrt{-1}$). The metaphysical issue is not the existence of such an imaginary number (my analogue here to language in its most encompassing sense) but the fact that one can do things with such a number. One can orient desire (intentionality) through objects and recognize the world as the object of desire. One makes worlds with the imaginary through such activities as interplanetary navigation with equations using "i."[1] The imaginary is thus that quality of thought that enables the intuition of essences upon which lifeworlds are formed. It is the noumenal corollary of sensory experience vital to the formation and reformation of the human lifeworld. However, it is not merely an aspect of consciousness (or indeed language) but in the Heideggerian sense what consciousness shares with being in general.[2] I stress that the imaginary is, in Dufrenne's terms, not simply the "imaginary" of an imaginary (i.e., unreal) number, but the imaginary in the sense of Staal's remark about such numbers being something with which one can do things. Of course, mathematical symbolization is a distinct form different from other aspects of language. However, as Cassirer (1957) argues in his comprehensive study of symbolic forms, mathematics shares attributes with other symbolic forms and indeed expands their potential to make worlds. In this sense, imaginary numbers, which are an important but by no means the only product of mathematical thinking, demonstrate their potential to make things better than other examples of "language" but nevertheless reveal this potential to be a characteristic of the imaginary in human beings.

One of the most potent expressions of the imaginary in human thought is the fantasy of origin or moment of emergence—the wakening of subjectivity and perception (Dufrenne 1987, 51). This is the primal fantasy that dwells most commonly in the realms of cosmogony and mythopoeia. It is the fantasy that appears driven by the force of duration expressing the attention of consciousness to itself through the projection of that moment (*in illo tempore*, as Eliade describes origin myths) when consciousness first appears as an intentional consciousness directed out into the world. What I explore in this essay is how the fantasy of origin is developed in the Hindu temple in order to capture or territorialize divinity as both the look and the thing seen through which the consciousness of the deity is ordered as a presence that then suffuses the space around it. I will demonstrate that, while all the senses are covered in Hindu temple aesthetics, the sense of vision or the gaze is the most important sense. Critically, this vision is both the devotional gaze as well as the gaze of divinity, both of which are carefully worked out by ritual to be complementary and expressive of the double movement of cosmic creation and return to the extent that I describe them, following Stella Kramrisch, as the mirror-gaze that "restates divinity" (Kramrisch 1981, 449) and thus presents to divinity an idea of itself. This is part of the nature of the temple as a territorializing machine that captures divinity, or puts it "in its own pasture" to borrow from the *Lankavatara Sutra*[3] and informs the power of such temples to act as nodal points in social (political and economic) space. I conclude my chapter with a brief consideration of this power of temples in order to make a case for an anthropology of aesthetics reducible to neither art appreciation nor the politics of representation.

I will show that the idea of capturing or ensnaring divinity is carefully worked out in temple aesthetics in both the subtle plan of the temple space as well as its gross material form of building and ritual practice. In this respect, the temple is an example of monumental architecture that according to Dufrenne (1973, 362) differs from other aesthetic objects for the way it draws the spectator into its form so that the aesthetic experience includes the spectator. There is no frame separating the artwork from the world of the spectator because the artwork becomes that world, drawing the spectator into a kind of dance. My central point is that, in the Hindu temple, this spectator is divinity as much as it is devotee. Hindu temple aesthetics cannot easily be grasped if one presumes an a priori idea of divinity and the sacred as something a temple simply represents (or, one might say, "embodies" while really meaning "represents"). Such a representational approach presupposes the existence of the sacred independent of its aesthetic forms and then treats these forms as merely representations. This is a flaw, for example, in the comparative religion approach of Mircea Eliade (1959), for whom the "sacred" is as much of a given as the "profane." While Eliade's contribution to comparative religion is enormous, his approach to the sacred is more ecumenical than comparative. This remains an ongoing issue for religious studies and the anthropology of religion, which rigorous attention to aesthetics can assist to overcome. It can do so by recognizing as a problem the idea of the sacred and, concomitantly, the idea of its aesthetic representation.

The analysis of temple aesthetics presented here derives in part from native exegesis, specifically from temple specialists at the Munneśvaram temple, mostly priests but also musicians, garland makers and other workers. It combines with textual studies, specifically the work of Stella Kramrisch (1946) and others,[4] to develop a phenomenological analysis that moves beyond exegesis to explore the problematic nature of Hindu divinity in ways not usually considered by a participant devotee for whom divinity and the temple are considered integral to the lifeworld. Thus, in developing an ontology of the Hindu sacred as an aspect of the imaginary via temple aesthetics, I necessarily move beyond exegesis in the same way that I move beyond Eliade's usage of the concept of the sacred. My criticism of Eliade, therefore, is not simply a criticism of his inadequate attention to specific or local variations of the idea of the sacred as expressive of a Western perspective that can be replaced by "the native's point of view." Rather, it is a criticism that offers a more radically deconstructive approach by the scholar.

The *Maṇḍala* Ground Plan

For Tamil Hindus (and specifically Śaivites), the Hindu temple represents the body of the cosmic man Purusa lying on his back.[5] One enters the temple through the feet, circumambulates the temple-proper—the body—along its inner road, then passes up the vertical axis of the body past four of the six bodily *cakras* to arrive at the chamber anterior to the inner sanctum, which corresponds to the head of the cosmic man. The passage up the bodily axis past the *cakras* replicates the movement of the energy of consciousness (*kundalini*) that rises through the top of the head in the body of the meditator. The head in the temple is the "womb" (*garbha*) and the "root seat" (*mūlasthāna*)—the source of consciousness or the third eye— where the most potent stone image of the deity is placed according to whose temple it is. At Munnesvaram, where I conducted the research for this study, the deity is the prime god of Tamil Śaivism, Śiva, and the core image in the inner sanctum is a *śivaliṅga*—a representation of the generative union of male (*liṅga*) and female (*yoni*). Only the temple priests are permitted to enter the womb chamber where they deliver private offerings (*arccanam*) and perform the routine daily rites (*nityapūjā*).

Shrines for other deities in the pantheon are located at prescribed points in the temple, including outside the temple-proper around its inner road. These deities include different forms of the same deity such as the dancing form of Śiva (Natesar, Nataraja), his mendicant form (Bhiksatana), his spouse (Ambal or Parvati), his sons (Murugan, Pillaiyar, Aiyanar, and Bhairavar), and others including the nine planets.[6] The entire temple space thus maps out the pantheon on the scheme of the cosmic body described by Kramrisch (1946) as the *vāstupuruṣamaṇḍala* (see figure 4.1). It describes a cosmogony as the emission into existence of the cosmos as the coming into being of Purusa from an originary formlessness. The term *vāstupuruṣamaṇḍala* can be translated as the ordered or measured representation (*maṇḍala*) of the cosmic man Purusa's dwelling or residence (*vāstu*). Its pattern is the subtle form of the temple, providing not only the blueprint of the gross temple but also its cosmic source as a representation of cosmic immanence. Thus, it is not merely a diagram of the temple ground plan, but an instrument of manifestation understood to contain abstract potentiality. Critically, the *maṇḍala* binds the variegated energy of the manifest universe by returning this energy to its originary undifferentiated source. This is the essence of the temple as a whole structure, as well as the basis for each shrine within the structure. Beneath each statue is a geometrical representation known as a *yantra* (from the root *yam* "to hold") that describes and thus binds the particular deity to the place.[7] These different examples of *yantra* are forms of *maṇḍala*, and the *maṇḍala* has the connotation of being mind (*manda*) and measure (*ma*). One can think of the entire temple, therefore, as a *maṇḍala* premised on the anthropomorphic form of the cosmic man, which also contains at specific points separate *yantra* designs that describe and thus hold on the *maṇḍala* various forms of divinity. *Maṇḍala* and *yantra* are thus more than mere representations. They are instruments of capture through their description or representation of an ordered cosmos. They constitute the conceptual apparatus of the temple.

Figure 4.1 The *Vāstupuruṣamaṇḍala*

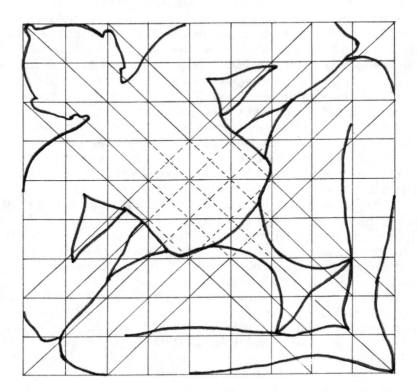

The design forms the basis of the temple groundplan.
Source: Ananth (1998, 41).

Daily Ritual

The ordered or measured space of the temple is described several times daily through the obligatory daily rites known as the *nityapūjā*.[8] The six rites held at Munneśvaram have variations as to their length and complexity as well as their physical starting point, but all share the feature of providing service to the deities in terms of making offerings of light, sound, aroma, and sustenance in the form of bathing and/or feeding. The common theme is one of elemental recombination whereby the five elements that comprise the cosmos (earth, fire, water, air and ether or space) are offered to the deity in different forms. Five types of fruit represent the earth; five types of sound the ether (made variously by bells, drumming, *mantra*, and/or the vibrating reed of the *nāgasvaram* instrument or the conch); and five types of fire from lamps (oil tapers or camphor flames in different configurations). Thus, not only are the five elements represented, but in some instances and depending on the degree of elaboration, five forms of the five elements are offered, thereby indicating in a unifying manner how creation is a complex process of manifestation, whose form can be likened to the process of multiplication in the *yantra* diagram. Emanating from a single central square, the number of squares grows as the overall diagram expands in a manner akin to the opening of a lotus flower (whose form is commonly used in several artistic styles for precisely this effect of emission).[9] In the rite of *pūjā*, this physical process of manifesting differentiation, is reversed through the elemental recombination of the essence of the physical world.

The rite of *pūjā* thus shares a logic of manifestation and recombination with the overall design of the temple premised on the theme of cosmogony evident in Purusa's self-sacrifice into being. This theme is well described by Richard Davis (1991) as the oscillating universe of cosmic emission and reabsorption (see also Curtis 1983). It is evident in the temple aesthetic of worship of black basalt images that contrast with the painted statuary adorning the temple extremities. The core image in Śaivism is the *liṅga*, which Kramrisch (1981) describes as meaning "sign" but is more accurately described as the signifier. Where the *liṅga* signifies form, the *rūpa* is the form or signification. In the same way, the *śivaliṅga* statue signifies immanent form at the point of creation. Emission is the process of differentiating formation whereby the *śivaliṅga* becomes first the carved and then the carved and painted statue. One thus moves from the formless stone in the inner sanctum to the brightly colored statues adorning the towers and the remarkable temple gateways (*gopura*) for which the south Indian or Dravidian temple is famous. In more elaborate temples than Munneśvaram, these gateways grow in size as one moves away from the temple itself; their height and elaborateness describe the panoply of manifest existence, but critically their source is the formless black image in the inner sanctum. Surmounting these towers are images of the *kirtimukha* or "face of glory," which command the keystones of the archways, mouths agape, swallowing existence in an act of reabsorption or eternal return (see figure 4.2).

As the movement away from the inner sanctum is a movement into form and differentiation, the movement toward the sanctum is a movement downward into dark formlessness. This is captured in the temple by what Kramrisch called "the aesthetics of piling down," which I have argued relate to the analogy drawn between the temple and a cave and also an anthill (Bastin 2002, 109). The inner sanctum in this scheme is the cave in the cave. It is a darkened airless space with a low ceiling lit only by the priests' lamps. The movement around the inner road can be thought of as a passage down a path to this cave, and this effect is achieved remarkably well at the famous Ramesvaram temple in south India, where the column

Figure 4.2 The Face of Glory that surmounts the tower archways to reabsorb the cosmic manifestation

Photograph by Rohan Bastin.

work on the inner road is renowned for providing a sense of tunneling towards the primordial source (see figure 4.3). There is thus a double movement in the temple that relates to the oscillation between emission and reabsorption, which is the nature of the cosmos. Radiating out from the center is an aesthetics of differentiating form and color. Moving into the center gives a sense of passage downwards to a condition of primordial nondifferentiation.

Through elemental recombination, the rite of *pūjā* creates the reabsorption or eternal return on a routine daily basis designed to reorder the space of the temple and the deities in that temple. The eternal temple can thus be likened to a cosmogonic event endlessly repeated in the circumstances of specific places and people. The temple as a whole is thus as much of a ritual as the rituals it contains. Like a ritual, it strives to create the conditions of possibility through engaging the primal fantasy that projects into existence that undifferentiated moment prior to space and time.

Curtis (1983) interprets the relation between the space of the temple and the *pūjā* ritual as an act of mediation between the manifest and the unmanifest, which is described in the pantheon through the contrast between different forms of Śiva. Manifest forms of the god are inscribed on the *cakra* points of the temple axis, while unmanifest forms occupy the space moving outward and upward from the inner sanctum. The number of forms varies between five and thirteen but is always a complementary opposition of even numbers mediated by a dual form—Sadaśiva, or Śiva as Light—who is both manifest and unmanifest.[10] The most common number is nine, consisting of four manifest and four unmanifest forms plus Sadaśiva (Curtis 1983, 92). The rite of *pūjā* elaborates on this relationship:

Figure 4.3 The Inner Road at Ramesvaram, south India

The famous column design accentuates the theme of tunnelling towards the temple's heart. Photograph by Rohan Bastin.

The *gurukkal* [priest] has completed the manifest-unmanifest progression to the focus of Sadaiva, the door to the unmanifest. From this point all progression can only find symbolic expression in the world. Thus the ritual turns back and proceeds to develop more and more physically as the symbolism of flowers, culminating finally in acts of offering which to all intents and purposes appear entirely physical. The *gurukkal* gives the furthest reaches of unmanifest activity symbolic expression in the world through the most violently physical acts of the entire rite. (Curtis 1983, 98)

What I have described to this point is how a Tamil Śaivite temple develops through both design and rite its status as a sacred space, articulating themes of cosmogony and macrocosmic and microcosmic relation. Thus it exemplifies what Eliade long ago described as sacred space and the idea of the world center or *axis mundi* evident in simple sacred poles as well as at such complex sites as Barabudur (Eliade 1990), which is also based on a *maṇḍala*. In the Hindu temple, the theme is explicit. The temple represents Mt. Meru, the center of the world and the world axis. The axis is shown by the temple flagpole, which corresponds to Purusa's penis and forms the focal point for the cycle of processions that comprise the annual temple festival. At Munneśvaram, this festival commences with a flag-hoisting and a veritable flood of milk and coconut water as the base of the pole is bathed.[11] This is followed by the first circumambulation of the processional deities around the pole, then by several days of circumambulation via the temple's inner road, before the processions move out to the road encircling the outer walls and then the extremities of the temple settlement. Again one can see the theme of radiating emission that culminates with the procession of the giant wooden chariots that represent the temple as a whole, but now the temple is, as it were, in procession around itself. Moreover, the chariot is also identified as a symbolic fire, the flame of a single camphor lamp used in *pūjā* and as such the point of mediation between manifest and unmanifest, and emission and reabsorption. What is daily done at an individual shrine to an individual deity is now being done to the entire temple complex with the kind of violent physicality Curtis describes. Indeed, the sheer physicality of the chariot processions then culminates with dramatic battles between deities and demons, cosmic unions of gods and goddesses, and bloody animal sacrifices to the ambiguous deity-demon guardians of the borders. Temple aesthetics thus enable the exploration of cosmic themes at multiple levels ranging from waving a *pūjā* lamp in front of a single statue to hauling a giant wooden juggernaut around the temple settlement. Each level shares a logic that relates to the fundamental cosmological relationship between emission and reabsorption (or manifest and unmanifest) and, in doing so, inscribes both divinity and humanity onto the cosmic scheme of the *maṇḍala* temple. This act of inscription develops through the "primal fantasy" of cosmogony as the creation of the world-body of Purusa.

Temple as Palace, Deity as Monarch

At another level of meaning, and one that often accords more closely with native exegesis, daily temple rites are also acts of servicing the needs of the deities; their treatment by servants in the manner of the treatment of royalty. The deity is like a monarch, and the temple is like a palace. Its common Tamil name *kovil* designates a king's seat, and devotion can be likened to having an audience with the monarch in order to receive blessings. The flag-hoisting that begins the festival marks the deity as in-residence, and the cycle of processions (*tiruviḷā*) mark the passage of the royal retinue (*parivāram*) as a regal conquest. Festival events are marked by a special rite of bathing called an *abhiśeka*, which involves in its most elaborate forms the use of special bodily treatments, oils, and perfumes prior to dressing the festival statues in fine clothing and jewelry and taking them on palanquins atop their special animal vehicles (*vāhana*) on processions with musicians and other attendants holding regal parasols and fans. At the conclusion of every night's procession, the festival statues are presented with metal images of regalia including weapons, fans, whisks, and flags. The link between deity and monarch is thus very clearly articulated. It establishes the sense of service as consisting of a full sensory and ordering repertoire that addresses the body of the deity as if the deity were a monarch and the priest a royal attendant.

It has been suggested by Fuller (1988, 52; 1992, 69–72) that the key to understanding all the devoted service to addressing the physical needs of the deity in temple ritual is the crucial and seemingly apodictic point that the deity does not physically need anything. This is partly because it is not actually the deity rather than an image of the deity as a piece of black basalt or a metal statue, and also because deities are deemed to be beyond physical needs. Therefore, all the feeding and bathing in *pūjā* must be symbolic of something the deity (as an abstract idea and not as an image) does want, and this is devotion; the act of giving rather than the gift. Some would argue that it follows that the link between deity and monarch is also symbolic and thus an expression of devotional servitude. I partly disagree. The notion that a deity is beyond physical needs, while true, does not distinguish between the deity as a transcendental entity (or abstract idea) and the specific manifestation of the deity in a specific temple, which is far more than simply a representation of the deity. The critical issue for the ritual specialists (priests and others) is to bring that presence or abstract idea into form in that space; to make this particular site, which is not the *axis mundi*, into an *axis mundi*. This involves localizing a deity through deterritorializing abstract divinity and reterritorializing it onto the *maṇḍala* / world body scheme. Fuller does not appear to appreciate this point, which is strongly evident in David Shulman's (1980) work on Tamil temple myths, because he appears to operate with an a priori idea of divinity that de-emphasizes the importance attached to locatedness. Somewhat in the manner of Eliade's approach to the sacred, Fuller's approach to divinity suggests an uncritical application of an idea whose roots lie elsewhere.

In terms of territorialization and the Hindu temple, Hindu kingship can be thought of precisely as deterritorialized divinity that reterritorializes space. The Munneśvaram temple is a *kovil* or king's seat precisely because it is a *pitham* (source) temple understood to have its roots in the age of the gods and the formation of the world. The critical point, though, is the theme of spatialization and capture, which can be considered in terms of a double movement of territorialization when framed in terms of the oscillation of emission and reabsorption. I will return to this point about temples, kings, and territory in my conclusion. Before doing so, it is necessary to return to the issue of aesthetics and the idea of the deity as spectator.

The Mirror Gaze

In addition to the careful tending of the deity's body and the offerings of the sensory repertoire with the theme of elemental aggregation, the critical feature for understanding temple aesthetics and their purpose of capturing divinity is the mirror that normally stands in front of the Munneśvaram inner sanctum (see figure 4.4). One does not automatically realize that the metal disc on a stand in front of the inner sanctum is a mirror, because it does not reflect; only upon asking about it was I told that the disc is a double-sided mirror whose two sides serve a distinct protective purpose. One side protects the deity from the harmful gaze of people, and the other protects the temple and the world outside from the continuous gaze of the deity. I am more interested here in the gaze of the deity. However, the fact that the deity needs protection from the gaze of the devotee is instructive for the way it demonstrates how divinity in the temple is not some abstract absolute, impervious to what occurs in a temple. Thus, what occurs in a temple is not merely symbolic of something else and is thus not reducible to an a priori idea of the sacred and of divinity.

Figure 4.4 The Temple Mirror in front of the Inner Sanctum

In the foreground, a priest conducts one of the routine monthly rites for the maintenance of *sakti*. Photograph by Rohan Bastin.

The importance of the mirror's other side, the side that protects the devotee from the deity, is further developed in the manner in which the area immediately in front of the temple is clear of habitation. As people say, no one would want to reside directly in front of a temple, because to be constantly in the presence of the divine gaze would be to risk injury or suffering of some kind. In a similar sense, devotees in the temple who fear the wrath of the deity from some wrong they may have done will not risk gazing directly on the deity during a visit to the temple and instead look to a mirror (in this case, a modern reflecting mirror) that faces the inner sanctum above the entrance to the adjoining hall. The point is that such a condition of incurring the deity's wrath is a possibility for anyone, so it is not wise to live permanently in the line of sight. The disc mirror, which serves to deflect the gaze, also controls this line of sight, as does the statue of the deity's principal animal vehicle—the only figure in the temple that is permanently in the line of sight. Moreover, the animal faces the deity and looks upon the deity with its pure gaze of devotion. Thus, the pure gaze of devotion looks back at the directed divine gaze and, like the gaze in the mirror, it thereby restates divinity to the deity (see figure 4.5). Mirror and vehicle do not simply block the line of sight; they direct it back upon itself. The double movement of emission and reabsorption that describes the Hindu cosmology is thus elaborated, as an intentional gaze, as both the look and the thing seen. It develops from the fundamental sense of the temple as founded on the cosmogonic act of Purusa that has at its core the idea of creation as resulting from the first stirring of consciousness directed out of itself as desire. To return to Dufrenne, this creates the condition of the imaginary as the opening of the relation between the image and the imagination that lies at the heart of the creative potential of consciousness and thus the world.

Thus, I argue that the essence of temple aesthetics is reflexive self-awareness designed to bring into existence and hold in place the presence of a deity, seduced into being in a specific tension of consciousness, who looks out into the world, suffusing that world with a presence aware of itself and aware of itself as a modality of consciousness. This is the beauty of temple aesthetics, where the "beautiful" and indeed the sublime is created as the supreme act of devotion. It is designed as service to the deity in the manner of service to the monarch, and its ritual repertoire is organized around meeting the physical needs of the deity not in an "as if" manner, wherein the service simply pretends that the deity has physical needs, but as a way of restating the nature of the deity to itself in order to establish the imaginary condition of the cosmos as a field of active potential specifically situated on that site. This is why I partly disagree with Fuller's argument that the offerings in *pūjā* are simply symbolic of devotion. They are devotion, but they are devotion because they restate divinity and as such constitute the physical corollary of the mirror gaze that enables the presence of divinity as more than a representation of divinity.

Figure 4.5 The Inner Sanctum at Thiruketheesvaram, Sri Lanka

Looking towards the dark recess of the inner sanctum, one can see the Nandi vehicle of the god Śiva whose gaze is part of the mirror gaze of devotion. Photograph by Rohan Bastin.

We are now in a position to consider the important Hindu idea of worship as *darśan* or seeing the deity (Eck 1985). As Diana Eck shows, *darśan* is more properly the act of bearing witness to being seen by the deity. It is the act of seeing being seen by the divine gaze; the act of being in the presence of the deity as that presence is expressed in basic measure as a gaze. Divine presence (in Tamil, *aruḷ*) is not only this gaze. It is also experienced in an embodied manner, which can take a variety of forms, some of which require physical ordeal, including dance and trance as well as pain.[12] In essence, though, *aruḷ* or presence is constituted as a gaze (in Tamil, *driṣṭi*); a gaze aware of itself and continually made aware of itself through the aesthetics of worship.[13] Its contrast is the demonic gaze, which lacks such self-knowledge and is, as such, a gaze of pure directed and unmediated desire. It is a lustful gaze that seeks only to consume. Kapferer (1983, 2000) explores such demonic gaze in the related cultural tradition of Sinhala

Buddhist healing rites, showing how demonic affliction or possession is the condition of being caught in the all-consuming passion of a demon. The task of the healing rites for such possession involves an act of seduction by the ritual specialists designed to capture the demon and subordinate it through nullifying its lustful consciousness. In a related sense, the act of worship for the Tamil Śaivite is designed as a nullification of ego consciousness (*anavas*) that establishes the proper relationship between humanity and divinity. The demonic is, in this sense, the extreme of ego consciousness as pure unmediated desire.[14]

Temples and the Sociology of India

In conclusion, I will return to the deity/monarch relation to say something about the value of considering temple aesthetics for a sociology of India. I do so to demonstrate the centrality of aesthetics for anthropology and with that the importance of the study of cultural forms and material culture for the study of the social imagination. I describe it as a *sociology* of India in order to evoke the important dialogue established in 1957 by Louis Dumont and David Pocock in their journal *Contributions to Indian Sociology*. In what amounted to a series of programmatic statements, Dumont and Pocock insisted that the study of religious texts as well as artistic works should be integral to the study of Indian society—a society with such a rich history of civilization, philosophy, science, and social theory that a more typical anthropology, accustomed to the study of technologically simple and illiterate societies, would be out of its depth. Especially through the contribution of Lévi-Strauss, such a disjunctive gap between the civilized and the noncivilized has been eroded. Nevertheless, the importance of Dumont and Pocock's directive for a sociology of India to look outside and beneath given sociological categories of human interaction remains pertinent.

The sociology of India that results remains marked by the colossal presence of Dumont and his highly influential and controversial work on the caste system, *Homo Hierarchicus* (1980, first published in 1966). Apart from criticizing Dumont's structuralist attempt to identify an underlying and pan-Indian caste system that transcends history and politics and forms the ideological basis for the incorporation of different caste groups, critics of Dumont attacked his notion of the superiority of the priest over the king as status over power. With his primary sources being the Brahmin-written classical texts and the colonial and post-independence ethnographic literature (when the power of kings had been drastically reduced), Dumont's critics argue that it is little wonder that the Brahmin appears on top of the hierarchy and that this hierarchy appears to be based on the ideological and structural relation of pure/impure.[15]

In the introduction to *Homo Hierarchicus*, Dumont describes the ideology of caste as essentially religious, but does not then examine Indian religion to any extent, exploring instead the nature of relations between social groups (*jajmani* or shares in the harvest, commensality, marriage, etc.). He does so because he feels the ideology of caste is identifiable from a small number of classical texts and that these must be set against a range of everyday practices that correspond, albeit with some measure of slippage, to that ideology. This easily lends itself to critique via contrasting ethnographic data where, for example, dominant castes or kings lord it over the priests or, more rarely, to the examination of the relevance of those ideological texts. Importantly, too, Dumont moved on following *Homo Hierarchicus* to the study of the history of Western thought, thereby leaving the field of Indian sociology for others to pursue.

There is much of value in the critique of Dumont's argument, and his influence in sparking such fierce debate has been tremendously important for producing high quality scholarship, both ethnographic and historical. However, to develop on Dumont and Pocock's manifesto and explore properly the Indian social imaginary requires more than the observation of the interaction of actual groups of actual people set against certain texts as ideological bearers. It also needs a close consideration of the imaginary spaces, which, certainly in south India, requires one to look at temples. Here, as Fuller (1988) demonstrates in a useful summary, the same status/power debate developed, now with more historians involved, as a debate about whether temples (status) made kings or whether kings (power) made temples. The debate has focused too heavily on the role of temple honors (*mariyātai*)—the keenly contested right to act as the patron of a ritual or festival—and, as Fuller argues (62), it overemphasized the transactional nature of relations between deities, priests, and kings. In its place, Fuller wants to highlight the differences between village temples and the grand urban temples patronized by the kings in order to show that, at different social levels, the temple functions in different ways. The village temple identifies the local community and draws a boundary around it, the city temple draws no such boundary. Thus, the "axis of the kingdom" (65) was irrelevant to the little community, and therefore, one must be careful about describing the temple too narrowly.

In my study of the Munneśvaram temple festival (Bastin 2002), I demonstrate how one local village articulates with the regional temple in its festival. Put simply, where the processions in the village temple festival that precedes the main festival involve processions from the outside in, the main festival involves processions from the inside out, with the villagers attending for their special *mariyātai*. The movement corresponds to the double movement of emission and reabsorption evident, I argue, in the architecture and daily rituals. The region now acquires the characteristics of a *maṇḍala*—a galactic polity as Tambiah (1976) insightfully describes the situation from the old kingdoms of Thailand (and Sri Lanka). When faced by such a double movement, chicken and egg arguments about status and power attain the absurd depths of debates like nature and nurture or mind and body. For the critical issue here is not who or what came first, but how is the double movement expressed as a process of territorialization.

What I have demonstrated in this essay is that a special relation to Hindu divinity and polytheism is emergent from temple aesthetics. The temple is like a palace because a deity is like a monarch, but at the same time the temple is not like a palace because it is the space through which the palace is imagined as the deity is called upon to imagine him or herself. For this reason, the temple must be inserted, as if it were a person, into the field of social relations through which the social imaginary is recast. Critically, the key to the temple is the manipulation of consciousness through aesthetics that brings consciousness into the world and the world into existence. By structuring unique spaces as temples according to this manipulation of the imaginary, the temple succeeds in creating not a priest-king relation but a deity-king relation, whereby the person of the devotee (priest, king, or ordinary worshipper) is able to restate divinity through his or her devotional gaze that provides the mirror of consciousness bringing the deity into the world. At the same time, the aesthetics of worship creates for the king an aesthetics of power that orders his sovereignty and turns him from being a highly ambivalent figure capable of extreme violence into a king capable of good government. Thus, the kingship is more properly the priest-king/ deity-king *relationship* and not simply the seemingly distinct categories of status or power. The aesthetics of power, so often examined in royal and state rituals as a mechanism of legitimation vis-à-vis the will of the commoners, must be recast here (and elsewhere) as the pomp designed to keep the king in line by restating kingship as if in a mirror.

The temple mirror is thus being held up for all to see—deities as well as humans. It utilizes all the features of what Dufrenne (1987) terms the aesthetic a priori. These are the fundamental qualities or attributes of aesthetic experience that inform the plastic arts and enable the relations between image, imagination, and the imaginary to emerge and be fully articulated. They consist of the elementary or natural, such as the immovable solidity of earth or the mobile ravenousness of fire; power as the manifestation of the elemental dynamics of Nature, and the spatio-temporal qualities such power elicits; depth as the concomitant of power, as that which is remote from both space and time, and that which is a primary link between objects and the interiority of the subject; and last, purity (and its obverse) as the direct communication of elements, power, dimensions, and associations (Dufrenne 1987, 33). Nature, power, depth, and purity combine as the characteristics of aesthetic experience to establish the ground of imagination—the imaginary. They are evident in the Hindu temple as the temple describes a cosmos and its genesis in order to describe divinity (and kingship and being) as a unique instance of an omnipresence.

The imaginary itself is anchored in this experience: if gods are true, it is not only because they are desired and express the desire of mortals who construct temples and 'images' to them, but also because they are captured in this first text of the world where what will be discerned as real has not yet been distilled, but where truth is nevertheless experienced. (Dufrenne 1987, 63)

Notes

1. My thanks to Douglas Lewis for enlightening me on the uses of *i*.
2. It must be stressed that Dufrenne is not subscribing here to the linguistic turn and to becoming one of the "voluntary prisoners of language" who treat language as "the new avatar of idealism" (1987, 57). Language and desire are basic to the imaginary, but the imaginary is reducible to neither.
3. Cited by A. K. Coomaraswamy in "Vedic Exemplarism" (Coomaraswamy 1971, 184).
4. See Michell (1988), Pieper (1980), Jouveau-Dubreuil ([1916] 1972), Shukla (1958, 1961), and Curtis (1983).
5. Śaivites are Hindus for whom the preeminent deity is Śiva. Śaivism is the most common form of Hinduism practiced in Sri Lanka, and in order to contrast it with Sinhala Buddhism I normally refer to it as Tamil Śaivism. For reference to the idea of the temple as Purusa's body, see Ananth (1998, 74) and Duraiswamy (1997, 5).
6. Statues of the planets Sun, Moon, Mars, Mercury, Saturn, Venus, Jupiter, Dragon's Head (Rahu) and Dragon's Tail (Ketu) are placed in a 3x3 grid as a freestanding shrine with a specific location in the temple precincts.
7. For an excellent discussion on the nature of *yantra* see Zimmer (1962).
8. Note that *pūjā* does not require a temple, but is the basic ritual act involving human and deity. Others have described it in these terms (Östör 1977; Courtright 1985; Fuller 1992).
9. See F. D. K. Bosch's (1960) excellent study of the lotus stem (*padmamūla*) as a recurring motif in Indian art. It does so in part because of this allusion to unfolding consciousness and manifestation.
10. Sadaśiva corresponds to the *śivaliṅga* as the master signifier and is represented as a column of fire with the anthropomorphic figure of Śiva emerging.
11. The polysemy of the temple flagpole includes the *yūpa* or sacrificial stake to which the victim is tethered (Hiltebeitel 1991, 117–52), the umbilical lotus stem rising from Purusa's navel, and also a simple flagpole in the palace of the regal god.
12. Daniel (1984, 256f.) discusses the link between pain and the experience of embodied divinity. My translation of the Tamil term *aruḷ* as "presence" rather than the more conventional gloss "grace" owes much to the intellectual generosity of David Shulman.
13. See also Eck (1985).
14. This point is illustrated by the frequency with which demon myths describe the demon gaining the illusion of omnipotence through acts of devotion that only on the surface appear to involve the surrender of *anavas*, as well as other myths where the vanquished demon is transformed into an image of devotion such as the deity's banner (Clothey 1978). Forms of surrender in worship include breaking a coconut where the nut is the objectification of *anavas* associated with the head and the "cool fire" of the camphor flame that burns without residue.
15. See Dirks (1987, 1989, 1996), Inden (1990), Quigley (1993), and Raheja (1988). For an excellent discussion of the status/power *relation* in Dumont's analysis of the Indian state, see Parry (1999).

References

Ananth, Sashikala. 1998. *The Penguin Guide to Vaastu: The Classical Indian Science of Architecture and Design*. New Delhi: Penguin Books India.

Bastin, Rohan. 2002. *The Domain of Constant Excess: Plural Worship at the Minnesvaram Temples in Sri Lanka*. New York and Oxford: Berghahn Books.

Bosch, F. D. K. 1960. *The Golden Germ: An Introduction to Indian Symbolism*. 'S-Gravehage, Netherlands: Mouton & Company.

Cassirer, E. 1957. *The Philosophy of Symbolic Forms. Volume Three: The Phenomenology of Knowledge*. Trans. Ralph Manheim. New Haven: Yale University Press.

Clothey, Fred W. 1978. *The Many Faces of Murukan: The History and Meaning of a South Indian God*. The Hague: Mouton Publishers.

———. 1983. "The *Yaga*: A Fire Ritual of South India." In *Experiencing Siva: Encounters with a Hindu Deity*, ed. Fred W. Clothey and J. Bruce Long. New Delhi: Manohar.

Coomaraswamy, A. K. 1971. *Selected Papers Volume 2: Metaphysics*. Ed. Roger Lipsey. Bollingen Series LXXXIX. Princeton: Princeton University Press.

Courtright, Paul B. 1985. "On This Holy Day in My Humble Way: Aspects of Puja." In *Gods of Flesh, Gods of Stone: The Embodiment of Divinity in India*, ed. Joanne Punzo Waghorne and Norman Cutler, 33–50. Chambersburg, Penn.: Anima Books.

Curtis, James W. V. 1983. "Space Concepts and Worship Environment in Saiva Siddhanta." In *Experiencing Siva: Encounters with a Hindu Deity*, ed. Fred W. Clothey and J. Bruce Long. New Delhi: Manohar.

Daniel, E. Valentine. 1984. *Fluid Signs: Being a Person the Tamil Way*. Berkeley, Los Angeles, and London: University of California Press.

Davis, Richard H. 1991. *Ritual in an Oscillating Universe: Worshipping Siva in Medieval India*. Princeton: Princeton University Press.

Dirks, N. 1987. *The Hollow Crown: Ethnohistory of an Indian Kingdom*. Cambridge: Cambridge University Press.

———. 1989. "The Original Caste: Power, History and Hierarchy in South Asia." *Contributions to Indian Sociology* 23, no. 1: 59–78.

———. 1996. "Recasting Tamil Society: The Politics of Caste and Race in Contemporary Southern India." In *Caste Today*, ed. C. J. Fuller, 263–295. SOAS Studies on South Asia. Delhi: Oxford University Press.

Dufrenne, Mikel. 1973. *The Phenomenology of Aesthetic Experience*. Trans. Edward S. Casey, Albert A. Anderson, Willis Domingo, and Leon Jacobson. Evanston, Ill.: Northwestern University Press.

———. 1987. *In the Presence of the Sensuous: Essays in Aesthetics*. Ed. Mark S. Roberts and Dennis Gallagher. Atlantic Highlands, N.J.: Humanities Press International.

Dumont, L. 1980. *Homo Hierarchicus: The Caste System and Its Implications*. Complete rev. Eng. ed. Chicago and London: University of Chicago Press.

Duraiswamy, Sivanandini. 1997. *Remembering Hindu Traditions*. Colombo: M.D. Gunasena.

Eliade, Mircea. 1959. *The Sacred and the Profane: The Nature of Religion*. Trans. Willard R. Trask. New York and London: Harcourt Brace Jovanovich.

———. 1990. *Symbolism, the Sacred, and the Arts*. Ed. Diane Apostolos-Cappadona. New York: Crossroad.

Eck, Diana L. 1985. *Darśan: Seeing the Divine Image in India*. 2nd rev. and enlarged ed. New York: Anima Books.

Fuller, C. J. 1988. "The Hindu Temple and Indian Society." In *Temple in Society*, ed. Michael V. Fox, 50–66. Winona Lake, Ind.: Eisenbrauns.

———. 1992. *The Camphor Flame: Popular Hinduism and Society in India*. Princeton: Princeton University Press.

———. 1996. "Introduction." In *Caste Today*, ed. C. J. Fuller, 1–31. SOAS Studies on South Asia. Delhi: Oxford University Press.

Handelman, Don, and David Shulman. 1997. *God Inside Out: Siva's Game of Dice.* New York and Oxford: Oxford University Press.

Hiltebeitel, Alf. 1991. *The Cult of Draupadi.* Vol. 2, *On Hindu Ritual and the Goddess.* Chicago and London: University of Chicago Press.

Inden, Ronald. 1990. *Imagining India.* Oxford: Blackwell Publishers.

Jouveau-Dubreuil, G. [1916] 1972. *Dravidian Architecture.* Varanasi: Bharat-Bharati.

Kapferer, Bruce. 1983. *A Celebration of Demons: Exorcism and the Aesthetics of Healing in Sri Lanka.* Bloomington: Indiana University Press.

———. 2000. "Sexuality and the Art of Seduction in Sinhalese Exorcism." *Ethnos* 65, no. 1: 5–32.

Kramrisch, Stella. 1946. *The Hindu Temple.* 2 vols. Calcutta: University of Calcutta. Republished 1976. New Delhi: Motilal Banarsidas.

———. 1981. *The Presence of Siva.* Princeton: Princeton University Press.

Michell, George. 1988. *The Hindu Temple: An Introduction to Its Meaning and Forms.* Second edition, first published 1977. Chicago and London: The University of Chicago Press.

Östör, Akos. 1978. "Puja in Society: A Methodological and Analytical Essay on an Ethnographic Category." *Eastern Anthropologist* 31: 119–76.

Parry, Jonathan. 1999. "Mauss, Dumont, and the Distinction between Status and Power." In *Marcel Mauss: A Centenary Tribute,* ed. Wendy James and N. J. Allen. New York and Oxford: Berghahn Books.

Pieper, Jan. 1980. "The Spatial Structure of Suchindram." In *Ritual Space in India: Studies in Architectural Anthropology,* ed. Jan Pieper. London: Art and Archaeology Research Papers.

Quigley, Declan. 1993. *The Interpretation of Caste.* Oxford: Clarendon Press.

Raheja, Gloria Goodwin. 1988. "India: Caste, Kingship, and Dominance Reconsidered." *Annual Review of Anthropology* 17: 497–522.

Rowland, Benjamin. 1954. *The Art and Architecture of India: Buddhist, Hindu, Jain.* Harmondsworth: Penguin Books.

Sartre, Jean-Paul. n.d. *The Psychology of the Imagination.* Secaucus, N.J.: Citadel Press.

Shukla, D. N. 1958. *Vāstu Sastra.* Vol. 2, *Hindu Canons of Iconography and Painting.* Bharatiya Vāstu Sastra Series. Volume 9. Lucknow: Vāstu-Vanmaya-Prakasanasala.

———. 1961. *Vāstu Sastra.* Vol. l, *Hindu Science of Architecture.* Bharatiya Vāstu Sastra Series. Volume 8. Lucknow: Vāstu-Vanmaya-Prakasanasala.

Shulman, David D. 1978. "The Serpent and the Sacrifice: An Anthill Myth from Tiruvarur." *History of Religion* 18: 107–37.

———. 1980. *Tamil Temple Myths: Sacrifice and Divine Marriage in the South Indian Saiva Tradition.* Princeton: Princeton University Press.

Staal, Frits. 2003. "Artificial Languages: Asian Backgrounds or Influences?" *International Institute for Asian Studies Newsletter,* March 2003, 15.

Tambiah, Stanley J. 1976. *World Conqueror and World Renouncer: A Study of Buddhism and Polity in Thailand against a Historical Background.* Cambridge: Cambridge University Press.

Volwahsen, A. 1969. *Living Architecture: Indian.* New York: Grosset & Dunlop.

Zimmer, Heinrich. 1962. *Myths and Symbols of Indian Art and Civilization.* Bollingen Series Number XXXIV, ed. Joseph Campbell. Princeton: Princeton University Press.

Chapter Five

WHERE DIVINE HORSEMEN RIDE
Trance Dancing in West Africa

Steven M. Friedson

I dance ... therefore I am.

– Léopold Sédar Senghor, *Freedom 1: Negritude and Humanism*

Léopold Senghor's philosophy of Negritude rethinks Descartes' ergo sum as an ontology of the body. This is not merely a substitution of terms, but a reversal of effect. A danced existence is always-already on the move, a coming and a going, a continual leaving and approach. To think that it ever ceases to be in flux is an illusion nurtured by the desire for narrative assurance. Cessation reinstates dystopia in the midst of worlds that no longer exist. A danced ontology moves us out of an interiority that projects a vision of certainty, and into a world that calls the body to recognize itself in the contours of musical experience. Cartesian metaphysics seeks to overcome gods who may be deceiving; danced existences embrace them.

Dance in Africa celebrates lives, commemorates death, consummates alliances, is part of the everyday lifeworld. We have nothing comparable in Western society, where danced bodies have been relegated to night-clubs, weddings, high school proms, and the occasional concert stage. In Africa, who you are often has much to do with how you dance. And nowhere is this more true than in dance's embrace of the other in its embodiment of a multiplicity of deities and spirits. This last dance—striking in its frequency (Bourguignon 1968)—is not merely the final item in a list, but marks the entire African continent. The Saharan divide—that somewhat suspect division of Africa—is not operative here. Trance dancing is an ancient practice that, to the consternation of both missionary and government official, persists to this day. Divine horsemen still ride in the northern savanna as well as the Guinea Coast, and drums of affliction continue to sound throughout Bantu-speaking Africa.

No doubt a danced religion was never far from Senghor's mind when he predicated his ontological turn on dance's fundamental difference; its orientation towards the other. Negritude was the "weak beat" in a dialectical negativity (Jeanpierre 1969, 451). Looking back, this Black Orpheus, as Sartre (1969) famously put it, offered a technologized West an aesthetic correction. If not for Africa, "who would teach rhythm to the dead world of machines and cannons?" (Senghor quoted in Vaillant 1990, 266). This parsing of vocations was part of Senghor's riff on a rhythmicized Africa that was always already different.

If all this begins to sound somewhat familiar—African participatory reason confronting European analytical minds, the regionalized equivalent of white people clapping on "one" and "three"—it is not surprising. The rhythmic vitality that is the core of Senghor's Negritude lent itself to a misappropriation aligned with oversexualized African bodies lost in a participation mystique. "Natural rhythm" was sympathetic to an arrested development attributed to the effects of puberty on bodies trapped in tropical climes. Yet despite all the advances in microbiology, we never have found that ever-elusive rhythm gene. Nevertheless, if you have been danced since you were in your mother's womb, rhythm can take on the dimensions of a cultural physiology, which Senghor understood as the psycho-physiological contours of a "Black soul."

Whether Negritude is ultimately an inverted philosophy, Cartesianism in disguise, or anti-racist racism (Senghor has been accused of all these; see Mudimbe's 1988 defense), it does not change its insight into African rhythmic praxis. This is not an essentializing of Africa, or rhythm, to reify its difference, as some have suggested (Agawu 2003), but rather an acknowledgement of the reality of a different way of being-in-the-world. Instead of suppressing the body as the antithesis of a translucent knowledge guaranteed by intellection, trance dancing privileges the body as the site of a gathering that declines into the world. What better place then to recover Senghor's ontological turn than in this dance that calls out to worlds that are both here and away?

But how do we retrieve ways of being-in-the-world so radically different from our own possibilities? What does it mean to be embodied by a deity, to be-there and not-there at the same time? If the people having such experiences can tell us nothing about it—possession is amnesic for those possessed—and given the fact that gods do not generally grant interviews to ethnographers, what kind of access can we have to such worlds? Is spirit possession inherently opaque, becoming a blank screen for our projections, power differentials cast before a silent landscape?

Possession trance variously has been taken as the local equivalent of multiple personality disorder, Freudian sublimation, Jungian archetypes, the formation of right brain personalities, Lacanian manifestations of the Real, peripheral strategies of marginal peoples, the working out of colonial and postcolonial disorders, Marxist illusion, and just plain good acting. What rarely happens, however, is for trance in Africa to be taken for what it is first and foremost: a danced existence, a way of being-in-the-world in a musical way. Long relegated to the back burner of ethnographic description, musical experience is treated as epiphenomenal to more important ongoing functionalist concerns.

We can pay attention to behavior, act, and word; learn of the gods, their attributes, and lineages; and investigate the everyday life of devotees. From these ethnographic facts, we then can extrapolate complex chains of causality. However, when facts are linked into narrowly defined sequences of cause and effect, the resulting analyses tend towards a stasis that is antithetical to the multidimensionality of spirit possession. Trance dancing is always on the move, withdrawing as it embodies, thus already open to other possibilities. Throughout Africa these possibilities are given first and foremost within the field of consociates, borrowing Alfred Schutz's terminology (1951), growing older together while making music together.[1] This is not an intersubjective musical sharing between isolated and bounded egos, an infection of subjectivities, but participation in a way of being, one that is precisely in-between such nodal existence. Happening in the in-between musical experience has a claim on us. And, in this claim, trance dancing reveals itself not in some diffuse way, floating above the thinly veiled grounds of shifting observations, but in the particular circumstances of specific sounds and locations.

What follows concerns a particular medicine shrine found amongst the Ewe-speaking peoples of the Guinea Coast, a *vodu* order I have been working with over the past ten years.[2] Writing about the Ewe, however, is a notoriously difficult task. More than one researcher has commented on a kind of Ewe chaos, a cultural style that defies textual description (Geurts 2002; Rosenthal 1998). There seems to be no getting to the bottom of things, especially those things having to do with shrines, leaving a distinct impression that, no matter how long you stay in Ewe country, you are never quite there. It is like the many clay Legbas, the god of the crossroads and thresholds, protecting the entrances to villages and houses. You only see the visible anthropomorphic figure, Legba's outward manifestation, not his power, the herbs, animal parts, and other things buried deep inside. Much in Ewe culture is similarly subterranean, not visible to the naked eye. Nothing is quite what it seems; everything feels submerged beneath at least two layers of clay.

A direct gaze that freezes Ewe religion into a silent tableau may make things more recognizable and thus more satisfying, allowing us to understand nuances and practices in a comforting way. However, this stable ground gives way under the weight of danced existences. A glance from the side, a fleeting glimpse of that which moves on the periphery, is much more in keeping with the phenomenon at hand, though it never will be as comforting as the cold discourse of certainty. This furtive vision, productive of understanding, is found in-between the being-there and being-away of fieldwork, the ethnographic truth that as long as we are in the field we are always-already leaving.

Being-in-Between

It was right before the old woman became possessed. I was looking at the ground, fascinated by the play of light and shadow on the dance floor created by the sun coming through the woven palm-leaf roof covering the open pavilion. We had been up all night wake-keeping, and I was feeling pretty tired. It was now late afternoon, and I found myself starting to doze but not quite going to sleep, a kind of twilight existence, when a type of synaesthesia set in, and the play of light and shadow started to take on a musical dimension. As this modality thinned, it simultaneously spread out and grew deeper. I was somehow between the light and the shadow, the sound of the drum and the rattle, between the call of the priest and the response of those who were gathered. Everything was on the move, including the ground, and I was suspended in-between the shadows, the sounds, the smells, the heat, the wind. And this was precisely when the old woman leaped out of her chair, transposed into the sublime countenance of a dancing god.

In the Brekete shrines of West Africa, ancient rhythms move bodies in spectacular ways. The power of repetition, inscribed in a soundscape of welcome and praise, calls northern gods to possess their devotees. These divine horsemen, so goes the trope, ride their mounts.[3] In the blink of an eye a person can become seized. Captured by their capacity to be taken, those possessed never know they are being ridden. They are no longer aware of their bodily existence for they are no longer themselves. It is not they who dance but Kunde the hunter, or Ablewa his wife, Sanya the first-born, or Bangle the soldier. Embodiments of virtuosity, these gods are virtuosos of being-there. Costumed in swirling saturated colors, they dance themselves into existence. And as long as the gods are there, someone always must be leaving. What is a being-there for a deity is already a being-away for a devotee. And this is exactly what had happened to the old woman when she became possessed. No longer a widowed fishmonger with arthritic knees, she was Bangle the avenging and thus protecting deity, the soldier and policeman, the owner of *dzogbe* (the desert), where hot deaths reside.

Ketetsi[4] (one of Bangle's many praise names) had been coming to her for a long time and was as familiar with being in her body as she was with being-away. It was after several miscarriages, when she was in her early twenties, that her husband first took her to seek the help of the gods. Shortly thereafter she became pregnant, and when she subsequently delivered a healthy baby boy, they were both, as it were, "born into the shrine." Not all members become *trɔsi*[5] (a spouse of the gods), but she was blessed, and shortly after she joined the shrine, the god joined her. Now, forty years later, Ketetsi was still working his way in her body.

He is but one of a pantheon of kola nut gods brought to southern Ghana from the northern region in the 1920s (Fiawoo 1968). There was a general belief that the north had resisted European domination more effectively, therefore their gods must be stronger, and these new deities were readily adopted. Although this was not the only reason, northern gods did find fertile ground in the disruptions of colonialism. Today Bangle and his family make up one of the fastest growing shrines in West Africa, found as far east as Nigeria and extending its reach in the west to Côte d'Ivoire and beyond.

Brekete—the name of the double-headed snared drum that accompanied these northern deities when they were brought south, and the one still used to call the gods to descend and dance—provides cures for all kinds of afflictions and offers protection against sorcerous attacks. For those who patronize the shrine, this help is inscribed in a moral code, referred to as "the ten commandments," that demands adherence. Retribution can be severe and swift if the code is broken. This contrasts with the many other *vodu* orders found along the Guinea Coast that offer their power without such a strong moral imprint. This, no doubt, is part of its appeal in the peripheral economy of a struggling Volta Region at the beginning of the twenty-first century, where a search for some kind of security is increasingly becoming a difficult and elusive task.

Probably of Hausa origin, Brekete (sometimes referred to as *gorovodu*, *goro* is the Hausa word for kola nut, the sacrament of these shrines) follows the typical contours of a Sahel-style possession cult (see Besmer 1983), with the gods situated in familial relationships and infused with an Islamic overlay. The coastal Ewes imagine the "North" as an Islamized region of "otherness," though the origin of the shrine is no doubt pre-Islamic. Even though the shrine is of foreign origin, the Ewe have domesticated it within a nexus of long-standing similar complexes found throughout the coastal regions. These shrines, populated by *orisha* and *vodu*, coalesce into a recognizable medico-religious form spread over a considerable portion of West Africa (Herskovits 1938; Rouget 1985; Rosenthal 1998; Blier 1995) and, as a result of the African diaspora, in much of the Western hemisphere (Bastide 1978; Deren 1953; Métraux 1972; Walker 1972). This is no local phenomenon but the workings of a world religion.

As with most gods in West Africa, Bangle manifests himself in a multiplicity of ways, such as in the many people he possesses, and as a god-thing, what Ewe still call fetishes. As fetish he is a collage of mineral, vegetable, and animal, shaped by human hands and brought forth through word and song. Bangle's most prominent feature is a cow tail that comes out of the

Figure 5.1 Bangle as fetish

Photograph by author.

end of an oval encasement that surrounds an iron bell (see figure 5.1). The tail is Bangle's beard, indicative of a wise and powerful man from the north. The fetish, however, is not a symbol "of" or "for" anything, nor is it a vessel for the god to inhabit. That is left to the *trɔsiwo* (pl.), those who become filled with the presence of the god. Bangle as fetish-thing *is* the god as a material manifestation.

Every Brekete shrine has at least one, usually two or more, of these Bangle fetishes. When I asked the head priest, the pope of all the Brekete shrines, how Bangle could be in so many different places at once, he asked me what happens when you put two atoms of hydrogen together with one atom of oxygen. It is the same for the gods. When the right combination of material is brought together under the necessary ritual conditions, as with water, you get gods.[6] It is to these fetishes, namely, the gods in their material manifestation, that animals and libations are offered, the very reason why we had gathered at the shrine.

Being-Away

When Adzo,[7] the fishmonger, became possessed, it was the third, and next to last, day of a *fetatrɔtrɔ* (literally, the year head turning), a triennial cow sacrifice.[8] No one had gotten much sleep, for at a *fetatrɔtrɔ* every night is a wake-keeping and every day a jubilation. What little rest we had managed consisted of short naps here and there. REM sleep was beginning to work itself out whether we knew it or not, and by that penultimate day we were all in an altered state; some, obviously, more than others. The almost constant music making, and three days of chewing kola nut and drinking *akpeteshie*, the locally distilled gin, more than contributed to the mood. A cow sacrifice, of course, is serious business: gods must be fed, libations poured, ancestors remembered, debts repaid, and pledges redeemed. Gods in West Africa, however, also simply love to celebrate with their children. Whatever else this sacrifice was about, whatever stories people were telling themselves about themselves, a *fetatrɔtrɔ* was always a good party, and this was no exception.

Although it had seemed like days ago, it was only earlier that morning when the fetishes were brought outside and "washed" in the blood of the cow. Inside the shrine-house, each god has his own *kpome* (literally, "in the oven" but here meaning the home of the god), a half-walled cubicle where sacrifices and libations usually are offered. For a cow sacrifice, however, the fetishes are gathered together, put into a large metal basin, and placed in the courtyard in the middle of the dance floor in front of the shrine-house. It is one of the only times when the gods are taken from their altars and displayed publicly for all to see.

As the gods were brought out that morning, several of the *bosomfo*, who are especially initiated sacrificial priests, led a large bull into the courtyard. After several tries they finally got the bull on its side and proceeded to lift it over the basin. One man put his fingers inside the cow's nose and pulled back the head so that the neck was exposed as the senior *bosomfo*, dressed in his blood-stained *adewu*, or hunter's shirt, emerged from inside the shrine with the sacrificing knife in his hand. He walked over to the cow and with several quick slashes nearly decapitated it. Blood gushed out of the jugular vein all over the fetishes. When the blood quit flowing into the basin, the cow was tossed to the side and the gods taken inside to be "polished." The cow was in its death throes for well over ten minutes, a propitious omen that the bull was strong and worthy of giving its life to the gods.

As always, there was an almost eerie silence when the gods were fed. There was no music, and most people kept silent. It is not polite to talk when the gods are eating. After the cow died and was removed, however, the special hunting songs of the *bosomfo* were raised as several small piles of gunpowder were set off. After these ritually charged songs were finished, the drumming and dancing began in earnest, continuing throughout the day with many *trɔsiwo* becoming possessed.

By late afternoon most of us were running on empty, moved on by the sheer energy of the music—and the continuing rounds of kola and *akpeteshie*. I was drifting in and out and had totally given up any pretext of being the resident ethnomusicologist. Fifteen or so *trɔsiwo* had appropriated the dance floor, taking up the entire space in the expansive and

highly articulated movements of divine horsemen. Visually it was stun-
ning: the gods' northern style dress, with its stripped cloth in primary
colors, highlighted by the stippled effect of the filtered light. Acoustically, it was overwhelming: songs of deep Ewe filled the air as they
played Bangle's music.

Befitting a soldier and policeman, his music is that of *agbadza* (literally,
"gunbelt"), the classic war drum of the Ewe. In the olden days, when it
was known as *atrikpui*, it was only performed on the outskirts of the village by returning warriors, or at the funerals of those who died a hot
death (Jones 1959; Alorwoyie 2003). Now it is mostly heard at wake-keep-
ings and burials, both for those who died coolly, in bed at an old age, and
those who died a hot death as a result of some kind of accident or other
misfortune. This music touches people deeply, seeming to embody core
features of an Ewe sensibility. At a wake-keeping, I have seen more than
one old man, inspired by memories past—and a bit of *akpeteshie*—dance to
this drum with tears running down his face.

Unlike other Brekete music that utilizes fast tempos and the stylized
dance movement unique to this shrine, Bangle's dance is the typical back-
breaking style for which the Ewe are famous. The beauty of this dance,
according to Ewes, is the action of the shoulder blades coming together,
focusing attention on the middle of the back. It is not the movement of the
shoulder blades but what happens in-between that is considered beautiful. While shrine members dance in this style, the gods are often twirling
around the dance floor in the expansive and exaggerated movements of
divine horsemen.

Among the possessed that afternoon, there were at least three or four
trɔsiwo manifesting Bangle at the same time, which seemed totally normal
to most Ewes, but always seemed a bit strange to me, especially when the
various Bangles would engage each other in animated conversation.
Eventually, however, I began to realize that Bangle in Adzo is something
slightly different than Bangle in someone else, which is different than Bangle as fetish. The gods are not a single entity analogous to a Western projection of personhood with a bounded ego and delimited personality, but
always a multiplicity of effect.

As I sat there watching the *trɔsiwo* dance, every once in a while one of
the gods would stop in front of me to offer greetings and give his blessing
with the typical handshake of the gods, a hard slap of the hand. In West
Africa you can shake hands with your gods, engage in face-to-face interaction, experience them in immediacy. If I had been daydreaming or
nodding off to sleep, which by this time was a frequent if not almost a
continuous occurrence, the hard slap would immediately pull me back
into my body and an awareness of my immediate surroundings. And just
as suddenly I would start to drift off again. The time between the shifts
became slower yet somehow closer together. I started getting confused
about which mode I was in. Being-away started feeling like being-there,

and in this liminality the texture of light and shadow, sound and movement, began to separate and coalesce at the same time.

Of course, we all have experienced being-there while being-away to some degree: daydreaming while driving a car, attending a lecture, listening to music, or in countless other ways. During those moments, we somehow manage to withdraw our conscious awareness of bodily emplacement even while we continue to do complex tasks, such as drive a car or even play in a symphony orchestra, as happens sometimes with professional musicians playing Beethoven's Fifth Symphony for the hundredth time. It is not something we willingly do; rather, daydreaming comes over us of its own free will. And just as suddenly, without warning, we are once more back in our bodies: someone asks us a question, a car pulls out in front of us, the speaker stumbles over her words, a string breaks. The dis-placement itself is displaced as it withdraws.

This is to say nothing of sleep, a much more radical attunement of being-away. When we are sleeping our bodies are not so much displaced as bounded in immobility. And, as with daydreaming, we cannot willingly go to sleep. This is evident when we nod in and out while dozing, but it is also true when we go to bed. As Merleau-Ponty reminds us, interestingly relating sleep to possession, before we actually go to sleep we assume the position of someone already asleep:

> I lie down in bed, on my left side, with my knees drawn up; I close my eyes and breathe slowly, putting my plans out of my mind. But the power of my will or consciousness stops there. As the faithful, in the Dionysian mysteries, invoke the god by miming scenes from his life, I call up the visitation of sleep by imitating the breathing and posture of the sleeper. The god is actually there when the faithful can no longer distinguish themselves from the part they are playing, when their body and their consciousness cease to bring in, as an obstacle, their particular opacity, and when they are totally fused in the myth. There is a moment when sleep 'comes,' settling on this imitation of itself which I have been offering to it, and I succeed in becoming what I was trying to be; an unseeing and almost unthinking mass, riveted to a point in space and in the world henceforth only through the anonymous alertness of the senses. (1962, 163)

We may call sleep to visit us, but, as with Dionysian frenzy and possession trance, the moment of its arrival is not under conscious control. I am not suggesting that possession trance is somehow an extreme form of daydreaming or some kind of sleepwalking, but rather there is a resonance that can bring us somewhat closer to an understanding of how someone entranced can be there and away at the same time.

No matter what the similarity may be, however, a gulf remains between the two that never can be bridged. In our dreams, whether they be of day or night, we hold on to who we are. We are always involved, in some way, with the dreamplay that unfolds. The trance of a *trɔsi*, however,

118 | *Steven M. Friedson*

entails a complete sacrifice of persona and a total concealing of ego in order to allow the unconcealing of the sanctified presence of the Other. This lack of present awareness characterizes possession trance, simultaneously projecting it within a temporal horizon. Possession trance is, in a sense, a time out of time. Ask a *trɔsi* after she has come out of trance how much time has lapsed, and she will invariably tell you that no time has passed: one minute she was sitting there singing, and the next she found herself drenched in the herb water (*amatsi*) of the god, which is poured on the possessed when the god decides it is time to leave.

This total being-away of possession also resonates with the captivation of animality, hence the widespread metaphor of divine horsemen found throughout West Africa. As horses are ridden enclosed in a disinhibiting ring of behavior, so those who are possessed are put through their paces by the gods. Animality, however, entails an open absorption into the self-encircling ring of disinhibition. In other words, horses are not aware of being ridden; it is something that happens when the necessary conditions are present, which is when the horse has been trained and there is a rider. Training a horse to be ridden is a matter of moving into the horse's field of instinctive drives. This manipulation happens "not in the so-called 'interior' of the animal, but in the ring of the interrelated drivenness of instinctual drives as they open themselves up" (Heidegger 1995, 255). A similar transposition, without the compulsion to open up, transpires in possession trance, when those who are possessed are temporarily released from their own rings of contextuality and are similarly ridden without knowing it. A lack of awareness, however, does not necessarily mean that there is no experience. Possession trance may not be amenable to a retelling because the happening is not linguistically encoded, but musically experienced. It is an example of why a logocentric bias blinds us to a hearing of what happens in spirit possession.

The happening of spirit possession always takes place in the lifeworld of shrines. Things, of course, can be in a world, stones and hammers, jugs and chalices, as well as cats and dogs, horses and cows; but being-in-the-world is the sole province of those who care, who can take up projects and reject possibilities within a temporal horizon, namely, predecessors, consociates, and successors (Schutz 1962). Northern gods also care, take up projects, and reject possibilities; however, they do this in a way different than that of people. Gods cannot exist within the "ekstatic"[9] temporal horizon of human comportment and therefore cannot fold back the possibilities open to them into having been. They cannot grow older surrounded by a field of finitude because gods cannot die. This does not mean that they necessarily live forever. If not taken care of, paid attention to through sacrifice and libation, they eventually may be forgotten and, as with old soldiers, just fade away.

Now and then, however, under special circumstances, gods can approach human temporality, can go along with it, when divine horsemen ride and those they have chosen are away. This ride is somewhere in-between the open absorption of animality and the being-there of human comportment. Neither present nor absent, they are world-possessing, in a continual state of *transition*, being-there in the in-between. They manifest themselves neither in disinhibiting rings of behavior nor in rings of contextuality, but are cleared in *trans*posing fields of existence, revealing *trans*actional ways of being in a musical world.

The Rhythm of the Crossroads

And that is where I found myself late in the afternoon when Adzo became possessed and Ketetsi stood up to dance, suspended in-between the symphony of drumming, dancing, and singing that takes place at a Brekete shrine. Everything was in slow motion; the cross-rhythmic density of drums, bells, clapping sticks, and rattles separating themselves out into distinct timbric bands. The play of light and shadow, color and costume, call and response was in a continual flux, coalescing under the weight of fluid synaesthetic boundaries. It was the rhythm of the crossroads inscribed in the flesh of the world.

Crossroads and cross-rhythms are sites of the liminal, where choices are made, paths taken up or discarded, doors opened and closed. Just as the crossroads, that resonant symbol of Africa, offers by definition multiple ways, cross-rhythms refuse to settle for one interpretive matrix. They are always open to other possibilities as different reads of phenomenological surfaces. Always in motion, the cross-rhythms of Brekete continually turn to that which is not there, and in this essential absence is danced to the core.

Such movement is not conducive to Cartesian certitude, the musical equivalent of "Where is one?"—the inevitable question Western musicians ask when encountering this music for the first time. Confronted with a destabilizing barrage of cross-rhythms, finding "one" can be an existential exercise. Not only do we want to know where "one" is, we need to know. Certainty can immediately relieve the distress produced by shifting metrical grounds that do not privilege beginnings. We want reassurance that there is a stable foundation—one meter, one viewpoint, a vanishing perspective that reveals a linear sequence of "nows" inexorably moving from past to future. There must be one beat that all players relate to, we reason; and though African musicians may not articulate this in Western terms, there must be, nonetheless, the equivalent to "one" somewhere. Everything else becomes a distraction that reifies difference. Yet the assurance of an *archai* somehow remains elusive in this rhythmic instantiation of a metaphysics of presence. In the cross-rhythms of Brekete, it is, as that old Indian story goes, "turtles all the way down" (Geertz 1973, 29).

Ask an Ewe drummer where "one" is, and he will tell you to listen to the bell. For *bangleza* ("za" is the suffix referencing shrine music), it is the

Figure 5.2 Bell pattern for *agbadza*

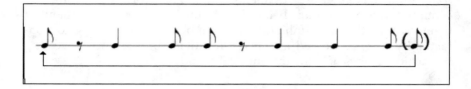

slow groove of *agbadza*, a piece of Ewe musical genius whose origins extend into a remote past. Its timeline is the hinge of a suspended musical world upon which all else turns (see figure 5.2). Heard from womb to tomb (the bell pattern is used not only for *agbadza* but can be found in a plethora of Ewe musical styles), it has assumed the contours of a naturalized aesthetic, which is part of a musical physiology that embodies a deep Ewe sensibility. Every drummer, singer, and dancer holds the bell's timeline in their body, and each part of the musical texture has the possibility to relate to the bell in a different way, creating a shadowed duet, what Pantaleoni (1972) calls a rhythmic silhouette. Significantly, not only do these parts rely on different metric schemes, but they begin at different places in the bell's pattern. When asked where "one" is, Ewe drummers tell you to listen to the bell because there is no "one."

Listening to the bell, however, can be a daunting task for a musician inculcated in a rhythmic approach that privileges a linear metrical scheme. In Brekete, there are always at least two metrical perspectives going on at all times, two rates of motion freely interacting in complex ways producing multiple layers of cross-rhythmic elaboration. The phenomenon of cross-rhythms, however, is something quite different than playing two rhythms together, regardless of their degree of complexity. Genuine cross-rhythms do something—they cross—and this crossing is only possible within the parameters of a polymetrical framework, when at least two contrasting meters are continuously present. Everything else is mere syncopation, which is what African rhythm is often reduced to in Western eyes and ears, thus masking its rhythmic vitality.

Bangle's bell is a paradigm of cross-rhythmic ambiguity, simultaneously open to multiple readings. Its seven-stroke asymmetrical patterning readily can be felt against a two-pulse or three-pulse beat background, with the inherent possibility of these beats combining into a dizzying array of changing meters that are both additive and divisive at the same time.[10] This bell pattern is probably one of the most written about aspects of African music, but I will not rehearse this considerable literature here. Suffice it to say that there is little agreement among scholars about the exact nature of this pattern; in fact, we still cannot even decide if, or where, "one" is.

The Brekete drummers take full advantage of the bell's ambiguity, effortlessly shifting metrical perspectives, while simultaneously keeping all possibilities in play. Instead of turning to the virtuosic music of the lead drumming—something essential, of course, but an entire study in itself—I want to concentrate on a place in the musical texture where shifting metrical schemes are transparent. Nowhere can this be more clearly heard, or seen, than in the clapping patterns of the *adehawo*, literally the "hunting group" but here meaning the shrine members.

Clapping, far from being the inconsequential accompaniment that most of the literature would lead you to believe, is, other than singing, the most direct way for a majority of people to participate in music making. It is, perhaps, the original musical instrument and deserves more attention from scholars than it has received.[11] Its deceptively simple structure foregrounds basic principles of Ewe rhythmic construction and is an important aspect of embodied musical experience. Within its confines we can begin to grasp the lived experience of an ecstatic musical time, a palpable sense of what it is like to be there in multiple ways.

Not everyone claps the same, not only rhythmically but also in physical terms, something that has been totally overlooked. Most Westerners clap one hand against the other, with the dominant hand usually hitting at an angle against the weaker hand. Although this is not an answer to that famous Zen *koan*, it does result in "one hand clapping." Most shrine members, on the other hand, clap with their two hands parallel to each other with flattened palms hitting together simultaneously. This tends to ameliorate the dominance of one hand, creating a rather sharp and loud percussive sound that engages both hands equally. This is to say nothing of the fact that we clap to the same beat, or at least try to, while Ewes always have the possibility of clapping to several different beats suggested by the structured ambiguity inherent in the cross-rhythmic texture of the music.

Some people clap four times to one cycle of the bell, other people clap six beats, and still others may freely mix the two, usually in a 3 + 2 pattern that can also be reversed (see figure 5.3). Therefore, it would seem to make perfect sense that those who clap in four, of course, hear the bell in four, and likewise those who clap in six hear the bell in six. In *agbadza* the four-beat clap is clearly privileged—most people do clap it, along with a second bell that also plays a steady four—but this does not mean that only one ruling meter predominates against which the other parts play, as Chernoff (1979), Locke (1978), and others have suggested. Quantity here does not dictate quality. If an abiding principle of Ewe rhythm is that there are always at least two beats going on at the same time, and there is plenty of evidence for this, then the bell would not be coincidental with the clapping but in cross-rhythmic relation to it. In other words, if you clap in four, then you would hear the bell in six (or in three at fast speeds) and vice

Figure 5.3 Clapping patterns in relation to the bell

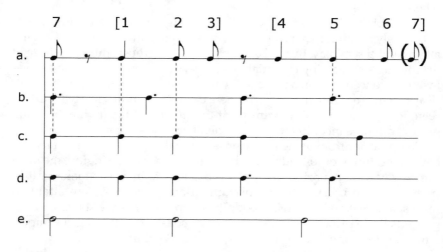

versa. It is a cognitive shift that foregrounds a fundamental difference in approach to rhythmic praxis.

From an African perspective, the trick, of course, is to hold all of these metrical possibilities suspended in the body at the same time. This suspension is not some kind of mental construct caught in the structural bones of a Lévi-Straussian binary opposition but is inscribed in the viscera of bodies that are both here and away. To enter the world of cross-rhythmic suspension is to enter the bodily realm of maintaining multiple beats in the body at the same time, something African dancers do as a matter of course. This bodily knowledge, what Merlau-Ponty calls a practognosis (cited in Kwant 1963, 28), cannot be fully grasped except through the medium of its offering. It has particular contours and grooves that can only be approached through a bodily practice. In the spirit of a performed aesthetics, I offer the following exercise as a set of phenomenological variations of the body.

Play the bell pattern with your right hand—I like playing it on my chest so that I can feel it more directly—and with your left hand beat the four-feel (figure 5.3 line "b"). One way to initialize this procedure is to figure out where the four beats match with the seven-stroke pattern of the bell.[12] Before doing this, we need to decide on a starting place for the bell. The first thing one notices about the bell is that the pattern groups itself naturally into two unequal parts marked at each end by double strokes (figure 5.3 line "a").[13] This marking of endings is typical of much African music, which seems to privilege endings over beginnings (see Blacking

[1973] and Jones [1959] on this point). As a pattern, two events (one stroke followed by a double stroke) are brought into close proximity to three events (two strokes followed by a double stroke). If we follow this initial grouping—and this is by no means the only possible one—and label the first long stroke as "1," then the four beats coincide with the bell on strokes 5 and 7. Synchronizing the parts in this way creates linkages, chains of coincidences that give you something to hold on to. It also highlights endings, giving the bell pattern a propulsive forward force. Once you feel somewhat comfortable playing these two parts, figure out where the six-beat feel aligns with the bell (figure 5.3 line "c"). Using the same starting point, they would come together on strokes 1, 2, and 7. After you have internalized this three-pulse beat, add the six feel to the other two parts by tapping your foot. (I often cut this in half and tap three [= three half notes, figure 5.3 line "e"], especially in fast tempos.) To summarize the basic orientation, four beats align with the bell at two points of articulation, and six beats with three points of articulation. Keep all these parts going on at once (do it in slow motion at first), and you have begun to enter the suspended world of Ewe cross-rhythms. Then, do as the Ewe say and "listen to the bell." Shift your inner listening to a focus on the repeating and incessant nature of the bell, while keeping the other beats going, and you will begin to understand that it is the bell itself that exists in a world in-between.

In keeping with the synaesthetic nature of this phenomenon, let me suggest that this suspended feeling is somewhat akin to the bodily sensation one gets when juggling. Tossing a ball into the air and catching it is not juggling, nor do we enter that domain when two balls are kept in the air, though both of these actions could be juggling in the hands of someone who can actually juggle. You always can work competence down. It is only when three objects are kept in motion by our two hands, which I take to be the essence of juggling, that we break into that realm. This act of motional balancing grants suspension, a particular kind of attunement—anyone who juggles is familiar with this phenomenon. What I am suggesting here is that there is something fundamental about the binary opposition of odd and even, twos and threes, which is rooted in the bilateral symmetry of the body.

In Brekete the possibility that six pulses can be evenly grouped into two beats of three pulses (1 2 3 / 4 5 6) or three beats of two pulses (1 2 / 3 4 / 5 6) is the lifeblood of a musical way of being-in-the-world, a basic orientation to the other that resonates beyond the merely acoustical.[14] As A.M. Jones points out, "If from childhood you are brought up to regard beating 3 against 2 as being as normal as beating in synchrony, then you develop a two-dimensional attitude to rhythm which we in the West do not share" (Jones 1959, 102). It is in this co-occurrence, this turn to the other that refuses to flatten the world to a single rhythmic perspective, that the music of Brekete finds its ontological significance.

These 3:2 configurations, as I have written elsewhere (Friedson 1996), create the possibility of Gestalt shifts in metrical perspective that has the possibility of decentering experience. The results are similar to the shifting that occurs in multi-stable illusions such as the Rubin goblet or the Necker cube series (see figure 5.4). Threes and twos, or their multiples, freely interact across the musical texture, producing shifting metrical patterns, acoustical illusions that are conducive to consciousness-transformations, such as those found in trance dancing. What is productive here is neither the "three" nor the "two" but the phenomenon of shifting granted through the suspension of polymetrical possibility.

This is not meant to imply that a direct connection exists between cross-rhythms and trance. If there were such a correlation, given its widespread occurrence, much of Africa would be in trance most of the time. Rather, cross-rhythms set up a kind of "habitus of listening" (Becker 2004) that, under certain circumstances, can lead to ways of being-there that are profound ways of being-away. One can start to get lost in the shifting and multiple perspectives of a Brekete ensemble, losing one's bearings in a swirl of cross-rhythmic ambiguity. The nature of African cross-rhythms, however, is not about three against two, nor two against three, not even about the shifts between them, though as I have just said, the shifts do seem to help decalcify minds locked on only one side of the silhouette.

Ultimately, African cross-rhythms are a boundary phenomenon. If both parts of the boundary are not firmly in place, then there is no in-between. It is something like the feeling when the positive nodes of two magnets are brought into proximity. That repulsive tension is analogous to the rhythmic tension introduced by polymeters, in part responsible for the amazing

Figure 5.4 Rubin goblet and Necker cube

 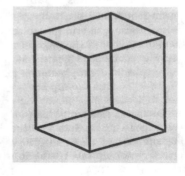

rhythmic consistency of an Ewe ensemble. Oppositional meters tend to keep themselves in check. It is this rhythmic suspension in-between the binary opposition of three and two, even and odd, that expands outward into the transposed world of gods and humans.

Being-There

As the late afternoon sun turned into that distinctive equatorial twilight that makes everything seem bathed in shadows, the gods decided that it was time to leave. Each *trɔsi* was washed in the special water of the deity who possessed them, instantly bringing them out of their trance and back into the quotidian world of everyday cares and concerns. The celebration was breaking up, and the brilliant colors of the afternoon were giving way to a more monochromatic hue. Most people started heading home, and the Brekete drums were taken inside the shrine-house and put away till the next ride. The only people remaining in the courtyard were some women and young girls, mostly the wives, sisters, and daughters of the head priest, who were cleaning up the courtyard and surrounding area.

Off to the side of the shrine-house, however, all by herself, was Adzo, who was still twirling around, dancing to music that no one else could hear. Bangle was not yet ready to let go, intent on taking one last turn with his horse. No one tried to stop her, nor seemed to pay much attention to what she was doing. After all, it was the god who was dancing, and gods do what they want. I, on the other hand, sat there fascinated by this silent dance, realizing in the moment of its happening that music for Adzo, Bangle, and myself was not, as I always had assumed, something dependent on the compression and expansion of air molecules. This was a musical experience born of its own ekstatic time, an original leap out-of-itself.

I think somehow Ketetsi knew that I too was listening, for he suddenly stopped his dance and came over to me. Welcoming me in Hausa, he knelt down and grabbed both of my hands, his right hand holding my right hand, his left, my left, thus causing them to cross. This is the traditional way Bangle's priests shake your hands after offering prayers to the fetish. It is Ketetsi's particular way of blessing. Then he did something that was not traditional and rested his head on our crossed hands. Adzo's breathing was so intense that her entire body was shaking in a kind of fine muscle tonicity. It felt like her body was giving off electrical shocks. I had learned from watching others that it is impolite to look directly at the god, so through all of this I was averting my gaze, only seeing Bangle off-to-the-side in my peripheral vision. Then, without warning, he took his leave and jumped up, dancing his way into the shrine-house. It was the last time I would see him that day, because twenty minutes later Adzo, the fishmonger, emerged dressed in her everyday clothes, walking slowly because of her arthritic knees.

Where Divine Horsemen Ride

When the gods dance, the then-and-there becomes the here-and-now. It is an opening where deities and devotees grow older together, projected into a future that folds back on itself, revealed in a continual round of retrieval, existing in-between the horizon of being-there-and-away. Here musical structure takes on the dimensions of an ontology of energy, the *force vitale* of an animated engagement with the world. It is nothing less than the heart and soul of a Black Orpheus, a rhythmic sensibility that is fundamental to African life. In this ontology, the rationality of certainty is transformed into the certainty of relationality. No rhythm stands alone; one part always invites another. To fill in the ellipses of Senghor's ontology quoted at the beginning, "I feel the Other Person, I dance the Other Person, therefore I am." In this dance, sound and object collapse. No distance separates call from response, color from sound, human from god, threes from twos. In the in-between of a danced existence, divine horsemen ride in musical fields.

Notes

1. Any separation implied here between music and dance is the result of the limitations of vocabulary.
2. I am following Rosenthal's (1998) terminology of *vodu* as an order.
3. While this metaphor is widespread throughout the Guinea Coast, and its analogies hold true for possession among the Ewes, it is not as forefronted in the indigenous discourse about trance as it is, for example, among the Yoruba and Fon peoples.
4. In the southern Ewe dialect "ts" is pronounced "ch."
5. In the Ewe language, "ɔ" is pronounced like "ou" in the English word "ought."
6. Not all gods, however, are manmade. Xebieso, the thunder god, and Da, the snake god, are found not made, a major classificatory node in Ewe cosmology.
7. In Ewe, "dz" is pronounced like the English "j."
8. In Ewe, "*f*" is pronounced like the English "p" but without completely stopping the consonant with the lips.
9. This spelling of "ekstatic" references Heidegger's ontological terminology (1996).
10. Jones (1959), in his transcriptions of Ewe percussion ensembles, uses multiple downbeats with changing meters. While my account is sympathetic to his analysis, I do not agree with his rendition of lead and supporting parts, which seems to be needlessly complicated.
11. One scholar who has paid serious attention to hand-clapping in African music is A.M. Jones (1964).
12. Locke (2002) describes a similar procedure for teaching the polymetrical feel of this bell pattern.
13. The second double stroke, which I have notated as an eighth note followed by an eighth-note rest, could also be notated as a quarter note for the bell sounds through what I am showing as a rest. I am relying on the kinesthetic sense of playing a double stroke for this interpretation. Even if this second stroke is taken as a quarter note, the eighth note before it still marks the bell pattern into two asymmetrical parts.

14. Fundamental to the cross-rhythms of Brekete, as it is to much of African music, is this binary opposition rooted in meters that are odd and even, the most basic of which is the simple ratio of 2:3, which in Western musical parlance is termed a hemiola. (A 1:2 ratio, like the phenomenon of the octave, is homological and thus unable to produce the necessary "cross of rhythms.") In African hands, however, the hemiola is much more than a technical device to be used on occasion to enrich the rhythmic life of a musical texture.

References

Agawu, V. Kofi. 2003. *Representing African Music: Postcolonial Notes, Queries, Positions.* New York: Routledge.

Alorwoyie, Gideon. 2003. Personal communication with author.

Bastide, Roger. 1978. *The African Religions of Brazil: Toward a Sociology of the Interpenetration of Civilizations.* Trans. Helen Sebba. Baltimore: Johns Hopkins University Press.

Becker, Judith. 2004. *Deep Listeners: Music, Emotion and Trancing.* Bloomington: Indiana University Press.

Besmer, Fremont E. 1983. *Horses, Musicians, and Gods: The Hausa Cult of Possession-Trance.* South Hadley, Mass.: Bergin & Garvey Publishers.

Blacking, John. 1973. *How Musical Is Man?* Seattle: University of Washington Press.

Blier, Suzanne Preston. 1995. *African Vodun: Art, Psychology, and Power.* Berkeley: University of California Press.

Bourguignon, Erika. 1968. "World Distribution and Patterns of Possession States." In *Trance and Possession States,* ed. Raymond Prince, 3–34. Montreal: R.M. Burke Memorial Society.

Chernoff, John M. 1979. *African Rhythm and African Sensibility: Aesthetics and Social Action in African Musical Idioms.* Chicago: University of Chicago Press.

Deren, Maya. 1953. *Divine Horsemen: Voodoo Gods of Haiti.* New York: Chelsea House Publishers.

Fiawoo, Dzigbodi Kodzo. 1968. "From Cult to 'Church': A Study of Some Aspects of Religious Change in Ghana." *Ghana Journal of Sociology* 4 (2): 72–87.

Friedson, Steven M. 1996. *Dancing Prophets: Musical Experience in Tumbuka Healing.* Chicago: University of Chicago Press.

Geertz, Clifford. 1973. *The Interpretation of Cultures.* New York: Basic Books.

Geurts, Kathryn Linn. 2002. *Culture and the Senses: Bodily Ways of Knowing in an African Community.* Berkeley: University of California Press.

Heidegger, Martin. 1995. *The Fundamental Concepts of Metaphysics: World, Finitude, Solitude.* Trans. William McNeill and Nicholas Walker. Bloomington: Indiana University Press.

———. 1996. *Being and Time.* Trans. Joan Stambaugh. Albany, NY: State University of New York Press.

Herskovits, Melville J. 1938. *Dahomey: An Ancient West African Kingdom.* 2 vols. New York: J.J. Augustin Publishers.

Horton, Robin. 1971. "African Conversion." *Africa* 41 (2): 85–108.

Jeanpierre, W. A. 1969. "Sartre's Theory of 'Antiracist Racism' in his Study of Negritude." In *Black and White in American Culture: An Anthology from The Massachusetts Review,* ed. Jules Chametzky and Sidney Kaplan, 451–54. Amherst: University of Massachusetts Press.

Jones, A.M. 1959. *Studies in African Music.* 2 vols. London: Oxford University Press.

———. 1964. "African Metrical Lyrics." *African Music* 3 (3): 6–14.

Kwant, Remy C. 1963. *The Phenomenological Philosophy of Merleau-Ponty.* Pittsburgh: Duquesne University Press.

Locke, David. 1978. *The Music of Atsiagbeko.* 2 vols. Ann Arbor: UMI Dissertation Services.

———. 2002. "Africa/Ewe, Mande, Dagbamba, Shona, BaAka." In *Worlds of Music: An Introduction to the Music of the World's Peoples*, ed. Jeff Todd Titon, 89–149. 4th ed. Belmont, Calif.: Schrimer, Thomson Learning.

Merleau-Ponty, M. 1962. *Phenomenology of Perception*. New York: The Humanities Press.

Métraux, Alfred. 1972. *Voodoo in Haiti*. New York: Schocken Books.

Mudimbe, V. Y. 1988. *The Invention of Africa: Gnosis, Philosophy, and the Order of Knowledge*. Bloomington: Indiana University Press.

Pantaleoni, Hewitt. 1972. "Three Principles of Timing in Anlo Dance Drumming." *African Music* 5 (2): 50–63.

Rosenthal, Judy. 1998. *Possession, Ecstasy, and Law in Ewe Voodoo*. Charlottesville: University of Virginia Press.

Rouget, Gilbert. 1985. *Music and Trance: A Theory of the Relations between Music and Possession*. Trans. Brunhilde Biebuyck. Chicago: University of Chicago Press.

Sartre, Jean-Paul. 1969. "Black Orpheus." In *Black and White in American Culture: An Anthology from The Massachusetts Review*, ed. Jules Chametzky and Sidney Kaplan, 415–50. Amherst: University of Massachusetts Press.

Schutz, Alfred. 1951. "Making Music Together: A Study in Social Relationship." *Social Research* 18 (1): 76–97.

———. 1962. *The Problem of Social Reality, Collected Papers, I*. Ed. M. Natanson. Boston: M. Nijhoff.

Senghor, Léopold Sédar. 1974. *Freedom I: Negritude and Humanism*. Trans. Wendall A. Jeanpierre. Ann Arbor: UMI Dissertation Services.

Vaillant, Janet G. 1990. *Black, French, and African: A Life of Leopold Sedar Senghor*. Cambridge, Mass.: Harvard University Press.

Walker, Shelia S. 1972. *Ceremonial Spirit Possession in Africa and Afro-America*. Leiden: E. J. Brill.

Chapter Six

SORCERY AND THE BEAUTIFUL
A Discourse on the Aesthetics of Ritual

Bruce Kapferer

> [T]he beautiful is the criterion that determines the true. But the true must
> be rooted in man.
>
> – Mikel Dufrenne, *The Phenomenology of Aesthetic Experience*

The efficacy of much ritual is founded in its aesthetics. This is especially so
in Sinhala demon exorcisms or healing rites (*tovil*),[1] in which the aesthetics of rite, the media of performance—the poetics of language, music,
song, dance, mime, masked drama, the various plastic arts—are crucial to
the ritual project. I address the aesthetic of these rites both from the cultural perspective of the ritual specialists who perform exorcisms and with
regard to the significance of the aesthetic practice of Sinhala healing rites
for wider discussions of aesthetics that may reach beyond the specific
ethnographic instance.

My argument concentrates on the thoroughgoing pragmatic force of
aesthetic processes in ritual. While I discuss some of the performance
aspects of ritual, my stress is upon what can be broadly described as the
dynamic logic of aesthetic processes that are variously realized through
performance. Furthermore, I address the power of aesthetic processes as
symbolically constitutive rather than expressive. While both aspects are
intimately connected, what may be described as performance perspectives in anthropology have tended to focus on the expressive features of
symbolic processes. This is especially so in approaches to ritual that stress
the way ritual practice reflects the social, political, and psychological
dimensions of processes that are present externally and independently of

the internal dynamics of rite. Ritual, therefore, is submitted to a logic or reasoning that, while relevant to the understanding of ritual efficacy, for example, is often at a distance from that of specific ritual practices. In such perspectives the cosmologies, logics, and internal intentionalities and orientations of ritual practice are given a reduced analytical significance, are frequently represented as mere "belief," and are subordinated to the more generalized analytic categories of the analyst.

The foregoing observations are why, in this discussion, I engage the concept of virtuality (see Deleuze and Guattari 1994). This is a concept, as I will explain, that focuses attention on the dynamics of the practice articulated by ritual itself. The virtual, in my usage here, is a concept that both argues for the specific reality of ritual practice and makes intensely problematic the question as to how ritual practice may relate to quotidian realities (the diverse, often chaotic actualities of the paramount world of everyday life). My chief interest in the concept here (see Kapferer 1997, 2001, 2003b, 2004) is in the critical direction it yields to the importance of aesthetic processes. The aesthetics of everyday life is gaining increased attention (see Burckhardt [1860] 1997 for an early and still unsurpassed perspective), but the idea of virtuality that I develop here accents, I suggest, a significance of the aesthetic that may not otherwise be so obvious. The aesthetic in virtuality manifests the thoroughly constitutive, rather than expressive, dimension of the aesthetic as quintessentially the potency of humanly produced symbolically sensuous processes.

One of the great contributions of Victor Turner's orientation to the liminality of ritual dynamics addresses this key aspect, but, as I will discuss towards the end of this analysis, the idea of the virtual enables a further development. Broadly, the attention to the virtuality of ritual extends an understanding of the construction of human realities (virtual and actual) as through and through the creation and invention of the world-making symbolic capacity of human beings.

A central issue of the analysis is a consideration of the grounded and pragmatic force of aesthetic processes. This is especially relevant to the specific context of Sinhala healing rites, where both aesthetic contemplation and immersion in the dynamics of aesthetic formation are joined to matters of life and death. No less vital in this process are ultimate questions of an aesthetic kind, such as the very nature of the beautiful and its relation to issues of Suffering, Truth, and Justice. These, as I will show, are as practical as they are apparently abstract, although one of my aims is to show that such a dualistic perspective (practical versus abstract) holds no significance in the pragmatic ritual contexts that I explore. Of course, the unity of the abstract and the concrete is integral to the Sinhala Buddhist cosmology within which the ritual practices I discuss develop and is fundamental in the ontological projection and organization of the whole ritual process.

The pragmatic orientation of the Sinhala Buddhist healing aesthetic opens up similar, if not identical, questions regarding the aesthetic in

European traditions stemming from the ancients (Plato, in particular) but finding new life in the post-Enlightenment idealist traditions, most notably of Kant and Hegel. Kant's connection of the issue of aesthetic judgement with matters of ethics and the problem of justice has resonance with matters at the heart of the Sinhala Buddhist healing practice that I discuss. I am particularly interested in Kant's discussion of the sublime as this relates to the formation and reformation of the conceptual categories involved in experience—a problem, incidentally, that seems to have guided Turner's interest in the liminal. Kant and no less Hegel are also concerned with the way aesthetic processes can, in my terms, be existentially transformational through their direction to ultimate value. Kant and especially Hegel ([1835] 1975) hierarchialize aesthetic forms and process accordingly, which is certainly relevant to the Sinhala case. Although I concentrate on Kant, I do not underrate the later importance of Hegel, whose argument is clearly relevant to the ethnography I present. This is especially so, for the dynamic aesthetic of Sinhala ritual articulates a progressive dialectic oriented towards the achievement of an ultimate aesthetic harmony, an absolute. Moreover, in the context of the processes I discuss, the emergence of such an absolute—even in art—is ultimately an impossibility. It, as life itself, is subject to fundamental contradictions that can never achieve a unity and against which even aesthetic artifice must collapse.

Sinhala Rites of Healing: A Sinhala Buddhist Aesthetics

Sinhalese ritual practice is directed within aesthetic conceptions firmly located within the historical development of religio-cosmic themes emergent in the Indian subcontinent. Thus, the concepts of *rasa* (taste, sense) integral to the musical and dance-drama of Bharata Natyam (see Kersenboom 1987, 1995) and refined in the work of the Indian medieval scholar, Abhinavagupta, are thoroughly vital in the artistic traditions of Sinhala exorcism. However, they are often quite distinct in their formation within exorcism practice (see Kapferer 1983) and bear only rough relation to the notions contained in classic texts, many of which are being revitalized in nationalist cultural revivals in India and Sri Lanka.[2]

Sinhala exorcism is founded in the idea that human realities are first and foremost human constructions. They are cognitive formations both generated and accessible through the human senses. Reality is no more nor less than that which is materialized through the senses. In accordance with this ontology, reality is *maya* or illusion; that is, reality cannot appear other than through the veil of the senses. There is no human reality that is not illusory—that is, constituted and sensible through the operation of the human perceptual faculties and rooted in the process of human symbolic construction. The aesthetic and artistic practices (consciously created symbolic forms that achieve their materiality in relation to the particular sense or combination of senses that govern their appearance) are par excellence those whose construction are composed specifically in relation to particular senses and their combination (sight, sound, touch, smell, taste).

A hierarchy of aesthetic value is involved in the structuring of Sinhala exorcism performance. This value is conditioned in the degree to which artistic forms, content, and style veil or cloud the order or "truth" of existence in their reality-creating dynamic: in their making of reality through their manipulation of the senses. The Buddha and his Teaching (*Dharma*) conditions the aesthetic hierarchy and in certain ways stands beyond or is located outside all aesthetic and symbolic formation. That is, aesthetic or artistic symbolic processes are valued in accordance with their capacity to achieve balance and harmony in their formation or dynamic by means of their orientation to the Buddha Teaching. The beautiful (*laksana*) in such a context is an index of balance and harmony. It is the object or materialization—as I will describe—that embodies the abstract and to which the aesthetic dynamic of rite is directed. Furthermore, through the developing and unfolding aesthetic processes of the rite, the participants at the center of the ritual action are led towards a realization of the truth of existence that yet is hidden by aesthetic formation (e.g., that suffering, *duka*, is its condition, one of the key teachings or Noble Truths of the Buddha integral to Buddha's reason).

In the rite I will examine, key participants are also brought to a point whereby they are enabled to constitute their realities, even the cognitive categories through which such realities are recognized and experienced.

Overall the value of aesthetic processes, the balance and harmony to which I have referred, depends on their capacity to manifest and produce a calmness or serenity of mind, of consciousness, and to open up mind and body so that reason, shaped after the Buddha's example, can flower. Aesthetic processes that impede or prevent or excite the passions, encourage Desire, Anger, Greed, or otherwise confuse, disturb, or excite mental action inhibiting the establishment of the clear sight of a reasoning consciousness, are regarded as being low in the hierarchy of aesthetic value.

The great artistic challenge in the figurative representations of the Buddha is to manifest a being who effectively does not act upon or activate the passionate senses of those who may gaze upon them, other than appeal to the highest mental consciousness (conceived as a sense, see Kapferer 2001). It is through such a consciousness that the Truth of the Buddha Teaching is directly revealed.

Particular Buddha representations are intended to produce a soothing consciousness for those who contemplate them and a mental orientation that is ultimately self-negating. The Buddha statue, for example, representations of the dying Buddha, unlike representations of Christ, should not activate the passion of pity. There is in this Buddhist aesthetics a logic in which the aesthetic dynamic itself tends to the destruction of its own force. In other words, it is an aesthetics of aesthetic negation, a motioning towards Nothingness or existential negation.

Dimensions of the hierarchy of aesthetic value I have outlined are evident in differentiations in ritual and religious practice and in the value placed upon particular kinds of aesthetic content. Practices centering on the key objects of Buddhist worship as well as the objects themselves (e.g., the Buddha statue or the central Buddhist edifice, the magnificent aesthetic, perhaps perfect, architectural form of the Buddha *dagaba* [*stupa, caitiya*]) express a simplicity and suppression of aesthetic excitement. The dominant color is white, a totally unsaturated or noncolor that does not excite the senses. The central Buddhist structures are intended to concentrate the mind, permitting its transcendence, and to encourage quiescence of the senses the other forms of aesthetic construction might activate. The shrines to the main Sinhala gods (who are regarded as guardians of Buddhism) are usually set aside from those focusing on the Buddha. They are full of color and intense activity. Their aesthetic, while it sets them apart, is always oriented in relation to the Buddha, from whom they receive their potency and towards whose idea and reason they typically tend. But returning to Sinhala exorcism, the hierarchy of aesthetic value to which I have been referring is integral to the logic and pragmatic effect of performances. Demons in both popular understanding and in that of ritual specialists are creatures who are so governed by their physical needs that they are not only incapable of mental concentration but also rendered thoroughly oblivious to the Buddha's Teaching. They are absolute victims of delusion, completely determined in their motivating passions. Their aesthetic formation, their appearance to the senses within and outside ritual contexts, express this. Their color is always that at the dark and saturated end of the spectrum; they are formed in foul fumes; their offerings and foods are the very essence of imbalance and disharmony; the demonic dance is furious and manifests a determining and polymorphic sexuality that, as frequently depicted, disregards gender distinctions;[3] the drumming of their music drowns out thought. The constitution of the body in unity with the movement of music and dance often manifests as demonic trance (*avessa*), which is expressed as the discordant movement of the body in disunity with the mind (see Kapferer 1983). Demons are called by the shrillest and sharpest of atonal sounds (the sound of the demon pipe or *vasdanda*); they are addressed in the crudest of poetic forms and through rough, obscene speech that knows no rule or convention. The aesthetics of demonic formation and realization manifests demons (*yakku*) as being at the very base of a hierarchy of aesthetic value. Their appearance, usually disgusting and ugly, defines the balance and harmony at the apex of the hierarchy (which Buddha encompasses) that the demonic threatens to subvert and topple.

Indeed, popular devaluations of the artistic worth of exorcism, especially among the urban middle class and elites, is closely connected to the hierarchical logic of value that informs much Sinhala Buddhist practice. This is so even though such class attitudes are also a product of the modernist rationalism born of colonialism and postcoloniality. Although dramatic events connected with Sinhala exorcism may be performed in the precincts of Buddhist temples (*vihare*), exorcism is conceived of as largely antagonistic to Buddha's teaching. Some ritual specialists of exorcism (*adura*), who are themselves devalued in a Sinhala hierarchy of caste (*kula*), will describe their ritual practice as an inverted ritual form associated with Hindu temple practice (*puja*) and, despite its conditioning within the authority of the Buddha's Teaching, inappropriate to Buddhist temple worship.[4]

What should be stressed is that exorcism works thoroughly in the realms of the senses, of *maya*. The victims of demonic attack who occasion an exorcism performance are in the grips of demonic delusion (*moha*). They are utterly given to the terrors of the senses through which their existential reality, a demonic reality, is constituted. One of the vital aims of the aesthetic process of exorcism is to work on victims by manipulating their sense experience, in effect reorienting their body and mind to reality. This exorcism does by aesthetically restructuring and reconstituting within the context of ritual the way reality is made to appear. The hierarchical formation of this reality—the plethora of beings, gods, godlings, demons, and other spirits (*preta*, both ancestor spirits and ghosts of former house occupants) that are in motion within it—is conjured through the aesthetic devices of the rite. The aesthetic dynamic engages the senses and organizes perception into ever changing and developing relations of balance and harmony. In this process the mental and physical orientation of patients is formed and reformed to the ritually defined terms of the appropriate Sinhala Buddhist cosmological scheme of things. The overall aim of an exorcism is to reveal, by means of its aesthetic, the delusionary aspect of demonic forces and their ultimate stupidity and distance from a world commanded by the Buddha's reason.

Sinhala exorcism can be conceived of as an aesthetic process that works in virtuality. The concept of the virtual I develop from the usage by Deleuze (see Deleuze 1989; Deleuze and Guattari 1995; Kapferer 1997, 2001). I employ the concept to depart from common approaches to rite, which often describe them as suspensions of everyday life (or its paramount reality; see Schutz 1967; Berger and Luckmann 1971) or else as their abstracted symbolic representation.[5] In this last perspective the symbolic is treated as an expression of nonritual social and political realities, a view that is common in sociology and is not the approach I take by regarding rite as a virtuality.

There is a connection between what I call the virtuality of rite and that which Victor Turner discussed as the liminality of ritual. Ritual conceived of as a virtuality, as in liminality, opens up a space within quotidian paramount reality so that new or renewed formations of reality (or orientations to lived experience) can be constructed. The liminal or the liminoid in Turner's analyses is outside the cognitive orders and relations of ordinary life or is dramatically deconstructive or subversive of the cognitive and other structures of life in which ritual participants have hitherto been embedded. Artistic forms or the poetics of rite in Turner's (1967, 1969) work achieve their force within liminal space as instruments of deconstruction and of reconstruction. The concept of the virtual has much similarity with this perspective. However, rather than conceive of it as a "betwixt and between" space, a space momentarily out of the space and time orderings and categories and constructs of cognized paramount reality, the concept of virtuality addresses ritual processes (such as the antisorcery healing rite that I will describe) as a descent into the very dynamic crux of reality formation. As I have explored elsewhere (Kapferer 1997), rather than a process out of time and space, the virtuality of ritual with which I am concerned involves an intervention in the dynamic formation of reality, repositioning, in this case, the victim in its flux. Thus in virtuality, ritual moves into the depths of reality formation, erecting and developing a simulacrum of it, by means of which focal participants are reoriented, repositioned, and reset within the ongoing processes of everyday life. Within the dynamics of reality formation that is virtuality, the aesthetic (the formations of the senses), as the quintessential dimensions of reality construction, is brought to the fore.

The art of exorcism developed in the virtuality of rite is nothing less than a direct engagement with the sensual forces that are thoroughly integral to the way human beings form and constitute their realities as an incarnated, embodied process. Thus, the power of exorcism is absolutely in its aesthetics or in the organizations of the senses through which reality in its multiple dimensions continually forms before and within embodied existence.

Sorcery, the Suniyama, and the Aesthetic

What I have discussed by way of introduction can be expanded through a consideration of the major Sinhala antisorcery exorcism, the Suniyama. There are five major demon exorcisms, and with the exception of one (the Iramudun Samayama or exorcism for the midday demon), the rites last through the night. Each engages distinctive episodes of poetry, song, music, dance, and drama relevant to the particular demon under whose primacy they are performed and whose name the exorcism bears (see Kapferer 1983; Kapferer and Papigny 2002). The principal demon addressed in the separate major exorcisms is generally a composite formation of numerous destructive demonic materializations or possibilities of one of the five principal elements from which all existence is constituted (*mahabhuta*) and central to the humoral theory of illness that informs exorcism. The main

demons and their exorcisms address specific illnesses or forms of embodied distress as signs of humoral imbalance. The one exception, however, is
Huniyam or Suniyam, a demon/god with a dual destructive and protective aspect (see Kapferer 1997, 2003a, 2003b).[6] Although he affects the
humors, he is not a manifestation of their imbalance as are the other major
beings of distress. Rather, he is the objectification of action, human action
(*vina*), and principally in its malevolent possibility.

Huniyam or Suniyam is the being of sorcery (*huniya, kodivina, vina*)
who, in the conceptions of exorcists, is an agency in all illness or personal
anxiety and distress. All exorcism rites will address his malevolence and
invoke his protective potential.

I stress Huniyam/Suniyam's critical feature, in effect, as a formation of
thoroughgoing human potency: the manifestation of that human causative
energy that is involved in the particular suffering of human beings, in the
suffering of self and other. Huniyam is generally regarded as the objectification of consciously motivated human destructive, disruptive force that is
directed at other human beings, their projects and objects of interest and
value. Suniyam, the higher form, articulates destruction with beneficence
and protection. Conceived as having godlike but intensely uncertain and
volatile potency, he has the capacity to intervene in the chain of human causation (*karma*), overcoming its malevolence and turning back the force of
humanly motivated destruction and disruption to its source. In the hierarchy of exorcism it is the rite to this demon/god, the ritual generally known
as the Suniyama, that is accorded pride of place in the ritual art of exorcism.

The ubiquity of sorcery in illness experience (the recognition that all illness is rooted in the human condition and in one way or another is the
result, if not entirely, of the action of other human beings) is a major reason
for this. This is so, I hasten to add, not merely because of the pervasive
character of sorcery as such but what is implicated in the factuality of sorcery as a foundational aspect of the human condition. The ubiquity of sorcery implicitly recognizes not that human beings are inherently destructive
or evil but rather—given the karmic universe of Sinhala Buddhist conception—that all human experience is grounded in human constructed
realities that must implicate the action of other human beings. Sorcery in the
Sinhala Buddhist context, as I have argued elsewhere at length (Kapferer
1997), implicitly extends towards central ontological problematics. While
these must be at the heart of the other exorcisms, it is to be expected that a
rite that deals thoroughly with sorcery—as does the Suniyama—will manifest, above all the other rites in the repertoire of exorcists, such issues to the
greatest extent.

Exorcists state that the Suniyama is their most highly regarded rite
because above all it is the original rite of exorcism; the rite that was
invented by the ritualist or grand sacrificer, Oddisa, who not only created
the Suniyama but also the other major exorcisms.[7] The exorcists claim that
the knowledge that underpins any performance of the Suniyama is in

large measure the key to understanding their practice as a whole. Those who perform the Suniyama, in the past members of the highest lineages among the *berava* (drummer) community, are considered to be the most skilled exponents of the exorcism arts. Exorcists look upon the Suniyama as being their highest aesthetic achievement. But this recognition of the aesthetic of the Suniyama is directly connected to the Buddhism of the rite, a fact that is stressed by the ritualists and that also underpins their reverence for the rite.

The other exorcisms are concerned with controlling specific demons, ending their hold over human beings and ultimately banishing them to the margins of human realities. The overarching objective of these exorcisms is to make demons conform to the proper Buddhist and human order of things. The authority of the Buddha is invoked to control and to remove them, but they are outside the capacities and reach of human reason. This is not so in the situation of sorcery. While the Suniyama addresses demons, its central concern is with the demonic possibility of humanity itself and with overcoming the forces integral to the human situation as a moral order. Here the arguments of Buddhism may be expected to receive the greatest elaboration and import because it is in the contexts of action between human beings that they experience their greatest challenge and potency. The other exorcism rites are referred to by exorcists as having little to do with Buddhism and even as being anti-Buddhist, for the arguments of the Buddha are beyond demon comprehension. This is not so in the human-centered practice of the Suniyama.

It may appear somewhat paradoxical to outsiders, especially those brought up in a relatively recent Western rationalist discourse on sorcery and witchcraft (see Kapferer 2003), that a rite dealing with sorcery should be considered to manifest the highest aesthetic achievement and knowledge by its practitioners and by many of those who demand its performance. However, it is precisely in the character of sorcery, as the Suniyama elaborates, that an understanding of the aesthetic achievement of the rite and the significance of its great Buddhist themes are to be discovered.

The Suniyama is a rite of reorigination of immense cosmological and ontological proportion. This is evident in the myth-narrative of the rite that underscores the Suniyama and that the ritual practice expands and reveals. The myth also indicates the key importance of aesthetic processes that the rite develops.

The Mahasammata/Manikpala Myth: The Ontogeny of Human Creation and the World Order

The myth, sung at the start and at intervals throughout the performance of a Suniyama, tells of the emergence of the world in the current age (*kalpa*), of how the great Being, Maha Brahma, came to earth climbing down the stalk of a lotus, and how humankind developed from his body. The myth concentrates on the parlous condition of human beings.

Among all the forms of life, only human beings are without order. They have no hierarchy, no ordering kings as do the other creatures of the sea, sky, and land. Human beings are continually fighting among themselves and consumed by greed. Their suffering is great. However, through this suffering they become conscious of the fact that other creatures, because of their order—because of the order that is natural to them—are living in relative peace and without suffering. Now conscious of themselves as human beings and thus aware of themselves as different from other creatures, human beings decide to choose a king from their number. He is called Mahasammata, the Great Elect, the most handsome of men from the lineage of the Sun. Mahasammata institutes the world order. He creates his cosmic city-state; a hierarchization of human beings into four castes or estates, encircled by defensive barriers that protect Mahasammata's cosmic city from the outside world from which it is now separated. Mahasammata then chooses his queen, Manikpala, the most beautiful of women, sister of Lord Vishnu. Mahasammata and Manikpala make love in their room at the heart of their palace at the cosmic center of Mahasammata's city. It is Mahasammata and Manikapala's erotic harmony that maintains the protective unity of the hierarchical order of the cosmic state. It is a just state within which there is no suffering. But this erotic unity is broken when Mahasammata decides to expand his authority and order beyond the borders of his cosmic city. He leaves his queen and engages in a war against the Asuras in a totalizing effort to bring all within his sway.

While Mahasammata (a *cakravartin*) is so involved, Vasavarti Maraya, the Great World Poisoner, sees Manikpala unprotected. He is filled with desire and lusts to possess her. He approaches the bedchamber of Mahasammata's Palace, and in so doing he takes the form of Mahasammata himself. Manikpala is confused, but a servant girl sees through the ruse and warns Manikpala, for she notices Vasavarti's foul stench, which is not Mahasammata's perfume of sweet-smelling sandalwood. Manikpala bars her door.

Furious at his discovery, Vasavarti revealed reaches into the hell of Ignorance (*avicciya*) and draws out a fire viper (*ginijala polanga*—firewater viper, generative essence, perhaps sperm?) that he flings at Manikpala. It breaks through the door and enters the queen's womb. Manikpala falls unconscious, and her body is covered in sores. Manikpala is the first victim of sorcery, and she is an innocent victim, although it is her beauty that engenders Vasavarti's destructive Desire. Her attack brings down what may also be regarded as Mahasammata's beautiful and protective hierarchical order, an attack made possible by Mahasammata's overambitious totalizing act to expand his order to encompass all of existence.

The overcoming of Manikapala's sorcery illness and her restitution to consciousness is also a world re-creative and ordering act, although not, of course, identical to the first act of world creation. I will explore later the implications of this fact for the ritual process of the Suniyama. For the present, I underline some key dimensions of the myth and therefore the rite as a discourse on the aesthetic.

The myth recognizes that the act of self-recreation by human beings is in itself a creative act, a constructive process in which the human order is imagined into existence. It is a mimetic act, ordered after the natural world of animals but reconceptualized, reimagined, as a distinct human creation (human by the fact of the conceptualizing imagination) in which human existence is reconstituted. This existence is no longer determined by processes outside human control and manufacture. The human world is created through a conscious, conceptualizing imagination.

The implication in this Sinhala Buddhist myth is paralleled in the Kantian a priori that is integral to certain Kantian notions of the aesthetic. I refer specifically to Kant's highly disputed contention that certain aspects of the force of the aesthetic occur outside of or independently of a conceptualizing reason. One aspect of the Kantian position—expanded in the work of Cassirer (1996) and especially Susanne Langer (1942) in her discussion of presentational symbolism—is that some features of the aesthetic, or the beautiful, are directly intuited and have their force independently of the mediation of conceptual or cognitive categories. The argument as I understand it does not rule out the importance of particular cultural conceptions, which so many anthropologists insist upon, but sees in different particularities an underlying universality.

The myth powerfully articulates the potency of order as an aesthetic synthetic and sensuous unity. The breaking of such a unity establishes a process of the loss of consciousness, and the reversal of the ordering process. Manikpala, the sensible body, is beautifully perfect in her erotic unity with Mahasammata, the being of Knowledge and Reason. Vulnerable in her separation, Manikpala loses her beauty, and Mahasammata, separated from her body, loses his knowledge and potency. Furthermore, power broken loose from its harmonic unity attacks its own perfection and manifests as the anti-just. Thus, Vasavarti Maraya assumes the appearance of Mahasammata.

The rupture in the order of human existence demands that Mahasammata seek the assistance of Oddisa, the arch ritualist, who has the necessary ritual skill but lives outside the human created order. He is a terrible figure, an arch-sacrificer, who embodies within himself the rupture that his artifice can heal.

The myth is concerned with existential extremes and has implicit within it an argument that the force of rite inheres in its aesthetic practice. In the myth, Mahasammata summons other healers, sages, persons filled with knowledge, to Manikapala's side. But they fail. Only Oddisa in possession of the artifice of rite succeeds. The implication in his success is that he comes from a position that is outside or marginal to the orders of existence. He is a liminal figure par excellence. In my interpretation, he is external to all structures of knowledge and power, indeed, threatening of them (for the gods tremble in fear at his presence, even the Buddha). Nonetheless, he possesses the technology that can bring forth the circumstances for the restoration of the orders of knowledge and power.

There is a further understanding that might attach to the myth, but realized in the performance of the rite and not in the myth. This is that the harmonies achieved through the aesthetics of ritual are momentary, that the circumstances producing anxiety and suffering must eventually return in the nonritualized actualities of ordinary existence. Moreover, intimated in the myth to be elaborated in the ritual practice are notions of the fundamental limitations of existence and also of power, order, and reason.

The Suniyama Performance

The performance of the rite is intended to close off the effects of sorcery, the potentiality of its recurrence, and to prevent the possibility of revenge or any other effort directed to cause a victim and his or her household harm.

The Suniyama is a composite and total ritual form, as are the other major exorcisms. Basically, it is an inventory of a set of ritual events both oriented to cause sorcery and to overcome it that can be performed independently, as rites in themselves, of this master rite. The Suniyama is a total rite in this sense, manifesting the poisons and antidotes of sorcery in all its manifestations. But more than this, and as I have indicated, it is a major cosmological intervention whereby the relations of space and time in whose junctures victims and their relatives may be caught (and so determined in their misfortune) are effectively readjusted. Indeed, it involves a descent into the Void, the living space of all realities, and an entrance into the forces of their generation.

The rite's overall structural thematic is that of sacrifice.[8] It is conceived by exorcists as being organized around sixteen events of sacrifice that in themselves are finishing acts of judgement (*tindui*), which cut the constraining bonds of sorcery, the ties of destruction, and free the victim to take once more an active role in reality constitution.[9] I note that these acts of judgement are explicitly grasped as involving acts of moral assertion. The aesthetic dynamics that lead to such acts or in which such acts are embedded—songs, poetry, events of dance and drama—declare the virtues (*buduguna*) of the Buddha's Life and Teaching. These virtues, I add, are themselves powerful instruments of force, judgement, and completion.

The performance of the Suniyama is a total act, a total sacrifice in the sense of Hubert and Mauss (1964). The conclusion of the rite is effected by the sacrificial destruction of the key ritual edifice, the Mahasammata Palace. This action in one of its vital aspects is understood as being a destruction of the total object of Desire (and of the very materiality of existence) that lies at the root of sorcery—indeed, of all suffering. The palace, moreover, is conceived as a lavish gift—a glittering edifice of wealth—and its destruction, much in the sense of the classic instance of the potlatch, can be seen as the action that paradoxically sustains the gift-ness of the gift (see Derrida 1994) and the restoration of the social and moral order that is the power of sacrifice.

The ritual performance, of course, constitutes an unfolding aesthetic, a hierarchy of aesthetic forms. This hierarchy, which is a structure of ascending value, is determined in accordance with ultimate Buddhist morality or the extent to which the realities formed by aesthetic events are conditioned in the virtues (*guna*) of the Buddha's Teaching. The progression of ritual events (usually discrete named ritual acts) is one that proceeds from lower to higher forms of aesthetic value: for example, from mantra and verses in demonic tongue (sometimes obscene and inchoate, manifesting a combination of different linguistic forms) to those expressed in Sanskrit or "pure" Sinhala of the medieval Elu form; from demonic dance to the dance of divinities, etc. A similar hierarchization operates within each particular ritual event and in the content and organization of gifts in the form of flowers, foods, smells.

The aesthetic focus of the whole rite is a building known as the palace of Mahasammata (Mahasammata *maligava* or *vidiya*), a supreme site of the Buddha's virtues and particularly of the ordering categories of the cosmos. It is a resplendent structure expressly made to appear beautiful and attractive to the gaze. Architecturally it represents the perfect cosmic city-state, the state as it was constituted by Mahasammata. As an aesthetic formation, to be gazed upon, Mahasammata's building is a representation before the senses of the dynamics constitutive of the realities of existence that human beings construct. It is the construction of constructive processes, an architectonic form, a representation of the potencies into which the sorcery victim will be progressively introduced. Perhaps it might be described as the "categorical imperative" in the aesthetic form of the cosmic state.

The façade of the palace embeds in its design the five elements (*mahabhuta*) of matter ingrained in all existence and the divine hierarchy (Brahma, Visnu, Siva). The right and left sides indicate the male (Sun) and female (Moon) principles of generative and harmonic union, and at the central apex of the façade, in mediate and commanding position, is a representation of Suniyam/Oddisa, bearing aloft his sword of sacrifice and judgement. In the contemporary popular imagination he is the mediating figure of justice and punishment.[10]

The victim, who is the center of most of the ritual action, is initially seated in a position confronting the palace and is enjoined to look upon it.[11] The victim is in the place of Manikpala and, regardless of the victim's gender, must wear Manikpala's shawl. At the start of the rite the victim is conceived to be located at the perimeter of Mahasammata's cosmic city and where the force of destructive sorcery is at its most intense. The victim must wear Manikpala's shawl both as protection and to cool sorcery's

Figure 6.1 The victim in Manikpala's shawl confronts the Mahasammata Palace

Photograph by Bruce Kapferer.

Figure 6.2 The Mahasammata Palace (the World of Desire)

Photograph by Georges and Marie-Claude Papigny.

Figure 6.3 The dance of the exorcist (Oddisa, the sacrificer)

Photograph by Georges and Marie-Claude Papigny.

destructive heat. Other cooling objects are placed close at hand, and the victim is told to keep his or her mind focused on the Buddha.

The object of the entire rite is to move the victim from where he or she is initially seated into the palace. This is achieved in the major event of the rite known as the *hatadiya* (seven steps).[12] The victim moves in slow stages progressively towards a small doorway set into the base of the palace into a space known as the *atamagala* (the place of eight auspicious objects) behind the palace façade. Here the victim is seated on a mat and turned around, reoriented, to face back into the world and back down the path already taken. The victim in this position is located at the axial center of world creation, simultaneously on the seat of Maha Brahma, Maha Purusa, and Lord Buddha. The victim is also conceived as being in the bedchamber of Mahasammata and Manikpala, in the erotic center of world (re)generative harmony. In some interpretations by ritualists, the victim changes into the balanced creative condition of Mahasammata and is no more in the condition of the afflicted Manikpala. Indeed, the victim is now poised to reenter everyday realities restored as a full participant in their ongoing creation.

The ritual journey of the victim describes a process that indeed spans the Void (*sunya*), the emptiness from which existence is perpetually emergent. The victim's progress effectively moves from that pole of existence where the potencies of life and death are in explosive originary emergence towards the point, within the palace, that lies at the edge of nonexistence (beyond life, death, and the perpetual cycle of existential emergence).

The rite's dynamic and the victim's movement towards the palace are effected, in the conception of exorcists, both by the victim's perceptual action and by the aesthetic construction of reality before the victim. This movement is intensified as the victim's body is cleansed of the destructive agents of reality formation (ghosts and demons), and a consciousness imbued with the Buddha's reason develops. In the understanding of exorcists, the victim's action of gazing upon the beauty, the glittering perfection of Mahasammata's cosmic city (the Mahasammata Palace), combined with the effects of the cleansing acts of the rite, operate to draw the patient into the palace. Simultaneously, the palace, as an aesthetic formation of cosmic order, draws the sorcery victim to it. The palace, therefore, is more than an aesthetic representation. It is an aesthetic form that has constitutive and motional force. In the course of the victim's movement towards the palace, the truth that yet lies hidden within the palace is progressively revealed to consciousness, a consciousness that is progressively embodied as it is recomposed (reborn) and freed from its bonds of anxiety and fear.

I interpret the victim's passing through the portal of the palace into the bedchamber as a breaking through the final illusion of reality's appearance, a movement beyond that façade to which Desire still clings and from which the suffering in the world emerges, of sorcery's anguish. The space within the palace reached by the victim is almost beyond the illusory field of *maya* and of the aesthetic formation of reality. In the view of exorcists it

Figure 6.4 The line of sorcery's viper and the seven lotus steps (*hatadiya*)

Photograph by Georges and Marie-Claude Papigny.

Figure 6.5 A victim (wearing Manikpala's shawl) seated within Mahasmmata's Palace

Photograph by Georges and Marie-Claude Papigny.

is the space of mind at the limit of illusion, a position from within which the victim can potentially constitute, like Mahasammata, the world anew.

The Suniyama and Kantian Aesthetics

There is much in this ritual discourse that can be brought into dialogue with other discourses on aesthetics. I refer specifically to the aesthetics that has its roots in the work of Kant and that continues to dominate, either in extension or rejection, discussions on aesthetics in Europe and North America. Perhaps the Suniyama extends an understanding of aspects of Kantian aesthetics as well as underlining the significance of the larger issues to which a Kantian aesthetics is oriented, specifically as argued in Kant's *Critique of Judgement* (1987).

I have described the victim in the Suniyama as moving between two absolute limits, which might have been recognized by Kant to be what he discussed as the Sublime. The Sublime for Kant is at the edge, at the very limit of human cognitive and conceptualizing capacity. It is the point where reason itself encounters its limit. The Sublime is where all cognitive categories break down (see Kant 1987; Deleuze 1995). But as Kant suggested (and I intimate that this is the powerful implication of the Suniyama), it is at the limits, at the points at the very edge of the orders of life, that the potencies wherefrom the conceptualizing categories integral to lived existence spring and take form.

There are two dimensions of the Sublime for Kant, or what he refers to as the mathematical sublime and the dynamic sublime. The former is the feeling of an immensity that lies beyond the measurements or symmetry of Reason, the point where Reason transcends itself, the Infinite. The power of Reason, it might be said, reaches its limit where the cognitive categories through which existence is known and is made sensible can no longer operate. Existence ceases to be. The latter notion of the sublime, the dynamic sublime, is the power of absolute origination, power in its volcanic, erupting, and motional force, of being in its becoming. In this sense, it is explosively generative, the energy of creative force as Desire, yet before the cognitive powers of reason through which its energies may be controlled and constrained. The dynamic sublime may be grasped as the energy of life that yet subverts and defies its further fruition and development.

Mahasammata and Vasavarti Maraya of the Suniyama might be conceived in this Kantian vein (as, too, Oddisa and the Buddha). Vasavarti is that immense explosive generative force that exists before the formations of existence, and the realities constituted through the differentiated categories of reason. He is the force that breaks down all categories, the limit that knows no limit and yet is mastered, if only momentarily, through the potencies of reason. Mahasammata is the power of reason at its ordering height. Yet he is at the limit of reason. The *atamagala* behind the palace is a transcendental space where reason through the passage of reason is itself transcended. It is the beginning and end point of reason, the place where reason itself is absolutely manifest or present, yet moving beyond the realities it constitutes and moving towards the brink of its own negation. A clear feature of the space of the *atamagala* is that it is a transcendental space. It is a space where reason, or the consciousness or mind that produces reason and the lived categories of a reasoning consciousness, becomes not just secluded but enclosed and cut off from existential realities. The victim in this space might be described as a transcendental ego, removed from the world even though the victim is at its most potent constituting point. Within the *atamagala*, described as a womb space *(gaba)*, the victim is intended to be removed from all sensory experience of the world, except that formed through the operation of the mind (see Kapferer 2001).

The *atamagala* is an awe-inspiring place. This seems to be the experience of many victims who enter within it. When they cross the threshold into the palace (or more accurately go behind the façade), they often shake and tremble.

It is critical that Vasavarti and Mahasammata are not understood as opposites. They are inextricably associated, and this, as I described, is explicit in the myth narrative. Vasavarti appears to Manikpala in the guise of Mahasammata. Thus he deludes Manikpala. But I think there is an implication in the myth that they do in fact form a unity in the sense that, while separate beings (never constituting a union of opposites, they are mutually repelling), they are inescapably the potential of the other. In the illusory realms of existence, consciousness and reason are tied to the constant reemergent energy and evanescence of life. Thus, Mahasammata as the reasoning, ordering power of existence is attached to Vasavarti, to Desire and eruptive, destructive potency. Each needs and must bring forth the other.

This is a basic message of the rite, vital in the tragic direction of its drama. The idea is embedded in the victim at the progressive center of the rite. It is a grounded abstraction, as it were, critical in the transformation of the victim out of the condition of sorcery that involves a commitment of the victim, an embodied commitment, to the force of Buddha's reason in subordinating and controlling the force of Desire, the energy of life. It is through such reason that life can be sustained and prevented from prematurely destroying itself.

Much of what I say here is condensed and elaborated in two closing events of the Suniyama that essentially form its dramatic denouement: a comic drama (the *vadiga patuna*) and the destruction of the palace (*chedana vidiya*). These are performed after the victim has attained the space of the *atamagala* and is liberated from the immobilizing bonds of sorcery that are literally cut from the victim's body by the presiding exorcist. Brought to the highest space of consciousness, the world constituting space of

Figure 6.6 A comic drama (the *vadiga patuna*)

Photograph by Georges and Marie-Claude Papigny.

Figure 6.7 Destruction of the palace (*chedana vidiya*)

Photograph by Georges and Marie-Claude Papigny.

Mahasammata, a situation of balance and harmony effected through the arts of the rite, the erstwhile victim is once more a creature of language and, in effect, a world creator and a constructor of order.[13]

In the comic drama of the *vadiga patuna*, life in all its fluidity bursts forth. The comedy ostensibly portrays the buffoonery of the sages who failed to cure Manikpala preparatory to Oddisa's successful invention of the Suniyama. The comedy has manifold import, among them the demonstration of consciousness as an object to itself. The pleasure of the comedy for the players and the audience alike derives from their submersion in the constitutive and deconstitutive dynamic of consciousness for itself (see Kapferer 1997, 2001). Comic speech reveals consciousness as itself an object of contemplation in the obscenities, spoonerisms, malapropisms that crowd the language and action of the drama. The Rabelaisian breaking of rule and convention of the comedy accentuates the very categories and boundaries that are integral within the realities of everyday life.

While the comedy affirms life it also demonstrates its interweaving with death.[14] Much of the comedy concentrates on sexual themes, making a mockery of the life-generating force of Desire, as well as the fact that such force underlies the potency of reason, is its nemesis as its necessity. Desire and Reason are unified in the comedy, but this unity through the comedy demonstrates its impossibility. The violence of so much comedy—and this is a powerful feature of the *vadiga patuna*—reveals the irresolute contradiction that comedy exposes, a contradiction, paradoxically perhaps, that is at the fount of life: its ultimate sadness or joke.

The comedy announces that the victim is about to return to the everyday world, and reconstitutively so. Within the *atamagala*, the victim is in the position of a *bhodisattva*, about to make a conscious choice to return to quotidian realities, alive to the excitement of life (facilitated by the comedy), freed from the pall of sorcery but made aware of suffering's inevitable connection with life. The comedy also indicates the impending destruction of the rite and the conclusion of the aesthetic processes that have hitherto formed its ritual realities and sustained them. The comedy ends with the final appearance of Vasavarti Maraya (the final joke of the comedy?), the supreme manifestation of Desire and of the world-destroying potency of sorcery's poison.

This is the *chedana vidiya*. An exorcist in the guise of Vasavarti bearing a sword and in a drunken stupor, a figure of absolute Ignorance and blind confusion, attacks the palace. Unreason and Reason, Annihilation and Nothingness, Vasavarti and Mahasammata, sorcery and the victim restored in the place of Buddha's Truth, the extremes of the Void of existence, all are brought into direct and defining confrontation.

Vasavarti in a rage hacks down Mahasammata's Palace. Effectively, he breaks down the edifice of illusion, reality as a construction before the senses that, while an object of order, is also the central object of Desire. Desire destroys its own object and, in my interpretation, could be understood as freeing the erstwhile victim, now incarnating reason, from Desire's embrace. More strongly, the victim as the embodiment of consciousness and reason at its height defeats Vasavarti, makes him rather than Manikpala, the creature of delusion and the victim of its artifice. Vasavarti's impotent destruction of the palace (which parallels the popular Buddhist story of Buddha's famous defeat of Mara, Death, and impassive concentration before the furies and temptations of Mara's demonic hordes at the time of His Enlightenment) signs the end of the rite. Most specifically it indicates the conclusion or limit of the aesthetic potency of the rite. While the force of the aesthetic processes of the ritual have brought the victim to reason's center, the blossoming of reason, the restoration of consciousness, has itself exposed the impotence of artifice before the potency of reason. In other words aesthetic forces have reached their ultimate limit. The victim is liberated by Vasavarti's destruction from what may be regarded as the false supports of rite, however functional they may have been.[15]

Now the victim is enjoined to constitute through the force of consciousness. This manifests as a series of sacrificial acts that bring the victim back once more into quotidian realities and outside the protective enclaves of ritual buildings and performance. Effectively, the erstwhile victim acts from outside the realm of the aesthetic. In essence, the victim restored to consciousness is situated independently of the realm of *maya* or of those constructions of human consciousness that have become vulnerable to the forces of delusion that are antagonstic to consciousness and the orders of reason.

In the rite's final events most of the ritual artifacts are cleared away. Indeed, a clearing is made, a space swept clean and purified of the decaying detritus of sorcery, within which the victim is now free to act and form anew his relation to ordinary realities. The exorcist-performers pack up, and the usually large gathering of spectators that have come to witness the events disperse. They leave the victim almost alone, apart from the guiding help of the presiding exorcist, whose skills in concluding sacrificial acts are effectively passed to the erstwhile victim. The victim becomes his own sacrificer and a being of order and justice. Using Vasavarti's sword—now transmuted into reason's sword—the victim engages it as an instrument of reconstitution and not destruction. In his own sacrificial action, the victim remakes his world.[16]

The transformational force of the aesthetic progression of the rite is achieved in virtuality, enabling an entry into the powers of the sensory realms at the heart of existential formation. To put it another way, the victim is drawn from the dreadful zone of death and destruction, from the edge of personal extinction—the living death of the ensorcelled—and drawn towards beauty and perfection. Here he finds a haven of peace and serenity where he is restored to consciousness and brought to the position where he can reconstitute an ordered and just world from which the disruptive forces of sorcery have been removed.

Interpreting the Homeric Odyssey, Elaine Scarry (1999) restores the importance of a Kantian perspective and his recognition of the aesthetic and the beautiful in underscoring the sensual as being at the heart of a universal human orientation towards justice and truth. This is a universality (grounded in human subjectivity within which cognition and reason are immanent) that perhaps widespread beliefs and practice of sorcery indicate despite their numerous particular cultural differences. In her wonderful essay, Scarry almost evokes the deep existential force of what I understand in the Suniyama.

She refers to the encounter of Odysseus with the beautiful Nausicaa. Nearing the end of his journey, the abject Odysseus, shipwrecked, alone, and naked, is confronted by the beautiful Nausicaa, who alone of all her friends is not frightened by Odysseus's wild appearance. Odysseus discovers a perfection and sanctity in Nausicaa. It is Nausicaa, beauty unafraid, who takes Odysseus to her father, King of the Phaeacians. He assists Odysseus finally to his home of Ithaca where, of course, Odysseus exacts his own life-reclaiming judgement. Scarry's interpretation of beauty as the mediator of justice and truth—Nausicaa's beauty is a kind of Kantian in-itself, a universal—compares with the import of the journey of victims in the Suniyama.

The very appreciation or awareness of something as aesthetic as something to look upon already depends on the emergence, in the very activity of such a look, of a synthesizing and unifying human mind. The pleasure in the sensible simultaneously gives rise to a cognitive and constituting capacity, which is not to reduce the cognitive to the sensual or subjective. But all thought of Kant aside, Scarry's commentary on the shipwrecked Odysseus is also suggestive of the sorcery victim in the Suniyama. The victim can be conceived of as "shipwrecked" on the verge of personal extinction as a consequence of the travail that sorcery implicates, but through the mediation of the aesthetic and beauty is lead back to the potencies of Truth, Reason, and Justice. The victim, as with Odysseus, is returned to a capacity to engage, once again, in the determination of his or her life chances.

Conclusion

The relation of ritual to art and aesthetics has long been recognized in anthropology. Recent and contemporary movements in the arts and much discussion of aesthetics in general recognize an identity with the diverse kinds of human problematics that are opened up in ritual. This essay has continued in such a concern but with a renewed emphasis on the particular force that artistic forms can achieve within the aesthetics of ritual practice.

There has been a tendency in some anthropological quarters concerned with art and the aesthetic to be removed from the great existential concerns that are at the root of so much ritual action and with which its aesthetic (and the pragmatics of such aesthetics) are enlivened. This in my opinion marks off the significance of the work of such major figures in anthropology for whom aesthetic forms and processes are crucial to the understanding of the diversity that is human being, as the work of Lévi-Strauss, Victor Turner, and most recently Roy Rappaport (1999) have all exemplified. In the studies of these thinkers—and specifically with reference to ritual—artistic practices and aesthetic forms engage thoroughly with the crisis that is human being. This is made intensely evident in the practical work of ritual, which, furthermore, reveals or manifests the vital potential within aesthetic processes and structures that may be obscured when "art is broken free from its ritual integument." When Turner made this observation he implied strongly that a distinction exists in the formations of the arts and aesthetic in rite from their realization *as art* independent from rite, even allowing for the many affinities between the several arts and ritual.

Turner's aesthetic focus with regard to rite (and more generally) is arguably the strongest among anthropologists. It was he more than most who insisted that anthropologists in their analyses of ritual had much to learn from the literary and performance arts. His aesthetic turn was not of the more reductionist kind epitomized in the focus on the "art" or "anthropology of art" orientations of some contemporary anthropology. Such perspectives these days tend to decline in the direction of a well-plodded "art and society" concern (often Durkheimian, less frequently Marxist) and despite some recent attempts at phenomenological or post-structuralist orientations (with of course exceptions, e.g., Munn 1973). Too frequently anthropologists wish to address their own aesthetic sensitivities rather than those of the peoples with whom they might more immediately be concerned.

This was not so with Turner, who along with an emphasis on the particular dynamics of aesthetic processes in rite showed how their practical concerns were connected with larger human existential questions of moral and ethical import. This is especially evident in Turner's early ethnography on rite, where he refused a too narrow philosophical and theoretical confinement that characterized the particular sociological Durkheimian directions of much British social anthropology of his time. One of the most poignant examples is his essay *Chihamba: the White Spirit*, in which he lays out many of the themes that he would later develop in his broad approach to ritual. In *Chihamba*, Turner shows that the practical concerns of Ndembu rites are wrapped up with the kind of great human questions that lie at the heart of other religious traditions and the literature that develops from within them. Thus he sees parallels in the discourses of Ndembu rites and those in Christianity. Turner, seizing on the multiladen values that the Ndembu place on "whiteness," engages with Melville's classic saga *Moby Dick*, finding in it the kinds of magnificent symbolic potency that Turner encountered in Ndembu ritual. Turner was not pursuing either a Christian-centric or Eurocentric perspective. Instead he was demanding a recognition from anthropologists that human beings everywhere manifest in their distinct and particular ways critical matters perhaps universally at the center of human being. His point, developing as much from Freud and Jung as from the neo-Kantians such as Susanne Langer, is that there exists a preconceptual, prelogical force emergent from human embodied existence in the world that develops differentially along particular cultural lines. These may not be reducible to each other but, nonetheless, they manifest a certain ontological universality underlying all human experience.

What is immediately apparent in Turner's discussions of the aesthetics of rite and of the art/rite relation is the vital conjunction and exploration of the existential forces at the ground of the formation of human beings and the cognitive construction of their realities. There is a clear Kantian direction in Turner's own early work. But he departed from the objectivist orientation in anthropology, possibly most strongly developed in various structuralist perspectives, that refused a consideration of the subjective and the sensual. Turner was influenced by another Kant, that which is at the heart of the philosophical and ethnographically sensitive work of Ernst Cassirer and Susanne Langer, figures of considerable importance for the development of symbolic anthropology. There are shades of Kant in Turner's approach to meaning (his discussion of its *orectic* and *exegetical* poles) and even in his, on the surface, most anti-Kantian developments of the concepts of liminality, antistructure, and communitas.

Kant's notions of the sublime as I have discussed in relation to the Suniyama have a definite bearing on these ideas. For Turner and Kant, it is at the limits, at the edge of reason and existence—when human beings are brought outside the forms of ordinary life and placed in situations of subjective intensity—that they can be brought to reimagine their circumstance and its orders and to reform and perhaps redirect their lives in original ways. At the limit, at the threshold, in liminal space, human beings can be brought to new realizations and break away from an endless repetition of the same.[17]

Regardless of whether Kant and Turner can in fact be reconciled, there is one aspect about which they agree. This is that aesthetic processes draw human beings towards major moral issues that are at the center of their existence. Here, too, the wonderful performance of the Sinhala Buddhist antisorcery rite, the Suniyama, should leave no doubt.

The Suniyama establishes the cosmological process within which a hierarchy of aesthetic value is both determined and has its effect. Within the course of the rite, artistic forms discover an aesthetic force, realize their value in effecting a progressive change in the victim. I stress the thorough pragmatism of the aesthetic dynamics directed as they are to the overcoming of the dreadful personal and potentially world-annihilating experience that sorcery holds for its victims. No less integral to the dynamic aesthetic

processes of the rite are what many readers might regard as highly abstract questions, matters of deep concern in Buddhist doctrine and philosophy. If not universal, many of these are yet apparent in diverse form
in widespread human practices separated in space and in time. Although
sorcery practices as they are often presented in anthropology would obviously seem to be very distant from such abstractions as those connected
with Reason, Truth and Justice, this is certainly not the case in the context
of the great Sinhala Buddhist antisorcery rite that I have discussed. Indeed, I contend that such issues—especially those of personal and social
justice—are implicit and immanent in sorcery practices in many parts of
the globalizing contemporary world, as the apparent increase in appeals
to sorcery ideas and practices might otherwise indicate (see Comaroff and
Comaroff 2000; Geschiere 1997; and a critique, Kapferer 2002). But my
critical point in this analysis is that the aesthetic of this Sinhala Buddhist
rite engages abstract matters to pragmatics, grounding them and their
emergence in the sensual world of human existence.

The ritual *as an aesthetic process* works in what Kant argued was the fundamental subjective (embodied) basis of human cognitive formation (an
argument developed in various phenomenologies, including the religious).
Through the manipulation of the sensual ground of human realizations
(constructions) of human existence oriented to the consummate values of
Buddha's Teaching, the aesthetic process simultaneously removes sorcery
victims from their particular suffering despair and feelings of injustice and
recenters them in the existential and experiential ground and position of a
Universal Subject in whom Reason and Justice, reached via the ever-
ennobling dynamic of the ritual aesthetic, are refounded.

The ritual discourse of the Suniyama resonates with an import that
reaches beyond the particular cultural and historical context of its production. Its celebration of aesthetic potency shares much with the splendor
of human artistic creations everywhere and in its difference manifests,
nonetheless, often a similar import. There is much in the Suniyama to my
mind that parallels, for example, Dante's progress in *The Divine Comedy*
as represented in Botticelli's splendid drawings. Despite the distinct
Christian cosmology of their context, there is yet, in the depiction of
Dante's ascent in the company of the beautiful Beatrice leading to the
breaking of the Devil's bonds, a similarity with the motioning of the victim in the Suniyama.

I have given some attention to Kant because I consider that the Suniyama enables a reflection from a different cosmological and cultural perspective on matters that have general import and that a discussion of the
aesthetic must enliven. The abstraction of the former as the pragmatism
of the latter reminds us of the crucial human issues and questions at the
center of aesthetics and, further, of that anthropology that attends to matters of aesthetic and symbolic process, whether in rite or other forms of
human practice.

Notes

I have discussed the arguments presented here with Angela Hobart, Tom Ernst, Jadran Mimica, and Roland Kapferer. I am most grateful to them and also to members of the workshop on aesthetics, performance, and ritual who met at Ascona in May 2000.

1. The translation of *tovil* as "exorcism" is problematic because of the ease with which it may be confused with exorcism in Christian traditions. Demons in *tovil* are not cast out in the way that they usually are in Christian exorcisms. Rather they are removed and placed at the margins of human social worlds. They are also transformed from malevolent to relatively benign and harmless creatures. In Sinhala conception, of course, the potential of the demonic is an ever-present dimension of human existence. These and other differences distinguish between *tovil* and Christian exorcism. However, there are broad similarities despite the differences.

   The word *tovil* specifically refers to Sinhala rites directed to demons (*yakku*). It is etymologically related to the Tamil for work or worker. In fact ritual practitioners (or exorcists) liken their rites to the noise and commotion of modern factory work where something new is hammered out of base material.

2. Exorcism in Sri Lanka is now increasingly being realized as a national heritage. Schools of dance and drama are being established catering especially for the middle class. The information presented is often being refashioned and made more and more consistent with classical Indian knowledge.

3. During the dance, which is oriented in terms of the dynamic of male and female principles, the dancers will play with convention, making a mockery of both homo- and heterosexuality.

4. Indeed, there is much in the structural organization of exorcism rites that explicitly relates to Hindu temple practice.

5. In my early work on exorcism (Kapferer 1983), I conceived of exorcism as involving a ritual suspension of everyday paramount reality. I note that this approach, common in ritual studies, allows for the equation of rite with modern theatre drama. While this may be appropriate in numerous instances, as far as exorcism is concerned, any such similarity would obscure significant differences. The use of the term "virtuality" conveys this. It is a thoroughgoing reality of its own that is neither a representation of realities external to it (symbolic in this sense) nor another reality altogether. Rather it constitutes a descent into the dynamics from which reality in all its multiple possibilities might be said to be constituted. I might add that, while there are clear theatrical dimensions of exorcisms that contribute so much to their delight, what could be called their "backstage" directions are also very much to the front. Exorcisms, like much ritual, constitute a complex of rules and directions into which participants are systematically introduced. If I were to continue with theatrical metaphors (which I have already indicated are not necessarily the best way to describe rite), I would say it is as if exorcism, as performance, is in a constant state of rehearsal.

6. Huniyam is the destructive demonic aspect. In Sinhala, "s" and "h" are interchangeable, although "s" is normally used for superior forms. Therefore, Suniyam is the encompassing form who transforms or articulates destruction with beneficence or protection, usually converting the one into the other.

7. Oddisa is presented in his origin myths as a demonic being who absorbs all the poisons of existence and then uses them to harm and to cure. He is presented as the great sacrificer whose knowledge outreaches that of Brahmanic astrologers and physicians. Oddisa lives outside human society, and it is from such a position that he has the ritual potency to reconstitute, for example, the orders of society.

8. The Suniyama shares much in its composition with the great ritual festivals and sacrifices of the annual renewal of kingship in medieval Sri Lanka, vestiges of which are still

performed today (see Seneviratne 1978). The Suniyama *as a sacrifice* is understood by exorcists to be composed of sixteen sacrificial actions (*tindui*) or completions in which the connection between the victim and sorcery is cut and the victim is reconstituted.

9. Events of drama and dance in the Suniyama are conceived by exorcists as sacrificial and finishing acts and are named by exorcists as part of the sixteen events of sacrifice that comprise the rite as a whole.

10. Shrines to the god Suniyam have been erected mainly in urban centers from the end of the nineteenth century. In these shrines he is a god who is represented as meting out justice or judgement, reward, and punishment to those who bring their problems before him. A popular cult would appear to be increasing around his worship. Problems with authority, state officials, or matters involving the law are frequently brought before him.

11. The gaze (*darsana*) is of central importance in the rite. To look upon the edifice of Buddhist order, the Mahasammata Palace, is to become part of its virtuous force.

12. This is a tantric rite. The victim is made to travel along the body of the snake of sorcery, which is simultaneously the snake of space and time, the spinal column, the world axis, etc. Marked along the line of the victim's journey in the rite are seven lotuses, or body plexuses, through which the energies of life renewal come. The *hatadiya* is the central rite of the entire Suniyama (see Kapferer 1997).

13. It must be stressed here that, throughout the rite, the victim remains silent. This silence is largely a silence wrought by the end of speech, which is one of the chief effects of sorcery. Sorcery kills the capacity of human beings to act in the world and to pursue their life projects. Language is, of course, the chief vehicle of such action. I note further that within the *atamagala* the victim is transformed from speechlessness into the silence of meditative quietude in which absolute consciousness and a moment approaching the transcendence of reason is achieved—reason in transcendence of itself being a condition at the very threshold of nonexistence. It is also, in the context of the Suniyama, a moment of the height of reason's potency.

14. The comedy elaborates on themes of life and death, and this is also its explosive quality, as Mary Douglas (1982) noted insightfully concerning the joke form.

15. Many Sinhalese Buddhists, laypersons, and monks will say that although ritual is necessary ultimately it cannot be used in place of the recognition and commitment to the power of the Buddha's reason. Such opinions undoubtedly are inspired in the great rationalism of a supremely modernist kind that has influenced present day appeals to Buddhism in Sri Lanka. Gombrich and Obeyesekere (1989) discuss this in their accounts of what they term Protestant Buddhism and what is generally described as the rationalism of recent Buddhist revivals spawned under the conditions of colonialism and after.

16. At this moment, or earlier in the rite, an effigy (*pambaya*) of the cause of sorcery is burnt, usually in a dark place and hidden from public view.

17. Turner's contribution through his development of the concept of the liminal must be emphasized in the overall context of the argument of this essay. Liminal moments are moments that stand outside conceptual orders, structures of interpretation (the categorical imperative) and, as Turner demonstrated in his Ndembu materials, are moments in which such categories or interpretative frames are actively demolished to give rise to new forms of meaning and position (status) in the orders of ongoing life. Here Turner broke away radically from that anthropology that saw in rite only conservatism and traditionalism. The liminal dynamics of rite are the vital clue to understanding how rituals can transform life situations. He effectively reassigned the significance of ritual in the anthropological imagination. He indicated why ritual action should persist through historical changes: integral in creating social and political ruptures, otherwise opening up social space, and facilitating the development of new or original orientations to the realities of experience. Within this move, Turner saw the potential identity between the liminal and the aesthetic and suggested why

artistic practice and aesthetic processes should be so vital in much ritual performance. The liminal in ritual gave rise to the creative, generative, and imaginative potentialities of the artistic and of the emergence of new orientations or an aesthetic reflective grasp on experience.

References

Berger, P., and T. Luckmann. 1971. *The Social Construction of Everyday Life*. London: Allen Lane.

Burckhardt, Jacob. [1860] 1997. *The Art and Civilization of the Renaissance*. London: Penguin.

Cassirer, Ernst. 1947. *The Philosophy of Symbolic Forms*. Trans. Ralph Mannheim. 3 vols. New Haven: Yale University Press.

———. 1996. *The Philosophy of Symbolic Forms: The Metaphysics of Symbolic Forms*. New Haven: Yale University Press.

Comaroff, Jean, and John L. Comaroff. 2000. *Millennial Capitalism and the Culture of Neo-Liberalism*. Durham: Duke University Press.

Deleuze, Gilles. 1989. *Difference and Repetition*. Trans. Paul Patton. London: Athlone Press.

———. 1995. *Kant's Critical Philosophy: The Doctrine of the Faculties*. Trans. Hugh Tomlinson and Barbara Habberjam. London: Athlone.

Deleuze, Gilles, and Felix Guattari. 1994. *What Is Philosophy?* London: Verso.

Derrida, Jacques. 1994. *Given Time: Counterfeit Money*. Vol. 1. Trans. Peggy Kamuf. Chicago: Chicago University Press.

Dufrenne, Mikel. 1973. *The Phenomenology of Aesthetic Experience*. Evanston, Ill.: Northwestern University Press.

Geschiere, P. 1997. *The Modernity of Witchcraft*. Charlottesville: University of Virginia Press.

Gombrich, R., and Gananath Obeyesekere. 1989. *Buddhism Transformed: Religious Change in Sri Lanka*. Princeton: Princeton University Press.

Hegel, G. W. F. [1835] 1975. *Aesthetics: Lectures on Fine Art*. Vol. 2. Trans. T. M. Knox. Oxford: Clarendon Press.

Hubert, Henri, and Marcel Mauss. 1964. *Sacrifice: Its Nature and Functions*. Trans. W. D. Halls. Chicago: University of Chicago Press.

Kant, Immanuel. 1987. *The Critique of Judgement*. Trans. Werner Pluhar. Indianapolis: Hackett.

Kapferer, Bruce. 1983. *A Celebration of Demons*. Bloomington: Indiana University Press.

———. 1997. *The Feast of the Sorcerer*. Chicago: Chicago University Press.

———. 2001. "The Sorcery of Consciousness: A Sinhala Buddhist Discourse on the Dynamics of Consciousness." *Journal of Cognition and Communication* 33, no. ?: 97–120.

———. 2002. "Introduction: Outside All Reason – Magic, Sorcery and Epistemology." In *Beyond Rationalism*, ed. Bruce Kapferer, 1–30. New York and Oxford: Berghahn Books.

———. 2003a. "Sorcery and the Shapes of Globalization Disjunctions and Continuities: The Case of Sri Lanka." In *Globalization, the State, and Violence*, ed. Jonathan Friedman, 249–78. Oxford: Altamira Press.

———. 2003b. "Sorcery and Renewal in Contemporary Sri Lanka." *Bulletin of the Royal Institute for Inter-Faith Studies* 4, no. 2: 1–25.

———. 2004. "Ritual Dynamics and Virtual Practice: Beyond Representation and Meaning." *Social Analysis* 48, no. 2: 35–54.

Kapferer, Bruce, and G. Papigny. 2002. *Tovil: Excorsismes Bouddhistes*. Paris: Editions DesIris.

Kersenboom, Saskia C. 1987. *Nityasumangali: Devadasi Tradition in South India*. Dehli: Motilal Barnasidass.

———. 1995. *Words, Sound, Image: Life of the Tamil Text*. Oxford: Berg Press.

Langer, Susanne. 1942. *Philosophy in a New Key: A Study in the Symbolism of Reason, Rite and Art.* Cambridge, Mass.: Harvard University Press.

Munn, Nancy. 1973. *Walbiri Iconography.* Ithaca: Cornell University Press.

Rappaport, Roy A. 1999. *Ritual and Religion in the Making of Humanity.* Cambridge: Cambridge University Press.

Schutz, Alfred. 1967. *The Phenomenology of the Social World.* Evanston, Ill.: Northwestern University Press.

Scarry, Elaine. 1999. *On Beauty and Being Just.* Princeton: Princeton University Press.

Seneviratne, H. L. 1978. *Rituals of the Kandyan State.* Cambridge: Cambridge University Press.

Turner, V. W. 1958. *Chihamba, the White Spirit.* Manchester: Manchester University Press.

———. 1967. *The Forest of Symbols.* Ithaca: Cornell University Press.

———. 1969. *The Ritual Process.* Harmondsworth: Penguin.

Chapter Seven

TRANSFORMATION AND AESTHETICS IN BALINESE MASKED PERFORMANCES— RANGDA AND BARONG

Angela Hobart

This chapter focuses on Galungan, the most elaborate and complex festival in Bali, which is celebrated every 210 days throughout most of the island and engages thousands of people. The festival is considered part of the traditional medical system, within which, it is important to stress, healing, sorcery, and art are intimately intertwined. During the festive period, ritual and dramatic performances create and recreate realities vivid enough to enchant, purify, heal, amuse, and beguile their spectators. The main actors of the performances are majestic masked figures, Barongs and Rangda. My concern in this chapter is with the nature of the aesthetics of the masked performances. What enables the diverse aesthetic modes—the music, songs, dance, and drama, the colors, the magical sounds and smells—to transform meanings and experience, so endowing the participants with the capacity to remake their worlds and extend their consciousness to the other and the life-revitalizing aspects of existence?

During the celebration the masked figures serve essentially as lightning rods, being considered momentary material manifestations of cosmic power. Barongs mainly take the form of wild animals, animated by two men. The actor in front operates the wooden mask, snapping the wooden teeth playfully, and the other moves the creature's hind legs. Another type of Barong is found in two towering figures that represent an elderly couple, Ratu Gede, who are dignified, as well as humorous in dance; each is performed by a single actor. The most important and majestic Barong throughout the island is the mythic, lion-like creature Barong Ket, Lord of the Forest (see figure 7.1). His consort is the wild-eyed Rangda, the volatile queen sorceress and Goddess of Power (see figure 7.2). Because of the dangerous powers associated with her, she is always danced by a man who has been initiated. Barong Ket's ancestor is probably the Chinese lion who entered South East Asia during the T'ang Dynasty (seventh to tenth centuries C.E.). Rangda resembles the fearful Indian image of Kali, "the Dark Goddess," whose name means time.

This chapter is divided into three parts. After offering an overview of the island of Bali, I will discuss briefly community and family life, with specific reference to the island's rural regions. This is crucial as the festival sets out to counteract the tensions and conflicts inherent in mundane existence. Moreover, the performances draw on symbolic forms and dynamic

Figure 7.1 Barong, Lord of the Forest, in the temple after his consecration

Photograph by Angela Hobart.

Figure 7.2 Rangda, the Goddess of Power, being carried to the dance arena

Photograph by Albert Leemann.

processes familiar to the people from daily situations. Second, I will look at origin myths of Barong Ket and Rangda and the making of sacred masks. Finally, I discuss the festival, focusing on the district of Tegallalang in the regency of Gianyar, where I conducted research on the healing power of masked performances.[1]

Bali is the only area in the Indonesian Archipelago that has remained predominantly Hindu. The population of the rest of the country is 90 percent Muslim or nominally Muslim. The island has a unique cultural heritage. It retains Hindu, Buddhist, and Tantric elements that have been intertwined with indigenous traditions of ancestor worship, spirit mediumship, and magic. In the last decades Bali has gone through rapid social and economic change in response to modernization and the influx of tourists. Progress and technology and biomedical knowledge have infiltrated all parts of the island. Yet the Balinese are known for their ability to blend the old with the new. Rituals and artistic creations, which are considered conducive to well-being, have remained integral to village life. My research took place in the Tegallalang district in rural south-central Bali that is reputedly the heartland of Balinese culture. The people seem to exalt the outward. Geertz has referred to their meticulous poise and etiquette as a "kind of dance," a "kind of worship" (1973, 400). This impression of serene beauty belies my own experiences when living in south Bali. Even the displays of bright faces and polite demeanors to which Unni Wikan (1990, 52) drew attention may be deceptive and transparent to the locals themselves. Certainly past events, such as the attempted coup in 1965, and the bloodshed that followed it in widespread purges of communists or suspected communists (during which hundreds of thousands were killed), and the protests and riots in 1998 that led to Suharto's stepping down, give a glimmering of the turbulence that potentially exists under the surface of social interactions.

Mundane Life: Outlets for the "Uncivilized" Passions

Sophisticated rules of etiquette and aesthetic standards guide the people in their transactions with other humans in mundane life. Yet, as elsewhere in the world, self-interest, envy, and greed are powerful driving forces. Above all, villagers fear anger, the furies that can poison consciousness. Family life is particularly acrimonious. Hildred Geertz (1995) is one of the few scholars who has drawn attention to the dissent that prevails in Bali, especially within the family, which only prolonged involvement with the people will bring to light. Tensions and difficulties are rarely divulged to neighbors, let alone outsiders. Friction and strife lead to chaos (*buwut*) when the family members are seen to plunge into darkness.[2]

In line with the need to give an impression of external harmony, the Balinese use a gamut of expressive possibilities and symbolic modes to displace meaning from one form to another. Here I will mention two institutionalized methods for coping with anger, irritation, envy, fear, the various "uncivilized" passions to which a person can succumb in public or private life.

In a similar way to the characters in Henrik Ibsen's later plays, the Balinese are adept at saying one thing while meaning another, and in razor-sharp exchanges made through evasive retorts and actions that can have lethal impact. This is evidenced by the following interchange. A villager sits at a stall with friends. Another villager, with whom he has recently quarreled, passes by. He snaps at a pig that he sees nearby wallowing in refuse, "you pig that does nothing but grunt" (*da nyake bungute celeng*). All know for whom the statement is intended, but face-to-face conflict has been avoided. Such incidents are frequent in the community.

Sorcery is another acknowledged form of action that is profoundly implicated in the anguish of human beings in their social worlds. Slaats and Portier (1989, 35) in their general discussion of magic as a social and legal problem in Indonesia, confirm that sorcery practices permeate all levels of the society. It is healers/sorcerers in Bali who make "black" (*pangiwa*) magic tools[3] or charms and give them to clients who wish to poison the consciousness of others, bringing illness, suffering, and misfortune in their wake. Sorcerers who set out to ensorcell victims pay special homage to the Goddess of Death, Durga. Yet all healers may call on her for she incarnates power, *kasaktian*, that can heal, destroy, and protect.

There are of course many ways that healers or sorcerer can harness power. Here I mainly want to emphasize how often indirect tactics, which include the manipulation of malevolent magic, are resorted to by locals when they find themselves in stressful or confrontational situations. With this strategy face-to-face social interaction is avoided. Veiled communication is also an intrinsic feature of Balinese ritual performances. However, as will emerge, aesthetic and contemplative qualities are suggested in these circumstances.

Rangda and Barong Ket: Myths and Mask Making

The most important figures during Galungan are Barong Ket, Lord of the Forest, and Rangda. Barong Ket is a magnificent hybrid creature. His shaggy coat is usually made of the fibers of pandanas leaves. Mirrors and gold leaf embellish the leather ornaments decorating his body. Peacock feathers adorn his tail and tinkle when he dances. The essence of his power is said to reside in his beard, which is made of human hair. (In Tegallalang this comes from the hair of a girl who has not yet menstruated to ensure its ritual purity.) Barong Ket is considered a vehicle of the god Siwa. Barong Ket is generally conceived to be a powerful protective figure with great regenerative potential. Nonetheless, one Tantric text describes him as having evil traits (de Zoete and Spies [1938] 1973, 97). Rangda, his consort, represents deepest obscurity and is to the Balinese, in Turner's ([1967] 1977) sense, a dominant symbol of the boundless power of destruction and transformation. Rangda, with her long, flaming tongue, tangled hair, bulging eyes, and dreadful teeth is to some scholars a "satanic image" who "evokes fear, as well as hatred, disgust and cruelty" (Geertz 1978, 30).[4] Other scholars have described her as a personification of "evil." However, in line with the recent scholar Lovric (1987), I would contend that these figures are best viewed as supreme demonic cult deities that are Tantric in orientation. As such they embody the ambivalent powers of sorcery that can simultaneously heal and destroy the lifeworlds of humans (Kapferer 1997).

It is relevant here to add a brief description of the prevailing stimulus of Tantric ideas on the traditional Balinese medical system and the culture more generally. While knowledge of Tantrism on Java and Bali is tenuous and speculative, the Dutch have long acknowledged its influence in the islands. Boon pointed out that, as far as Tantric texts cohere, they revolve around the ecstatic union between Siwa and Siwa's bride. A well-developed Tantric philosophical doctrine did not develop in Bali; rather, as Boon (1990, xiii) writes, "Tantric values were propagated through rites, texts, and tactics that are seldom doctrinal." They are reflected in the prominence given to the cemetery and death temple, the Goddess of Death or Goddess of Power, as she is often called in south Bali, and the origin myth of Barong Ket and Rangda. This myth is summarized below as it is crucial in understanding the significance of these figures during the festival.

The myth recounts the radiance of the Supreme God who created the world of humans. He then requested Siwa and his consort Uma to inspect his creation. Uma descended quietly to earth by herself. She gazed at the myriad things around her and was carried away by the beauty of the forests, flowers, and rice fields interspersed with human habitation and lost her equilibrium. The Demon King Kala penetrated her consciousness. Her perception became distorted, and she began to destroy human realities. Suffering and illness broke out. Siwa looked down from the heavens and was consternated at the affliction that his consort was bringing to earth. However, passionate desire inflamed him as he approached her, and he too lost his bearing. Possessed by the demonic, the couple was transformed into Barong Ket and Rangda, wild-eyed, with flickering fangs. The gods Wisnu, Brahma, and Iswara realized that the couple was entrapped by the illusionary world of appearance. They descended to earth and performed a story about the consummation of the marriage of Siwa with his spouse Uma. This soothed the divine couple, and the demonic lost its hold on them. They regained awareness of the unity of being-in-the-world and the illusion of one-sided clinging. They returned to heaven; order, harmony, and prosperity were restored to earth.

This myth was probably superimposed on an older story, prevalent throughout the Archipelago, of how Father Sky, stretched upon Mother

Earth, impregnated her (Hooykaas 1961, 268). These creation myths are so important because they become lived reality, their existential force being discovered as a property of the underlying dynamic of the rites and performances given during the festive period. It is then that the power embodied by Barongs and Rangda is manifest as a reconstitutive energy enabling individuals and social groups to remake their worlds and the land to prosper.

In order to explain how these masked figures materialize such immense power in the eyes of the locals, I shall describe briefly how they are made. I have written about this in depth in my 2003 book, *Healing Performances of Bali* and hence will now only say a few words about their craftsmanship. Surprisingly little has been written about the art of making sacred masks; most scholars focus on their iconography and symbolic input. But these approaches ignore the process whereby principal actors and participants interact. It is important to stress that it is through the process of making the masks and costumes that Barongs and Rangda come to embody totalizing power that can galvanize social reality to the locals.

Barongs and Rangda are referred to as "vehicles of gods" (*palinggihan ida batara*).[5] A consecrated masked figure takes about three months to make and involves up to four thousand villagers. Because of the great variety of materials used, a new mask costs several hundred dollars to make, and the coat or costume several thousand. The resources of the community are pooled for the creation of a new figure. In contrast a costume for Barong or Rangda intended for performances before tourists only takes a few weeks to make and is not initiated. The craftsmanship of these is fairly slapdash.

Rituals punctuate the entire creative process. The simplest rite is carried out when chopping down the wood for a mask. The choice of tree is considered important. A *pule* tree (*Alstonia scholaris*) that grows near the cremation grounds is often used for ceremonial masks. Offerings are secured to the tree and dedicated to the God of Inspiration, Taksu. Healers and actors pay homage to this god before performing. Barong Ket himself is associated with the God of Inspiration. This is one reason he is considered the sublime World-maker during the celebration (Hobart 2003). The most elaborate rites are carried out at night in the graveyard when it is said to be electrically charged and dangerous, once the figure is complete. The priests then invite the gods to enter the masks. These few lines from a mantra chanted during the rite of *pasupati* (a Sanskrit term referring to Siwa as "Lord of Animals") give an idea of its orientation.

Ong, God Sang Hyang Pasupati bring well-being.
May the gods animate (*angurip*) the mask.
Ong, may the Supreme Gods Siwa Sakti, Sadasiwa Sakti and Paramasiwa
    Sakti,
empower it with consciousness (*teke urip*).

In the meantime, hundreds of villagers sit huddled together some distance away from the graveyard. Tension builds up as the night progresses, and the unseen ritual activities produce an atmosphere of subdued excitement. The darkness and secrecy of the rites tantalize the beholders and stress the authority and power of the mythic masked figure that is being created.

Once made, the sacred masks and costumes are stored in temples until needed. Rangda and Barong Ket always reside in the death temple, which lies outside the village and, being connected with the vital forces of life and death, is a site of vital transformation.

The Religious Festival Galungan

Healing is a spectacle in many societies. This also applies to Galungan, where a wide range of ritual and dramatic performances are presented. Most of these involve Barongs who are simply called Ida Batara, god. The locals say that Galungan is a time to pay homage to the ancestral spirits and gods, and the unpropitiated demonic beings, *buta/kala,* are banished from the environment. It is interesting that, in relation to Galungan, the official Balinese calendar explicitly affirms the importance of intertwining well-being, beauty, and morality, implying individual and cosmic order, *dharma.* In passing, this refutes Geetz's (1973, 400) contention that what matters to the people in both daily and ritual life is aesthetics, not virtue. Ritualistic activity is seen as creating an embodiment of the cosmic forces of moral order, purity, and beauty, which infuses social reality, the individual, and human group. Galungan is in fact considered one of the main means to counteract the "ills" in the society—the acrimony that can arise when uncivilized passions are not contained, and the confusion and tension brought on by modernization and corrupt government procedures.

The festival proper continues for ten days, following the actual day of Galungan, but continues on for another twenty to thirty days. It peters to an end when the temples hold their annual anniversaries, *odalan.* The arrangements for the festival are largely in the hands of village priests, *pamangku,* and the headmen of the different sociopolitical groups. Yet it is important to stress that the center of gravity during the celebration is at the level of the community. During the festive period processions with Barongs and Rangda cover more or less the entire area. They essentially demarcate the sacred space involved. Interestingly, some learned villagers refer to this orbit as a mandala, a term that Zoetmulder (1982) translates as the district or sacred circle in which (perhaps Tantric) ceremonies are held. Obeyesekere (1984, 51) points out that "mandala" has also other meanings in ancient Hinduism: among other things, it represents a dance hall where the gods are invisibly present and constitutes the circle of their influence.

Humans and gods are drawn into this "magic circle." Galungan in effect enacts a cosmic journey or passage that ends at the temples, which are at the core of the village community.

Because of the plethora of visual and auditory images presented to the villagers during the celebration, I will limit my discussion to just three performative events: processions with Barongs, the lofty couple Ratu Gede singing and dancing, and the Calon Arang drama. In addition, a few words on the preparations and the ending of the festival are necessary to give a flavor of this complex celebration.

Preparation for the Day of Galungan

During the preparation days the villagers separate themselves from everyday life. Offerings are made to purify consciousness. These are brought to all household shrines and temples.

Tall bamboo poles are erected along the paths, where they remain until the end of Galungan (see figure 7.3). Shrines are often set up next to the poles with runners of palm leaf showing stylized female figures.[6] The poles and runners form a unit symbolizing, among other things, Father Sky and Mother Earth, Siwa and Uma. Throughout the festival humans and Barongs pass under the arcades formed by these gracefully curving poles that allude to the creation myth of Rangda and Barong Ket mentioned earlier.

Processions with Barongs

The days following Galungan have all the elements associated with liminality, implying an aesthetic and metaphysics of indeterminacy and fragmentation when various types of playful, solemn, and ludic events are presented. High-spirited processions of up to 400 people, with Barongs and Rangda at the end, travel through the hamlets and winding paths in the district. They may travel up to eighteen kilometers per day. The priests and headmen determine their paths and ensure that processions do not collide with one another. The processions include women carrying offerings (see figure 7.4) and musicians beating drums and cymbals. The latter have the explicit purpose of banishing hostile demonic spirits, *buta/kala*, from the borders and establishing harmonious relations with the spirits or energies that guard and generate the crops. Barongs through their movements exert their territoriality over the district. This would have been especially important in the past, when intense rivalry existed between kingdoms. Moreover, unappeased *buta/kala*, to learned Balinese, epitomize the cravings of the world, the passions and furies to which the human being can succumb. Together with witches and sorcerers they are often implicated in destructive actions on others. Hence, it is crucial that these malignant agents are brought under control.

Figure 7.3 Ceremonial bamboo poles with runners, set up in all villages during the festival Galungan

Photograph by Urs Ramseyer.

At intervals Barongs sing, dance, and enact episodes from folk tales in village squares or on the roadside, and the entire procession comes to a standstill. How long they perform depends on how much money is collected from the villagers who line the paths. Rangda (in Tegallalang) never dances on these occasions. She is carried in a basket next to her consort Barong Ket, with only her scarlet tongue lolling out.

The Couple, Ratu Gede, Sing and Dance

In this section I will briefly describe the towering, elderly couple, Barong Ratu Gede (see figure 7.5), who are beloved and revered in Tegallalang. They are associated with Wisnu, the god of water and fertility, and therefore peasants pay special homage to them—and 87 percent of the inhabitants

Figure 7.4 Ceremonially clad women carrying offerings to the temple during the festival Galungan

Photograph by Urs Ramseyer.

Figure 7.5 Ratu Gede, the towering couple, walking in procession during Galungan

Photograph by Albert Leemann.

are peasants, many of whom remain dependent upon irrigated rice for their livelihoods. The male is a black and martial-looking figure, with large buckteeth, while his partner is elegant, prim, and coy. During the festival these towering figures sing ludic songs while dancing seductively to a small musical ensemble. The first two lines are deliberately obscure in order to draw attention to the veiled sphere of life, *niskala*, and to show respect to the figures that manifest divine powers. I offer the following two songs as examples:

Ebe Dengdeng, sampi tua,
kekrupukan belulang emeng.
Adeng adeng peturu tua,
angkuk mangku matane nengeng.

Beef that is old and has dried in the sun,
crisp thin cakes (*krupuk*) made of cat's skin.
As we are elderly our loins move slowly [when we make love],
and our eyes remain wide open.

Esok pecok pedemin cicing,
memula lateng di Bankiangsidem.
Nyaka bocok nyaka tusing
lamun suba anteng ajak medem.

A dented basket slept in by a dog,
planted nettles in [the hamlet] Bankiangsidem.
I like her whether she is ugly or not
provided that she will sleep with me.

These bawdy, humorous songs and comic dancing, which induce peals of laughter from onlookers, entertain and heal by providing an outlet for pent-up emotions. After singing together the couple may dramatize episodes from well-known folk tales. These short dance-dramas, which attract beholders from near and far, are distinguished by a tone of pathos that is radically different from the songs. The tragic love story of *Jaya Prana* has attained special popularity, as it is based on a legend that alludes to the emancipation of the common peasant after World War II. The poem also highlights the strength of individual love and concomitantly the flexibility inherent in the society that adheres to principles of caste and status relations (Boon 1977). The story tells of the murder of *Jaya Prana* by a demonic king, who lusts after the innocent young man's beloved wife. In sorrow, she stabs herself to death. The verses of the poem (see Hooykaas 1958) are replete with poetic allusions and metaphors, as illustrated in their romantic encounter.

[Giving homage to the king Jaya Prana spoke:]
"Your servant I am, most humble I am,"
and thereupon he clasped his hands,
begged leave to go and went his way;
arriving at the Outer Court
his eye now roved
at girls who went to the market.

And then there came one from the south,
adorned with a costly scarf;
her, but lightly tied, yet showed
the tail that fell upon her neck;
a slender waist, her body straight,
small pointed breasts
the peer of ivory coconuts.

Her nails were long and pointed too,
her step was slow and quivering,

supple, like a sapling swaying;
brows drawn sharp, as far her temple,
her eyes were kind but yet afire,
her smile was sweet,
her gums as a *rijasa* flower.

Just like an image made of gold,
I Layon Sari was she called,
I Jaya Prana nearly swooned,
beholding such a wondrous girl.
(Hooykaas 1958, 41)

As some of the words sung are in the archaic language, Kawi, or are drawn out, the stories are only partially understood by the audience. Villagers point out that stories such as *Jaya Prana*, if well acted, purify and cool mind and body by touching on fragile and sensitive memories and motivations. The towering Barongs emerge as mediators par excellence between cosmic and social dualities, between self and other, inside and outside, order and chaos, the solemn and the playful.

The Calon Arang Dance-Drama

These days in Tegallalang, my research area, the Calon Arang dance-drama is the most spectacular ritual performance during the festival. (It may also take place during temple anniversaries.) This dance-drama, more than any other, brings to expression existential awareness of the inevitability of suffering and the paradoxes of life. A performance is given at night outside the death temple. It is accompanied by the full gamelan ensemble. This genre of theatre has been extensively studied by a number of scholars (Belo 1960, [1949] 1966; Bateson and Mead 1942; Geertz 1978, 24–40). Hence, I will focus just on performances that I witnessed during the celebration. It is worth noting, though, that while details of the dance-drama vary considerably, there are common scenic elements in performances across the island. In Bali performances usually involve entranced dancers with krisses (Balinese daggers) in their hands, and strikingly, this feature is totally absent in my research area.[7] Like the performances enacted by the towering couple, Ratu Gede, the Calon Arang dance-drama does not present an argument or commentary; rather, the aesthetic forms intrinsic to this form of theatre engender poetic tension and drama that can simultaneously move artistically, psychologically, and physiologically dancers and beholders alike.[8]

The story is based on events set in East Java in the eleventh century. The legend tells of the queen sorceress and widow (*rangda*), Calon Arang, who is identified with the Javanese queen Mahendratta. No one wishes to marry Calon Arang's lovely daughter for fear of her mother's evil reputation. In revenge, the enraged sorceress transforms into Rangda, a fearful manifestation of Durga, the Goddess of Death. Together with her six female pupils she strikes the kingdom with a terrible epidemic. Rangda is finally appeased and purified by the powerful sage Mpu Baradah, who has been summoned by the king to help in the desperate situation. In my research area two main acts can be distinguished. These are summarized below.

In the first act the elderly widow-witch summons her six beautiful pupils (*sisya*). Their long hair hangs loose, and they are clad in white skirts, with yellow and black bodices. They pay homage to the Goddess of Death at a small temporary shrine set up for the occasion, requesting malign power with which to inflict the land with suffering and illness. This is granted. Throughout they speak Old Javanese, Kawi, the archaic literary language. A few comic scenes follow, performed by villagers and witches. A wrapped up object (representing a corpse) is carried onto the stage. Torches are lit as the group makes their way to the cemetery. The king consults his prime ministers and the sage Mpu Baradah is sent to vanquish the sorceress. He succeeds because the potency of life-regenerating power is considered greater than destructive demonic power. The former, though takes longer to acquire. Calon Arang and the other actors leave the stage.

In the second act Calon Arang transforms into Rangda, who enters the stage. Her long fingernails quiver and her pendulous breasts sway to and fro as she dances. Barong Ket prances onto the stage. He is a magical creature whose moods and dynamics are ever changing in tune with the gamelan orchestra. He has a particular affection for the drum, which, like that of a shaman, binds together the elements of the ritual dance-drama. The two protagonists enter into combat, but their struggle ends without resolution and in Tegallalang is playful and short. The show ends.

The music, together with the arousing imagery and setting, draws the participants into the performance reality. The sanctity of the occasion is intensified as the dance-drama takes place during Galungan, which is orientated to the gods whose radiance the two protagonists, Rangda and Barong Ket, embody. Of course the participants may not all experience the same significance or efficacy. Yet all villagers say that the dance-drama has regenerative potential. How do we account for this? The performance is clearly multifaceted, but a few comments are worth making in the space of this essay.

Consider, for example, the magical white cloth (*kudrang* in low, and *kekerab* in high Balinese) that Rangda flourishes when dancing (see figure 7.6). It is an inseparable adjunct of the mask throughout Bali. Nothing has been written about the cloth. Psychoanalysts, especially those adhering to the Kleinian perspective, would have a heyday interpreting the meaning of the figure drawn on the cloth (in Tegallalang).[9] However, I feel it is unsatisfactory to use Western psychodynamic models on a completely different culture. The figure is derived from the sacred palm-leaf manuscripts. To learned Balinese, she is the Goddess of Power who actualizes

Figure 7.6 Magical drawing of Rangda, the Goddess of Power

Drawing by I Gusti Sudara (original in palm-leaf manuscript).

Rangda's potency. They explain that the full, drooping breast contains poison, and the minuscule breast honey. Poison is associated with the destructive power of sorcery, and honey with traditional medicine that revitalizes. Most people are driven by their "animal" passions and desires. Hence, the breast containing poison is large enough to satisfy them all.

The Goddess of Power, in other words, is a totalizing figure who unites poisonous and reconstitutive forces, but she adjusts to the directional trust of human beings. Most villagers are unaware of the deeper meaning of the figure, but they too view the cloth as symbolically condensing and extending Rangda's paradoxical power. It emerges that the enigmatic and fearsome imagery associated with Rangda expresses the striving of people to find an acceptable explanation for the human being's nature. It is suggested that "evil," which gives rise to suffering and anguish, is the propensity of all humans and capable of breaking out at any time, in any place; in fact, the propensity for evil outweighs that of good. This resonates as a universal problem, but one that is represented differently around the world. So the Calon Arang performance as it unfolds may prompt new sensibilities and encourages participants to reexamine their lives and to reflect on their orientation towards the ever-shifting horizons of existence. In this context it is relevant to stress again the fact that all theatrical presentations in Bali have moral import.

The play culminates with the ritual contest between Rangda and the Lord of Forest. He too has a magical cloth, which is often flung over his shoulders when he dances (see figure 7.7). The drawing on his cloth, like that of Rangda's, has great significance to the Balinese. The naked figure

Figure 7.7 Magical drawing of Barong, Lord of the Forest

The Supreme God Tunggal, surrounded by the serpent Basuki. Drawing by I Gusti Sudara (original in palm-leaf manuscript).

in the center represents the supreme god Tunggal (also called Acintya). He is encircled by the cosmic serpent Anantaboga, a dynamic image of trans-formation in both Southeast Asia and India. So the drawing objectifies and actualizes the magical creature's great reconstitutive potential, which reflects his role as supreme World-maker in the festival.

Villagers explain that Rangda experiences joy when she dances in the visible realm, *sekala*, in a ritual setting. This is of course intensified when she is joined by her splendid partner. During the dance-drama the two majestic figures are said to "play" (*macanda*) with the dangerous, ambigu-ous forces in the world. The joy transfigures Rangda, in particular, so that her dark energies of sorcery are converted into ones that heal and protect. The dramatic tension of Rangda and Barong Ket's encounter infuses the environment and captivates the beholders. They may then perceive the richness of every aspect of life when nothing is rejected, nothing accepted. This encourages awareness of the flux of moments without clinging, with-out seeking to bind them into fixed structures.

A full-scale Calon Arang dance-drama is a complicated and flamboyant performative event. Yet it is crucial to reiterate that it is only one of many ritual events during the festival. Processions with Barongs and Rangda who sing and dance are constantly traveling through the district. The var-ied dance-dramas, with their spectacle and humor, are differently articu-lated and accentuated at specific moments in the ritual progression. The audience itself also warrants brief comment. The elusive, loosely knit qual-ity of the performances enacted by masked figures is in tune with the way the spectators engage with a ritual event. Their attention and commitment to the performance fluctuates as people come and go. Nonetheless, the spectators are acutely aware of the aesthetic merit of a performance. A good performance is said to enchant, *ngelangunin*, spectators. Interestingly, this concept has affinity with *(a)lango*, an Old Javanese term that conjures up the idea of both "enraptured" and "enrapturing" (Zoetmulder 1974, 173). Rapture implies surrendering oneself to the aesthetic experience, when the distinction between subject and object becomes blurred. The scholar Zoetmulder points out that prose treatises (*tutur*) in Java and Bali suggests that this practice takes the form of a particular kind of Tantric yoga that developed on the islands in the thirteen and fourteen centuries with special reference to religious poetry (1974, 179).[10]

Intrinsic to this form of Tantrism is the veiled and indeterminate nature of the performances enacted by Barongs and Rangda. As mentioned, the stories narrated are partly in Old Javanese or chanted, and hence, remain inaccessible to most of the spectators. Ludic songs are deliberately obscure. Earlier I alluded to the importance of indirect, suggestive speech and tac-tics in situations of conflict in mundane life. Yet to the locals this feature attains aesthetic and spiritual significance in the ritual context. The people stress that the words have literally to be unpeeled (*melut*), unraveled, in order to understand their sacred essence. On the one hand, the "blanks" and "negations" (Iser 1978, 182) explicitly draw attention to the unseen world of the gods, spirits, and energies, and on the other, the nebulous nature of the performances excites the senses, stimulates the memory, and entices the imagination. Moreover, this dynamic creates spaciousness and encourages reflexivity, whereby the multiple voices, forms of knowledge, and moral stances can be drawn together and thus sense can be made of the events. Attitudes, moods, and relationships may then be shifted.

However, from an overall perspective, transformation in meaning is primarily effected by the participants experiencing aesthetic images and symbols as part of their journey during the festival. Interestingly, the locals themselves describe the processions with Barongs and Rangda as "circulating" (*malindar*) around the district. The figures, as it were, propel the expanded social universe, the mandala, into motion during the celebration. Through their movements the demonic is expelled and the paramount reality of everyday life reified. Within this magical arena, where colors, scents, movements, and sounds are reconfigured, human perception can be reorganized and action restructured.

Temple Anniversaries

The festival gradually ends after about twenty-five days. Fittingly, the holistic process set into operation by the processions culminates with the anniversaries of temples that are figuratively at the center of the village community. Rangda and Barong Ket deserve special mention. Together they repose regally in their elevated shrines in the death temple before being dismantled. Because of the anniversary's brevity, their presence is fleeting. Their quiet dignity as they gaze down from their shrines brings to mind the myth of their creation: once Siwa and his consort Uma have attained freedom from the bonds of earthly desires, they unite again in heaven. The conjunction of the male and female principles, Siwa and Uma, sky and earth, is a theme that runs like a shimmering thread through the festival. Their harmonic unity (Kapferer 2000, 25) has ontological dimensions. It testifies to the sociality of the occasion when the human transcends the bounds of individual existence and realizes that extending consciousness towards the other in a ritual context leads to unity of being-with-others. Prosperity, order, and fertility in the land follow.

A few words should be said about offerings that are brought to the temples during the celebration and accompany all ritual performances. All households are actively involved in making offerings during the festive period. They are made from natural ingredients—flowers, leaves, rice, fruit, and so forth. They are anonymous and by intention transitory. Locals consider offerings the purest and most refined art form on the island. They are symbolic transformations of experience that imbue life with aesthetic value, beauty, and well-being. Elaine Scarry's evocative words come to mind: through their "symmetry and generous sensory availability," offerings help direct human attention "towards ethical equality" (2000, 109), when self-lessness and mindfulness are reinforced. This is in tune with the festival's orientation that supports the Balinese contention that the community is fundamental to existence and is constitutive of it. It is interesting to turn for a moment to Western thought. Kant (1973, 109), in his critical ethics of the late eighteenth century, conjoined beauty and virtue, aesthetics and ethics. The Balinese approach echoes these ideas. It is evident that the locals are aware of the beauty of virtue, which responds to the dignity of human nature. However, order, beauty, and harmony are fragile and transient. Hence, Galungan is celebrated anew every 210 days of the Hindu-Balinese calendar. This is consistent with a religious system that envisages the cosmos in a condition of constant flux, process, and transformation.

Conclusion

This essay reveals the power of the aesthetic formed through practices unfolded during the festival Galungan. I am not interested here in the category of "aesthetics" divorced from the ritual life of the people involved. The focus is on how the varied aesthetic forms structure and organize the perception of the participants, enabling transformation of meaning and reflection on experience to occur that is healing in intent. In this context it is relevant to recall that the people themselves view the festival as intrinsic to the traditional medical system. As we have seen, the festival, as processions with Barong and Rangda singing and dancing at the rear travel through the countryside, sets into motion dynamic processes that aim to rebalance, recenter, and purify the village community. Exploring these processes extends our understanding of the importance of aesthetic forms in ritual and performative activities.

A few final words should be added about the Barongs and Rangda who are the main actors in the ritual performances. Made by the community for the community, they embody totalizing power that can galvanize social reality. During the celebration this power is actualized and harnessed by the participants and directed to regenerating the village community, by encouraging human beings to become open to the others. As the Balinese poetically say:

> Chained consciousness is like a tarnished closed flower. Its odor is putrid.
> On the contrary, the efflorescence of consciousness (*kembang pikayun*) is like
> a blossoming flower. Its scent imbues the surroundings with fragrance.

Notes

I would like to acknowledge the financial support that I received from the British Academy and the Social Science Nuffield Foundation for the research upon which this chapter is based. I thank Albert Leemann and Urs Ramseyer for the lovely photographs, and the Balinese craftsman I Gusti Sudara for the detailed drawings. The originals are in sacred palm-leaf manuscripts.

1. This chapter is based on my ethnographic fieldwork, conducted in Bali intermittently between 1990 and 2000. For an in-depth discussion of the indigenous medical system, see my 2003 book, *Healing Performances of Bali: between Darkness and Light* (New York, Oxford: Berghahn Books). A number of points brought up in the chapter are elaborated on in the book.
2. According to villagers, conflict in the family is especially virulent over inheritance problems and the negotiation of new patterns of relationships between family members after marriage, when young in-marrying women enter households.
3. Magical "tools" (called *pakakas*) and charms have multiple purposes, apart from ensorcelling victims. They can be used as protection, to incite love in someone, to produce rain during drought, and so forth. Such objects or tools may be burnt, pierced, entwined, wrapped up, or buried in the house compound. Neither healers/sorcerers nor clients ever talk about these objects, for their power is then said to wane.
4. Such views of Rangda are erroneous. Statues of her are found in palaces and temples that are protective in intent. The sacred mask and magical cloth are revered and regarded as benevolent in community life. In line with this, it is unsurprising that the masked figure can be used in dance-drama to represent the god Siwa.
5. The head is the most elevated part of Barongs and Rangda. The mask is literally said to manifest the "footprint," *tapak*, of the gods. Unsurprisingly, spirit mediums who are mouthpieces for celestial beings are also referred to as *tapakan*.
6. These decorative items and symbols are used throughout the island during Galungan and point to common themes. In the north, however, there are few Barongs because of the impact of Islam.
7. Entranced male dancers with krisses often support Barong in Calon Arang performances in south-central Bali. On approaching Rangda, she waves her magic white cloth in front of the men, whereby they perform (*ngorek*) – a ritualized choreography in which they turn their daggers against themselves. The villagers in my research area called such performances *barong dan* (from the English word dance), saying that tourists primarily enjoyed this drama.
8. Geertz argued that the inconclusive struggle between Barong Ket and Rangda was a "model of" and a "model for" core religious beliefs of the people: Barong Ket incarnates the Balinese version of the comic spirit and Rangda, above all, fear. This approach does not take into account the fact that the participants are drawn into the performance reality, which allows them to experience a way of being in the world. For a more comprehensive discussion of the Calon Arang dance-drama with kris dancers, see Belo 1960.
9. Kleinian theory places great importance on the child's resolution of his or her ambivalence towards the mother, that is, the "good" and "bad" breast. The child's development involves constant oscillation between powerful feelings of hatred and love towards the mother, referred to as the paranoid-schizoid position. In Klein's view, failure to leave this position leads to psychological disorders and obsessional difficulties.
10. According to Zoetmulder (1974, 173), Indians refer to the common element in both subject and object as *rasa*; this innermost element, purest essence, or flavor makes mystic union possible. The Old Javanese court poetry indicates that a beautiful view, object, or person can incite rapture. Beauty moreover appeals to the aesthetic sense by being veiled, apparently inaccessible. Thus, the seeker of beauty is consumed with longing for it and the desire to experience it. These ideas still resonate in Balinese religious ceremonies.

References

Bateson, G., and M. Mead. 1942. *Balinese Character: A Photographic Analysis*. Vol. 11. New York: New York Academy of Science.

Belo, J. [1949] 1966. *Bali: Rangda and Barong*. Monograph of the American Ethnology Society. Seattle and London: University of Washington Press.

———. 1960. *Trance in Bali*. New York: Columbia University Press.

Boon, J. 1977. *The Anthropological Romance of Bali 1597–1972*. Cambridge: Cambridge University Press.

———. 1990. *Affinities and Extremes*. Chicago: Chicago University Press.

Geertz, C. 1973. *The Interpretation of Cultures*. New York: Basic Books.

———. 1978. "Religion as a Cultural System." In *Anthropological Approaches to the Study of Religion*, ed. M. Banton, 1–46. A.S.A. Monographs 3. London: Tavistock Publications.

Geertz, H. 1995. "Sorcery and Social Change in Bali: The Sakti Conjecture." Unpublished conference paper, University of Sydney.

Golomb, L. 1993. "The Relativity of Magical Malevolence in Urban Thailand." In *Understanding Witchcraft and Sorcery in Southeast Asia*, ed. C. W. Watson and R. Ellen, 27–45. Honolulu: University of Hawaii Press.

Hobart, A. 2003. *Healing Performances of Bali: Between Darkness and Light*. New York and Oxford: Berghahn Books.

Hooykaas, C. 1958. *The Lay of Jaya Prana*. London: Luzac and Company.

Hooykaas, J. 1961. "The Myth of the Young Cowherd and the Little Girl." In *Bijdragen tot de Taal-, en Volkenkunde*, 267–78. The Hague: Martinus Nijhoff.

Iser, W. 1978. *The Art of Reading: A Theory of Aesthetic Response*. Baltimore: Johns Hopkins University Press.

Kant, I. 1973. *Observations on the Feeling of the Beautiful and Sublime*. Trans. J. T. Goldthwait. Berkeley: University of California.

Kapferer, B. 1997. *The Feast of the Sorcerer: Practices of Consciousness and Power*. Chicago: Chicago University Press.

———. 2000. "Sexuality and the Art of Seduction in Sinhalese Exorcism." *Ethnos* 65, no. 1: 5–32. Stockholm: National Museum of Ethnography.

Lovric, B. 1987. "Rhetoric and Reality: The Hidden Nightmare, Myth and Magic as Representations and Reverberations of Morbid Realities." Unpublished Ph.D. thesis, University of Sydney.

Obeyesekere, G. 1984. *The Cult of the Goddess Pattini*. Chicago: Chicago University Press.

Scarry, Elaine. 2000. *On Beauty and Being Just*. London: Gerald Duckworth.

Slaats, H., and K. Portier. 1989. "Upholders of the Law, Practitioners of Magic: A Social and Legal Problem in Indonesia. *Indonesia Circle*, no. 47 and 48: 29–36.

Turner, V. [1967] 1977. *The Forest of Symbols: Aspects of Ndembu Ritual*. Ithaca: Cornell Paperbacks.

Wikan, Unni. 1990. *Managing Turbulent Hearts*. Chicago: Chicago University Press.

Zoete, B. de, and W. Spies. [1938] 1973. *Dance and Drama in Bali*. Oxford: Oxford University Press.

Zoetmulder, P. J. 1974. *Kalangwan: A Survey of Old Javanese Literature*. The Hague: Martinus Nijhoff.

———. 1982. *Old Javanese-English Dictionary*. The Hague: Martinus Nijhoff.

Chapter Eight

A CONCISE REFLECTION ON THE BRAZILIAN CARNIVAL

Roberto DaMatta

> He was surprised that the wondrous, which in his infancy was so close
> that he had almost touched it with his own hands, had been resurrected
> now in such a profuse and noisy way and was soon, nevertheless, to dis-
> appear and everything turn back to the old rules.
>
> – Anibal Machado, *João Ternura*

Despite all the real and alleged changes, Carnival continues to be a topic
difficult to take seriously—especially for us Brazilians, for whom this
annual satirical farce has a sustained and systematic presence (perceived as
good or perverse, positive or negative, intimate or distant). Thus, in order
to write about Carnival, one must also touch upon an even more complicated reality: our perennially fleeting, untamable, and paradoxical Brazil.

The complex link between Carnival and Brazil has many masks. Carnival belongs to Brazil—one cannot deny a "Brazilian Carnival," with its
history, gestures, spaces, objects, style, music, and many other elements
unique to the Brazilian festival—but Brazil also belongs to Carnival (as I
have systematically pointed out in my work—see DaMatta 1973, 1979,
1981, 1991).

This Carnival, with its generous leniency, with its magnificent anti-
bourgeois spirit, with its attitude resolutely opposed to utilitarian reason,
with a tendency towards ambiguity, mythical transformations, and, above
all, with the possibility of making people and social groups change places
and points of view, has no rival as model of a Brazilian "social contract"
and cosmology.

Notes for this chapter begin on page 193.

Figure 8.1 Ambiguity and paradox in the Brazilian Carnival

In the context of the Brazilian Carnival, ambiguity and paradox are not considered to be a perversion but something to be watched and laughed at. Note the positive, surprised faces and the presence of children in what would be a serious morals case in other societies.
Photograph by João Poppe.

In this sense, Carnival has a twofold dimension, being both constituted by and constituting of that which we call nonchalantly "Brazil" or "Brazilian reality." After all, what would Brazil be without Carnival, *cachaça* (sugarcane rum), *futíbol*, *macumba* (Afro-Brazilian religiosity centered on spiritual possession), and the animal game *jogo do bicho*;[1] without political patronage, roguery, shrewdness and craftiness, and the iron laws, written on paper, designed to control the country's inhabitants; without the *mulata*, samba, the beach, and *sacanagem*? Where would it be without this handful of institutions orphaned of academic pedigree, which precisely because of this fact helps define Brazil as a relatively (dis)integrated and unknown and disturbing reality?

How many of us would be able to characterize and interpret Brazil without mentioning Carnival? And how many of us have used Carnival in an attempt to describe Brazil?[2]

If my memory does not fail me, I was the first (at last a marginal!) to take Carnival seriously, studying it in its multiple manifestations and implications—as a popular celebration, as a drama of equality, as a political and institutional ideal against the hierarchical practices of daily life, as a ironical moral footnote designed to remind Brazilians that they are also free individuals capable of finding enjoyment outside of family and house—from a sociological, symbolic, and comparative perspective (see DaMatta 1973, 1979, 1981). Despite the fact that Carnival has been systematically absent from our official historiography and sociology, its presence in Brazilian social life was always striking. This is so much the case that nobody better expressed this intimate bond between Brazil and Carnival than one of the greatest Brazilian popular composers, Lamartine Babo, in a *marchinha* composed in 1934 entitled "History of Brazil," in which he significantly asks:

Quem foi que inventou o Brasil?
Foi Seu Cabral ... Foi Seu Cabral!
No dia 21 de abril
Dois meses, depois do carnaval![3]

Who invented Brazil?
It was Mr. Cabral, Mr. Cabral!
On the 21st of April
Two months after Carnival!

Is Lamartine Babo miraculously anticipating postmodern thought? Of course not! To suggest this would be to offend the composer, who did not have philosophical presumptions but only expressed one of those trivialities that, by virtue of being so deep inside, requires a naïve and unguarded outlook to be brought to light. Mary Douglas called these things "implicit forms of communication" (Douglas 1975, ix). The American sociologist Robert Bellah attributes to Alexis de Tocqueville, founder of a political sociology that compares by contrast and not by similarity, the beautiful expression of "habits of the heart" (Bellah 1985, vii). And Brazilian writer Nelson Rodrigues (1993) used to call this the plane of things near, but invisible, the *óbvio ululante*, or the "crying obvious."[4] To paraphrase Jorge Luis Borges: in Rio de Janeiro, in spite of their feeling of defeat, some people were discovering eternal truths (Borges 1977).

In the case of Carnival, the "crying obvious" is not its analysis as an "alienated" or "prepolitical" popular festival, by nature and essence an opium of the people; or as an innocent celebration ready to be digested by stupid people; or as a smart invention of cultural producers, controlled and capitalized by the media in order to make a huge amount of money; but rather (also) as one of the threads with which social identity is constructed in Brazil.

Indeed, in Brazil, the currency fluctuates and changes, the stock market and government enter crises, constitutions are invented, corrected, and perfected, new political pacts contrived, regimes transformed, and new cities built. But good old Carnival stays as it has always been.

Brazilians could not trust much in a currency that has changed its name and lost its value many times. But they can always count on the samba school and the permanent *loucuras* or craziness—the "follies" beyond mere play of the Carnival balls, which display inverted, licentious, and grotesque behavior—that lie outside the conduct appropriate for the real world. And yet it would be absurd to claim that Carnival has not changed over the years. For one thing, it is not an obligatory event that requires certain clothes, motions or attitudes, or the participation of all Brazilians.[5]

Nevertheless, Carnival continues as a beautiful and paradoxical rite of inversion, a moment sandwiched between time periods that the Catholic tradition—which is no longer the official religion of Brazil—defines as symmetric and inverted: Advent (when Christ is born) and Lent (marked by the passion and death of Jesus). Located in the middle, and before a moment of constraint and world renunciation, Carnival marks a transitory moment when the ethic of "everything is possible" comes into being.

As such, even in this world marked by the dictatorship of economic rationality and the tyranny of globalization and bureaucracy, Carnival continues to honor costumes (fantasias), masks, gestures, music, the free gesture of popular creativity, and, through all this, freedom and equality. In other words, the festivity has been able to survived ruthless massification and continues to profane, as Bakhtin (1984, 106; see also 1987) would have it, our bourgeois life style based on the sacralization of equilibrium, on superficial morality, on rampant individualism and isolation, on historical linearity, on all kinds of savings and, last but not least, on the accumulation of money as a symbol of prestige and success in this and the other world.

All this is in clear opposition to family name, skin color, state innovation and empty institutional experimentation at the cost of society and culture, and family and class hegemony. In Carnival, Brazilians become

Figure 8.2 Transvestites in the open

This "immoral" gesture expresses how in Brazilian Carnival the world is womanized. Note the position of men in the background. Photograph by João Poppe.

Figure 8.3 The Dead at "play" in the Brazilian Carnival

Here we see the Dead carrying Death's coffin in a most improbable but revealing carnivalesque gesture. Photograph by João Poppe.

individual citizens capable of joining the groups and associations they want. Free from kinship and household links, they frantically compete and dispute in a land where hierarchical social definitions often stand at odds with individual autonomy and voluntary movements. From this point of view, Carnival provides substantive citizenship to Brazilians. That is why "Carnival time" is perceived and translated by Brazilians as *uma loucura*, a sort of madness.

I must emphasize, however, that the freedom associated with Carnival is not the liberty and equality celebrated by the bourgeois code of conduct whose model and agency was the French Revolution—a model of normative and formal liberty and equality, sanctioned and explained by a rational, abstract, and deductive code of conduct, defined by a set of individual rights and duties before the law, the government and the state. This is the civic and formal freedom of being "in favor" or "against," which Isaiah Berlin called positive and negative in a classical essay (Berlin 1969).

Carnival freedom and equality do not deny civic values but go well beyond (or in-between) it. Indeed, as Bakhtin writes: "These Carnivalistic categories are not abstract thoughts about equality and freedom, the inter-relatedness of all things or the unity of opposites. No, these are concretely sensuous ritual-pageant 'thoughts' experienced and played out in the form of life itself, 'thoughts' that had coalesced and survived for thousands of years among the broadest masses of European mankind" (1984, 123).

What Carnival presents and conveys is the temporary abandonment of these abstract values, based on individualism and almost always conflicting amongst themselves in their applications, by proposing its substitution with what I would like to call a substantive or holist liberty, a freedom not centered on the individual as a bundle of rights and duties that escapes beginning or end, bottom or top. It is a freedom not against or for, but with; a freedom that does not refuse civic rights but assumes the concreteness of the human body and is addressed to what is classified as "irrational," "marginal," or "incorrect." Its focal point is located in the area situated below our body's equator: the legs, the thighs, the navel, the buttocks, the genital organs, and all that is below the waist, such as the hips and the feet. All that refers to the sexuality and vulgarity of the common people, who have, as we say in Brazil, *os pés no chão*, their feet on the ground and may have *pés sujos, pés de barro ou pretos*, dirty, muddy, or black feet, is fair game. It is the foot—but notably not the hand, which represents manual, or obligatory, labor and thanks to our slavery past is equated with punishment—that Brazilians, most of whom have never read Bakhtin or any other classic sociologist, know as a fundamental body part in the theory and practice of the samba.[6]

The hands symbolize routine, duty, domination, and control. The feet, emphasized by Carnival, are instruments of dance and mobility. They reveal and express performance, movement, and action, allowing for a crucial inversion, for in Carnival what counts is not family name and inherited, or external, fortune, but concrete internal capacity given in talent perceived as a *dom* or gift. Thus, the Brazilian saying that samba resides in one's feet; as in football and capoeira, which is a martial arts dance in which practitioners use their feet, changing their bodies' center of gravity.

Another area that this liberty puts into focus is that of concealed flesh: the orifices and innards that are only revealed in open or libertine sex, or at the moment of childbirth. These openings substantively connect one person with another. They are also the "inverse" of the "right" dimension of the body (and of society). Thus, abominable openings banned by etiquette, and by bourgeois routine that chastises and fears them, are revived in Carnival in what Bakhtin calls "grotesque realism" (1987). In Brazil, perhaps more than in other places, during Carnival the product and practice of this freedom simultaneously makes us feel shame and laugh, while it fills our televisions, parades, and ballrooms.[7] These are "liberties" that obviously escape from modern legislation as things to be avoided, repressed, or denied.

But this is not all. One can add to this freedom to show the bare body and use it as a revelation the freedom from sadness, pain, finitude, family (from father, husband, wife, daughter, and son), sin, death, sincerity, sickness, responsibility, and even the liberty of escaping one's own sex. For, in Carnival, the world not only becomes free of biological and moral sexual restrictions, allowing the change and switching of sexualities and also creating in-between sexes, but the social universe becomes feminine. Thus, a society of "machos" and pater familias, a system dominated by men with balls, transforms itself into a place marked by all kinds of womanhood, a world whose reference points and styles of gesture, dressing, dancing, and singing are not tough and masculine but soft, delicate, and feminine.

I call these "mobile freedoms" because they are not dependent on social or political position. In Brazil, popular wisdom (whose ideological paradigm is ritualistic even in Carnival) understands that "money does not bring happiness," as money,—equated to faeces,—as Noel Rosa and a legion of popular composers would say, "does not buy happiness," or pain, talent, courage, honor, or, above all, passion and love.

For middle- and upper-class Brazilians, one of the major surprises of carnival lies in observing the masses of poor and marginal people, as well as some friends, celebrities, and domestic servants, parading as gods, angels, clowns, and heroes on the black asphalt of the avenue. Carnival leads to the sometimes contradictory awareness that poverty is not, after all, an obstacle to the explosion of cheerful sensuality—in a ritual movement that turns misfortune and misery into laughter. It is as if everyone finally understood that everything in life, including money and secular power, were not ultimate goals as religious creeds preach, but merely arbitrary conventions.

Let me elaborate a little more on this basic topic. In (and with) Carnival one remembers that money is not everything, that money is not the only

Figure 8.4 Undefined sexuality

In Brazil, where conventional masculinity is equated with rationality and dominance, gender distinctions are often blurred during Carnival.

Photographs by João Poppe.

Figure 8.5 A rare moment of total inversion

criterion of social classification. The festival opens society to multiple possibilities by which people and situations may be read, related with each
other, and ranked.[8] If one suppresses the power that comes with money,
one is able to "see" what the sheer power of money suppresses: *luxo* (ide-
alized aristocratic wealth and manners), music, happiness, and fantasia.

Joining these are other kinds of liberty, such as that of breaking with the
behavior limited by the bank account, as well as that of transcending the
schism between house and street, between young and old, and, principally, the abysm between masculinity and femininity—between man and
woman. The carnivalesque ritual opening—in which words are substituted by singing, labor by freedom, work by laziness, purposeful, firm
walking by aimless dancing and in which the soul is represented by the
body—even dilutes the opposition between life and death, and God and
the Devil, whom, during Carnival, are called to "play" and mingle with
local *foliões* (follies), changing their cosmic places.[9]

Because of all this, Carnival shapes itself as a truly regular and cyclical
ritualization of utopian practices, as they are defined in Brazil. As also
occurred in some messianic movements, Carnival takes the task of creating
another social reality. But in Carnival—in contrast to what happens in urban
violence, in banditry (social or otherwise), and in religious escapes from the
world, typical of Brazilian messianic movements—one moves towards the
plenitude of life, now encompassed by laughter, by a focus on the beauty of
the body, by music, and by the fantasy that allows allegorical change.

The great carnivalesque tradition—to which Brazil is heir on a national
and international level—is brief but ambitious. It intends to encompass
everything, even the utopian gesture of class societies: an escape from the
social segment in which we are trapped, not to mention—from the work
that makes us packhorses, that fleeces and enslaves us, despite the imposing universal prestige of the noble Protestant work ethic.

In this way, the carnivalesque ethic subverts values that modernity sit-
uates as public, rational, and unquestioned. If in our daily lives we have
to be individual citizens compulsively trapped by political correction and
by our financial means, during carnival, we dissolve ourselves in a group
(*bloco*, *escola*, or *cordão*). We are ritually (at least and last!) to escape from
rational econometric logic, and practice wealth as aristocracy and excess
defined by the Brazilian expression *luxo*, which means the possibility to
enjoy life and refuse work.

How can such a poor people carry out a festival so sensual, beautiful,
and luxurious, asks an astonished bourgeois rationality circumscribed by
the consistency and discipline of the links between means and ends? A
symbolically oriented popular rationality would respond that the festival
exists precisely because the people know that poverty is a relative concept.
Besides being a situation, it is also a state that transcends the economic
sphere and can be existentially and ritually relativized, serving as a motive
for playfulness and laughter—and, sometimes, indifference.

Moreover, to a society of patrons (*coroneis*, *medalhões*, and *figurões*)—and rulers who govern by virtue of their academic titles,—Carnival commands by example and performance. Quite an inversion in a system in which *o povo* (people) are always the victim of inadequate laws, of unfair taxes, and of the "Do you know who you're talking to?" of those who control society or believe in their own social superiority. It is impossible not to perceive the reversal of official routines founded on "do as I say, but not as I do," of hierarchies that promote distance, fear, and the reverence of the people, in stark contrast with the sincerity of the carnivalesque game that promotes the exact opposite, unmasking the rich and the powerful—as it did with at least one emperor (Pedro II received a lemon in the face at a celebration in Rio de Janeiro at the end of the nineteenth century) and one president (Itamar Franco was photographed in the presidential box beside a young lady dancing with only a T-shirt covering her body in a Carnival parade at the end of the twentieth century).

This power of dissolving and desacralizing arises because, in contrast to other rituals that cannot do without a center, a motive, or a subject, in Carnival everything is decentralized. We can miss a birthday, an inauguration, or a graduation, but there is no way to miss a Carnival endowed with multiple centers and without an owner or absolute event. Within Carnival live community and competition, individual and group, solidarity and conflict, sin and purity, individualism and holism. Thus, here one finds the radical contrast between the "festivals or celebrations of order"—distinguished by the presence of a center, of bosses and landlords, real and supernatural, such as the saints and gods—and the Carnival that dissolves hierarchies and creates a substantive equality between all individuals. In fact, if solemnities glorify power, Carnival—in contrast—laughs at the rich and powerful. The result is seen in Brazil's history: neither a powerful dictator such as Vargas nor the military dictatorship that ruled the country from 1964 to 1985 was able to use the revelry politically.

Concluding these reflections, which could continue endlessly, I would like to recall a notable observation by the wise Josias, one of the characters of Anibal Machado, who uselessly tries understanding, from a theoretical perspective, the cosmic Carnival described his 1965 book, *João Ternura*: "It is preferable to do Carnival than to define it" (184).

Notes

1. I recently wrote, with Elena Soárez, an essay on the "jogo do bicho" soon to be published in English by the University of Notre Dame Press. See also DaMatta and Soárez 1999.
2. Let me take this opportunity to repeat that I am not an expert on Carnival. One has only to read my work in order to realize that I have a triple interest in the festivity. First, I have taken it as a window through which I can "read" Brazil in a sort of first-hand,

unguarded, and unbiased way, free of all sorts of economic, political, historical, and ideological manipulations and "defenses," which as we know are part and parcel of most of the so-called interpretations of Brazil. Secondly, as I remarked in my book *Carnivals, Rogues and Heroes*, I take this farcical festivity to reveal a society simultaneously attracted by the parodies of Carnival and by rigid ideological recipes and legal formulas and institutions. Finally, I look at Carnival as ritual, not as folklore or an innocent celebration, following the steps of Lévi-Strauss and in a dialogue with the theories of Arnold Van Gennep and their reinterpretations by Max Gluckman, Victor and Edith Turner, and Sir Edmund Leach. But, I must add, the whole point of my book was to show that Carnival is only one instance of a dilemmatic society, a system caught up between the ideals of modern freedom and equality (and individualism) and the practices of patronage and holism. In doing so I was inspired by the work of Tocqueville, Max Weber, and, most of all, Louis Dumont.

3. This song was an immediate success. It refers—in a parodic, farcical way, typical of the inversions of Carnival—to the Portuguese Admiral Pedro Álvares Cabral, who commanded the fleet that, so the Brazilian foundational myth goes, "discovered" Brazil on April 21, 1500. By doing so, Lamartine Babo, who also wrote songs glorifying the beauty and seductive power of the "mulatto," proposes the encompassment of Brazilian official history by Carnival. The point I have made is reiterated here: it not Brazil that invented Carnival, but Carnival that invented Brazil.

4. These positions bring with extraordinary clarity a local way of thinking about the world, and its style of facing challenges and answering problems and paradoxes. In the case of Brazil, it is worth noting that the local answer was always suffocated by "modern," "enlightened," less naïve perspectives that interpreted social life as governed by universal laws and values born in France and other "advanced societies" taken as the final end of all social processes. In the Brazilian case this final historical point was socialism; today it is globalization. That is to say, the same "historical laws" that would produce socialism are taking us now to the inevitability of globalization.

5. Marcel Mauss was one of the first to reveal the social exigencies demanded in such well-marked social situations as parties and solemn moments. We dress "in full" in hot summer days in order to attend a formal invitation; we listen with false attention and interest to the boring speech of politicians at an inauguration party; we show a sorrowful face at the funeral of our worst enemy and laugh at the marriage of the woman we love. In Carnival we are forced (obliged) to be merry, to participate and be accomplices to its "madness." Here, I am transposing the Maussian idea (Mauss [1921] 1969) of "the obligatory expression of sentiments" to the ritual sphere in order to show that some rituals encompass society because they are obligatory forms of celebration. Today Carnival and Catholic celebrations are also "holidays," but in many instances and places they have retained their obligatory aspect. From that point of view, some Catholic celebrations and Carnival share only partially the modern idea of "leisure" with its bias towards choice and individual freedom. Twenty years ago Carnival used to find us everywhere; today we sadly look for it. Even in societies such as the United States, it would be unconceivable to commemorate the Fourth of July only as a holiday and not as a "civic ritual" as well. It is true that the "holiday dimension" is basic in most modern celebrations but so is, for some groups or corporations, its obligatory, ritualistic component.

6. Dancing, as we say in Brazil, "the samba in the foot" ("*o samba no pé*"), which puts emphasis in concrete action or practice and, above all, in performance, disconnecting the dancer from such previous socially inherited attributes as social position, skin color, or family name. Writer Anibal Machado says that this Carnival dance style caused "blacks to be in a state of levitation," his hero envies "(their) body falls and the acrobatic round turns" (see Machado 1965, 173).

7. I have discussed this subject in detail in my 1981 book *Universo do Carnaval* (The Universe of Carnival) through a series of beautiful photographs taken by João Poppe, some of which are reprinted in this chapter. There, the set of images revealed this grotesque

theme that dislocates the centrality of privacy of some intimate and unspeakable and sacred acts and states, such as defecation, urination, menstruation, and sex that Bakhtin, with surprisingly evocative power (he never witnessed Carnival anywhere), with rare sociological sensitivity, located as part and parcel of Carnival. This Carnival one once thought was gone, consumed as it was by the enlightened bourgeois, or in his case Stalinist, rationality. See Bakhtin 1987.

8. I mentioned this "multiple classification of the social world," a mode of classification that transcends the hegemony of the economic dimension as a singularity of the Brazilian system, when I study the authoritarian rite "Do you know who you're talking to?" in my book *Carnavals, Rogues, and Heróis* (DaMatta 1979, 130).

9. In the novel *João Ternura* [John Tenderness], Brazilian writer Anibal Machado ends the story using images of a cosmic Carnival in which God Himself descends to Rio de Janeiro to participate in the festivity. He commands a rain of pastries called *pasteis* and *empadas* (patties with thick [in *empadas*] and thin [in *pasteis*] shells filled with meat, shrimp, chicken, cheese, or vegetables), hors d'oeuvres highly appreciated by Brazilians, to appear in the context of the narrative as manna in several areas of Rio de Janeiro.

References

Bakhtin, Michael. 1984. *Problems of Dostoyevsky's Poetics*. Ed. and trans. Caryl Emerson. Minneapolis: University of Minnesota Press.

———. 1987. *A Cultura Popular na Idade Média e no Renascimento: O Contexto de François Rabelais*. São Paulo: Hucitec.

Bellah, Robert N. 1985. *Habits of the Heart: Individualism and Commitment in American Life*. New York: Harper & Row.

Berlin, Isaiah. 1969. *Four Essays on Liberty*. Oxford and New York: Oxford University Press.

Borges, Jorge Luis. 1977. *Prólogos con un Prólogo de Prólogos*. Buenos Aires: Agüero.

DaMatta, Roberto. 1973. *Ensaios de Antropologia Estrutural*. Petrópolis, Brazil: Vozes.

———. 1979. *Carnavais, Malandros e Heróis: Para uma Sociologia do Dilema Brasileiro*. Rio de Janeiro: Rocco.

———. 1981. *Universo do Carnaval: Imagens e Reflexões*. Rio de Janeiro: Pinakotheke.

———. 1991. *Carnivals, Rogues, and Heroes: An Interpretation of the Brazilian Dilemma*. Notre Dame and London: University of Notre Dame Press.

DaMatta, Roberto, and Elena Soárez. 1999. *Águias, Burros e Borboletas: Um Estudo Antropológico do Jogo do Bicho*. Rio de Janeiro: Rocco.

Douglas, Mary. 1975. *Implicit Meanings: Essays in Anthropology*. London and Boston: Routledge & Kegan Paul.

Machado, Anibal. 1965. *João Ternura*. Rio de Janeiro: José Olympio Editora.

Mauss, Marcel. [1921] 1969. "L'Expression Obligatoire des Sentiments (Rituels Oraux Funéraires Australiens)." In *Oevres*, vol. 3, *Cohesion Sociale et Division de La Sociologie*: *Présentation de Victor Karady*. Paris: Les Éditions de Minuit.

Rodrigues, Nelson. 1993. *O Óbvio Ululante*. São Paulo: Companhia das Letras.

Chapter Nine

BUREAUCRATIC LOGIC, BUREAUCRATIC AESTHETICS
The Opening Event of Holocaust Martyrs and Heroes Remembrance Day in Israel

Don Handelman

My concern here is with logics and aesthetics that organize rituals. I will argue that the logics of ritual organization are intimately related to practice, informing practice with its shaping of goals, action, movement, direction. So, too, aesthetics are crucial to practice; for that matter, perhaps practice works best, if I can put it like this, when given its senses by aesthetics. Aesthetics are crucial to practice; while logics of organization hardly exist without practice. Logics, in the terms used here, are the ways that inform how the practices of connecting, of fitting together—people, things, worlds—are done. Aesthetics, on the other hand, enable the very connecting, the fitting together, to be done in practice. Aesthetics are informed, obviously, by cultural logics. The logic of ritual organization and the aesthetics of practice form a set without which there is no such phenomenon that might be called ritual. However, I do not intend that there be any clean-cut conceptual distinction between "logic" and "aesthetics." Perhaps because through practice, logic and aesthetics mesh together epistemology and the sensuous, their relationship is vague. In my view, the relationship between logic and aesthetics is teleological rather than lineal—if logic is present so are aesthetics. Perhaps logic generates its own aesthetic as it is practiced into being by that aesthetic.

I want to argue more generally that aesthetics are crucial to all practice—to the very practice of practice—in the regularities of mundane living; and that in this sense the aesthetics of ritual practice may not be radically distinct from those of everyday practice. To make these arguments relatively straightforward, I will discuss aspects of the state ritual that officially opens Holocaust Martyrs and Heroes Remembrance Day in Israel (*Yom HaShoah v'HaGvura*), a day popularly if facetiously known as Holocaust Day. Officially, the ritual is called a Memorial Gathering (*atzeret zikaron*). The logic of organization of this event I will call bureaucratic logic, and its aesthetics, bureaucratic aesthetics. I will argue that this ritual, despite its empathic and emotive sacralization in Israeli society, is an extension of the logic and aesthetics of mundane bureaucratic order. The military logic of organization is continuous with the logic that organizes the performance of the Holocaust Memorial Gathering. Here the logic and aesthetics of ritual are organized as a continuation of mundane, bureaucratic practice.

Underlying my argument is the claim that in the history of modern Western thought, the conceptualization and treatment of "aesthetics," as a higher-order condition of value and knowledge, took a terribly wrong turn, in its thorough and unrelenting identification with beauty, art, truth, reflection, and so forth. To save the significance and the inestimable value of aesthetics in the mundane, and in the ritual living of lives, aesthetics should not be severed and parted from the grounding of social and personal practice.

The Aesthetic "Feel" of Practice

My understanding of the aesthetic in mundane living is quite rough and ready—for that matter, murky—and again is not given to any neat definition. My sense of the aesthetic is something like the "feel" that one has for that which one is doing; the feel for that which can only be called the "rightness" of how one is doing what one is doing, or how this is done in concert. The aesthetic in mundane living is related to Bergson's idea of "habit memory," which is a way of attending kinesthetically to one's own body, monitoring that which one is doing. As Sheets-Johnstone (2000, 360) points out for the individual, "this is memory etched in movement," providing unconscious ways of behaving that "engender a *felt sense of rightness* in doing what one does ... we feel at home in our bodies ... because we resonate with a familiar dynamics, a tactile-kinesthetic dynamics that we have come to establish as our own way of doing something, whether brushing our teeth, throwing a ball, playing the violin, or walking" (Sheets-Johnstone 2000, 360–61, my emphasis). This sense of rightness or "fitness" (Hardin 1993, 12)—kinesthetic, sensuous, and interpersonal—indexes the aesthetics of living unselfconsciously, in the main. No less, this sense of rightness is one of feeling—unselfconsciously, one monitors affectively. This is a sense of rightness not in moral terms but in the sense of how one does that which one is doing.[1] The aesthetics of mundane living are forms of autopoiesis, of self-organization, that produce and conserve personal and intercorporeal awareness through feeling the rightness of action, of practice, inside oneself, outside oneself, and between oneself and others (see also Inglis and Hughson 2000, 289). To put this otherwise, the everyday aesthetics of practice are feelings of rightness-in-doing, of feeling that which feels right in doing that which we are doing. In Michael Polanyi's (1966, 17–23) terms, one could say that mundane aesthetics are a kind of "indwelling" of tacit knowing, a knowing that, as he puts it, always relates to or includes more than we can tell, were we able to relate this knowingly. Paraphrasing Polanyi, Jack Katz (1999, 314) argues that "effective action requires that we disattend our body as we act, focusing away from the point at which our body intersects with the world." In my view, tacit knowing is the feeling of disattending/attending that enables the exterior world of practice and the interior world of experience to be unified as the exterior world of experience and the interior world of practice (see also Dufrenne 1973, 446). Mikel Dufrenne (1973, 377) argues that to feel is to transcend. The aesthetics of practice transcend practice by enabling practice to communicate "more than we can tell," while feeling the rightness of not needing to, or not being able to, tell this. The aesthetics of practice integrate us with that which we do, in ways that self-produce and self-organize this integration as more than we can tell and as feeling the rightness of this.

This positioning, as Katz (1999, 314) points out, "leads quickly to an appreciation of the essential place of aesthetics in all behaviors, however mundane or esoteric." In mundane living, it is the aesthetics of practice, in my terms, that enables people and social orders to naturalize their own arbitrariness, to know their worlds tacitly as "natural," as "taken for granted" (see Bourdieu 1977, 164; Garfinkel 1967; Geertz 1983, 86–91). Without the aesthetics of practice/experience there is no feel of rightness in practice, no feel that this is how doing is doing, how doing is done, how done continues on into doing.

Aesthetics, then, are crucial to the naturalness of the feel of mundane practice as more than we can tell, indeed, as more than we can know, self-consciously, self-reflexively. Practice is inevitably the fitting together of person and world, person and person, person and action, action and action—their fitting into, yet through one another. Aesthetics—the synesthetic, sensuous feel of things fitting together (and not fitting together)—is that which enables us to proceed coherently, perspectively, and prospectively in the hereness of nowness, as it were. Simmel (1994a, 10) wrote that "the human being is … the bordering creature who has no border." I would add that the bordering creature in kinesthetic movement is always on the edge of coming into being, and so is always creating borders in order to cross them, in order to move. The aesthetics of practice have something intimate to do with the creation and crossing of borders, and how these are done. It is by creating and crossing borders, the sites at which exosmosis and endosmosis (Simmel 1994b, 11) of the fluidity of selfness and otherness occur, that fitting together is accomplished. To put this yet more emphatically, without the mundane aesthetics of practice, there likely would not be self-integrating individuals nor, for that matter, social life. The aesthetics of practice not only enable practice—they are the persuasive grounds, the grounds that persuade us that practice is in the process of being done as the kind of practice it is (or is becoming). Perhaps this could be called the persuasive self-embodiment of the truth-claims of practice. Aesthetics may be more like an ongoing gestalt, in the sense of a "coherent entity" (Polanyi 1966), or an entity whose coherence is continuously coming into being, fitting itself together self-persuasively, even as that which it fits together ruptures and breaks.

Since we must know ourselves indirectly, through interaction, through others and their mediation, through what might be called the "practice of betweenness," there is always a break (perhaps an ongoing break) in any aesthetics of mundane practice. The very feel or sense of rightness also constitutes a temporal lag, however small; a lack of synchronization with oneself and with others. As Katz (1999, 315) puts it, "I see, hear, feel, and express myself through actions that in part always remain behind myself, always just beyond the reach of my self-awareness." In this regard, we are always trying to catch up with ourselves and with others. This is integral to the sense of mundane aesthetics as more than one can tell. But this is also the break between a ritual and mundane social order—the possible shift from an aesthetics of mundane practice to something else; the world catching up with its rituals and their visions of (and dynamics of) order; the break that may open towards radical shifts in aesthetics of performance or that may continue to hone its aesthetics, but in different venues.[2] Here, my concern is with the latter, as it organizes the opening ritual of Holocaust Remembrance Day.

Bureaucratic Logic and the Event of Presentation

Earlier I said that cultural logics inform us as to how practice fits together people, things, and worlds. Bureaucratic logic indexes how certain kinds of cultural taxonomies are organized and practiced. Recent studies of modern bureaucracy and its origins recognize clearly that it is constructed of premises about how worlds are put together, how they work, and how this knowledge may be known (Brown 1978, 373; Morgan 1986; Astley 1985; Melossi and Pavarini 1981). Nonetheless, not recognized is the premise that the epistemology of bureaucratic logic is to intimately engage in the invention and practice of taxonomy that is lineal, exclusivist, and hierarchical in character. Bureaucratic logic is a mentality of the modern world that consciously invents and deploys lineal taxonomy to create, to control, and to change order. The conscious control over processes of classification is a most powerful means through which to shape social order (Handelman 1995; Shamgar-Handelman and Handelman 1991, 308).

The use of bureaucratic logic encourages the invention of forms of classification that are hierarchical and exclusivist. In true Linnean fashion, the boundaries of categories of classification on the same level of abstraction are mutually exclusive and are organized in hierarchies of subsumation and exclusion. This lineal logic of classification—of membership that is permitted, exclusively, in one and only one category on the same level of abstraction within a given taxonomic scheme—is powerfully implicated in the making of "difference" in modern life. That is, it is implicated in our mechanistic capacities to make infinitesimal and infinite distinctions of difference that mutually exclude whatever they fragment, while insisting on the significance of these divisions. (On this logic, see Wyschogrod 1985.) In hierarchical terms, we perceive levels of difference to nest quite neatly and naturally within one another, thereby encompassing difference within yet more subsuming difference.

Bureaucratic logic informs institutions how to continually invent and implement new taxonomies by reimagining and reorganizing the social categories of everyday life. This logic informs consciously how to consciously create social categories that can be made to divide, to fragment, to reclassify, and to reshape members of any social unit—group, community, family, relationship. This logic informs how to perceive that the making of division through the creation of a boundary is also the demarcation of differences that are naturalized on either side of this border. Therefore, bureaucratic logic foregrounds the significance of boundaries that separate mutually exclusive categories from one another.

No less than any other mode of informing the organization of realities, bureaucratic logic is enabled by its own aesthetics of practice that give to its use the feel of rightness. In keeping with the significance of ocular centrism and the gaze in the modern epoch (Foucault 1973, 1979; Jay 1992a), these, one may say, are the aesthetics of anatomization—of laying out, defining, classifying, specifying, inspecting, and enumerating all of the parts from which some totality is constituted. In modern bureaucratic society, in the modern bureaucratic state, these aesthetics of bureaucratic logic are performed in public most explicitly in rituals that I call events of presentation (Handelman 1998). The organization of performance in the public event of presentation often (but not necessarily always) is pervaded by aesthetics of bureaucratic logic. Again, I am arguing that it is aesthetics that enable us to sense the rightness of organization and practice; and so, too, of performance (which, as noted, I understand as the heightened consciousness, and perhaps the morphogenesis, of practice). In other words, the logic and aesthetics of events of presentation are strongly continuous with the logic and aesthetics that organize so many domains of mundane life. There is no radical shift in logic and aesthetic from the mundane to this kind of ritual.[3]

The event of presentation often shapes, puts into place, and demonstratively shows social taxonomies. To a high degree, taxonomies are put on view, their categories filled, and members of these categories are used to perform a repertoire of symbolic actions. Perhaps there are here taxonomies in motion, a spectacle of bureaucratic logic whose aesthetic feel of rightness enables their performance. Events of presentation may be societal icons, fully open to the inspection of the public gaze. These rituals rarely conceal any mysteries, nor is their atmosphere particularly mysterious. Their purpose may be to assert the determinacy of the significance that they enclose within themselves. Such rituals are ocular centric, their symbolism arranged often in the form of a relatively static tableau, or a tableau in motion. The actions of performers (like the categories they embody) rarely overlap and are carefully allocated, measured, and often synchronized. Order is continually seen to be practiced during the event.

The opening ceremony of Holocaust Martyrs and Heroes Remembrance Day is held in Jerusalem at Yad Vashem, the Holocaust Memorial Authority, which is the national site of Holocaust memorialism in Israel. The ceremony, televised in its entirety, is a major ritual occasion of the state, the first of the three major "ritual days" legislated after Israel's declaration of independence.

I have chosen this Holocaust occasion to press my arguments on bureaucratic logic and bureaucratic aesthetics in statist public events especially because the Holocaust is a highly emotional and volatile subject (and increasingly so) in Jewish Israeli everyday life (Friedlander and Seligman 1994; Young 1990; Handelman and Shamgar-Handelman 1996; Handelman 2004: 171–199; Feldman 2000; Kidron 2000). In Israeli discourse, popular and academic alike, the ritualization of the Holocaust is attended to primarily (and often solely) in terms of moral, philosophical, theological, historical, and political valences and their consequences, as if the logic and aesthetics of ritualism and commemoration are irrelevant to how these valences are expressed and conveyed. Yet it is the logic of ritual organization that in no small measure is shaping the significance of the Holocaust in Israeli society.[4] And in no small measure it is the practiced aesthetics of this logic that enable such events to take, naturalistically, the presentational, taxonomic form that they do, and to be appreciated as such.

The Memorial Gathering

My concern here is to show how the Memorial Gathering is performed as a taxonomic tableau of categories, one that embodies in its organization ideas of bureaucratic logic and aesthetics, as discussed earlier. I do not closely interpret the symbolism of this event (as I have done so elsewhere for the opening ceremonies of Israeli Remembrance Day for the war dead and Independence Day; see Handelman 1998, 191–233).

The gathering lasts approximately one hour. The setting is the Warsaw Ghetto Plaza (dedicated to the revolt staged in the ghetto) at Yad Vashem, dominated on one side by a high brick wall (called the Wall of Remembrance; hereafter, the Wall), within which are embedded reproductions of Nathan Rapoport's original sculpture and bas-relief that stand on the site of the razed Warsaw Ghetto (see Young 1989). The sculpture and bas-relief effectively divide the Wall into sections, two categories; and during the ceremony itself attention is shifted from one to the other (from right to left, facing the Wall, the direction in which Hebrew and Yiddish are written).

The Taxonomy of the Wall of Remembrance

The large bronze bas-relief of the last march is embedded within the right side of the Wall. The bas-relief depends through a horizontal, longitudinal axis that depicts Jews—all older men, women, and children who look like they are from a ghetto or *shtetl*—clustered together, eyes averted from the viewer, bent beneath the burdens they carry, appearing to walk into a strong wind, sorrowfully marching to some unknown destination. Whatever this destination, it leads to their annihilation. To the left of the bas-relief is a sculpture of the fighters of the Warsaw Ghetto uprising, one that emphasizes verticality and height. Recessed within the Wall, these fighters, most of whom are young, stand tall and strong at the ready, grasping rifles and grenades, facing the viewer and looking straight ahead at a distant horizon. In the Warsaw original, the bas-relief is placed on the reverse side of the ghetto uprising sculpture, so that bas-relief and sculpture cannot be seen together. At Yad Vashem, the bas-relief and the sculpture are placed in a lineal relationship of two scenes. The bas-relief (given this genre of art) has less depth of figuration and more sketchiness than does the more fully formed sculpture.

These two scenes constitute a taxonomy of the sequencing of narrative history, one that more cleanly divides Jewish perceptions of history into a before and an after, into categories of destruction and ascension, and that shifts one into the other. As I noted above, at Yad Vashem these two scenes should be looked at from right to left—from the driven despair of the breaking edges of generations of Jews, of the very young and the old on the bas-relief, to the fierce determination of the ghetto fighters, the maturing of embattled but powerful strength. The scenes move from the horizontal stretch of the bas-relief, an even plane of suffering that extends indefinitely without relief, to the unbending verticality of the sculpture, which stops movement through posture, gesture, and positioning (even bending the lineality of the Wall), communicating a message of this far and no further. These are all themes of the dominant narrative of the Holocaust in present-day Zionist Israel, and, so too, of Yad Vashem. It is this narrative framing that dominates the taxonomic shift from catastrophe to regeneration that is enacted within the ritual gathering. I first discuss the visual placement of social categories along the Wall, and then their performative sequencing during the ritual.

Since its inception, the plaza has been used as the venue for the ritual gathering. The Wall itself is made to frame the performance. The major social categories of the performance are laid out, in lineal fashion, along the breadth of the Wall. The vertical, recessed sculpture of the ghetto fighters is used to break this tableau into two segments. To the right (facing the Wall) of the vertical sculpture, the area of the bas-relief, the catastrophe and sorrow of the Holocaust dominate the performance tableau. To the left, the fighting response dominates.

For the ritual, a central memorial beacon is placed between the bas-relief and the ghetto fighters sculpture—but more to the right side, identified with the Holocaust catastrophe. In 1991, the gas flame of this beacon reached to the very top of the Wall. The flame emerged from a cone set atop a squared base, rising high through a spiral of barbed wire, searing and transcending the barbs that tore the flesh, heart, and the very life of the Jewish people. To the right of this central beacon are two podia that are used by the announcers of the ceremony (who also perform the memorial readings) and by those who deliver speeches and prayers. Still further to the right are situated the choir and orchestra. The right side, then, is identified more with what could be called civil/religious (as opposed to military) order, as well as with Holocaust suffering.

By contrast, the categories of the left side are identified primarily with military order. Immediately to the left of the central beacon stands the Honor Guard of the Israel Defense Forces (IDF), with naked bayonets fixed to automatic weapons. Further left, atop a lower extension of the Wall, are placed six memorial beacons in memory of the six million Jews who perished in the Holocaust. During the ritual the beacons are lit ceremoniously by persons chosen by the Yad Vashem administration. The beacon lighters are assisted by Gadna paramilitary youth in uniform who hand them the lit torches with which they kindle the beacons. Framing the entire tableau at its extreme left is the flag of the state. Thus, the fighting response to the Holocaust—the IDF Honor Guard, the beacon lighters, the paramilitary youth—is itself framed, enclosed on its right by the ghetto fighters sculpture and on its left by the state flag. The sequencing of the ritual shifts from stateless Holocaust victims driven fatedly, to Jews standing their ground, focused for battle, intergenerational, national.

Thus, during the performance, the narrative—or, more accurately, the visual sequence of taxonomy, of bas-relief and sculpture—is extended from World War II into the present. This sequencing of categories shifts the Jews from that of uprising (signified by the sculpture) to that of the State of Israel (signified by the national flag). The fighting response extends into the present, within the state. During the ritual, the entire Zionist version of recent history is taxonomized as a classification of historical events laid bare and explicated before the gaze of the audience.[5] The audience sits facing the Wall, dignitaries and speakers in the first row.[6]

In terms of the sequencing of the ritual, the initial focus of activity tends to cluster around the bas-relief, with its figures bent beneath tribulation—the unredeemable tragic side of the Holocaust tableau. However, with the lighting of the six beacons, the focus of activity is shifted to the fighting response. The beacon lighters are often living heroes and heroines of the Holocaust—the living embodiments of the Warsaw Ghetto sculpture—who stand above the level of the audience, on the low wall of beacons, to the very left of the tableau. By contrast, the Jews depicted in the bas-relief no longer exist in this version of history—either they have been turned into survivors and perhaps fighters (who live in Israel), or they are dead "martyrs," in the language of this day of remembrance. In any case, there is no mimetic embodiment of the category of martyr within the performance of the ritual—only the ghostly outlines of figures long past, frozen in the bronze of the bas-relief. When all the taxonomic categories are added together, category by category, they constitute a version of history that connects the annihilation of the Holocaust to the fighting response in the face of oppression, and connects the fighting response to the active, armed protection offered to Jews by the State of Israel (which is embodied by the Honor Guard and paramilitary youth, who protect the beacon-lighter survivors, all of them grasped within the protective envelope of the IDF, which safeguards the entire site).

Taxonomy and the Three Generations

The section of the performative tableau that I am calling "the fighting response" is embodied in three distinct categories that are no less metaphysical and historical in their temporal linkage. These categories are those of three generations of fighters, which can be likened to the grandparental, the parental, and their offspring. The beacon lighters are analogous to the grandparental generation who, born in Europe, survived the Holocaust (often heroically), and made the decision to "ascend" to Israel, thereby making this their future, through which they aligned themselves with the generation of founders and pioneers.[7] They light the beacons of remembrance that are also flames of destruction and sacrifice, rising and transcending, as it were, their own pasts. The Honor Guard of the IDF, standing near the beacon lighters, fixed bayonets at the ready, is composed of young soldiers who are doing their compulsory military service. They are analogous to the generation of children of the survivors, who have grown to maturity within Israel. They serve the state directly, in its uniform modality, honoring and protecting the generation of Holocaust survivors who themselves pioneered the Jewish fighting response in Europe and who later joined their efforts to those of the pioneers in Israel. The beacon lighters are handed their torches by the uniformed (but unarmed) paramilitary youth. The youth are analogous to the generation of Israeli Jewish grandchildren to whom belongs the more distant future. As they hand over the lit torches, the paramilitary youth (the still-unformed future) enable the beacon lighters (the past) to remember and to commemorate, all the while protected by the Honor Guard (the fighting present).

The narrative structures and the three-generational paradigm of re-membrance are at the heart of the symbolism of the gathering; and they are encoded through the aesthetics of temporal rhythmicity, of low to high. I emphasize the aesthetics of temporality because, in terms of my earlier argument, it is aesthetics that enable the natural feel of the right-ness of practice. The experiencing of the organization of categories in sequence as temporal—in a relationship of low to high—feels right in a fully natural sense in monotheistic cosmologies.

Neither the rhythmicity of Jewish time nor the paradigm of three gen-erations is explicitly recognized in the ritual. The bureaucratic logic for the composition of symbolic meaning seems to require the specification and description of discrete taxonomic elements and categories. But be-yond this, bureaucratic logic should enable the arbitrary combining or joining of categories to one another, in somewhat arithmetical ways, by bringing them into conjunction—added to, subtracted from, or mixed together. Yet, aesthetically, these taxonomic elements and categories are enabled to be practiced, felt, and experienced as a moral rhythmics of time. And, though in practice we recognize the rightness of these rhythms of temporality, they are also "more than we can know," and therefore they encompass us aesthetically in ways that in their fullness of becom-ing are beyond our ken.

Bureaucratic Logic and the Planning of the Ritual

The presence of bureaucratic logic is plainly evident in the comments of a planner and organizer of the early opening ceremonies of remem-brance at Yad Vashem, which first used the Wall of Remembrance. He stated that the arrangement of taxonomic categories, in my terms, along the length of the Wall was primarily a matter of practicality, of a some-what arbitrary positioning according to available space. Thus, one listed the elements needing to be included, without particular attention to the consequences of their particular positioning in relation to one another. So, once the decision was taken to use the Wall and the taxonomic cate-gories I have mentioned, the only space sufficient for the six beacons was on the left side. Therefore, since the national Honor Guard defended celebrated the beacon lighters, it too went to the left side. The national flag, then, also went to the left side; and, of course, the paramilitary youth whose task it was to hand a lit torch to the beacon lighters. But then, all space on the left side was taken up, and the choir had to go to the right side, and so, too, did the orchestra. This disposition, said the organizer, "has no meaning."[8]

The distribution along the Wall of categories of participation was done, approximately, according to the following thinking: first, decide which elements should be included in the ritual; second, arrange them in relation to one another so that they all fit into the available space/time. In this there is the arbitrary character of bureaucratic logic, yet also the tacit aesthetic perception (which accords with this logic) that like goes together with like. Once the beacons were positioned arbitrarily, the beacon lighters, Honor Guard, paramilitary youth, and flag also joined the beacons. All these elements fit together naturally; they belonged together without much thought. Once they were brought into conjunction, their positioning in relation to one another—their symbolic interaction—immediately began to make emergent, perhaps even unintended, meaning (see Handelman and Shamgar-Handelman 1993). One result of this interactive making of meaning was the structuring of the doubled visual narrative; another was that which I am calling the paradigm of the three generations, clustered about the flames of sacrifice, remembrance, and freedom. Relatively unrelated symbols brought serendipitously near to one another within contexts officially defined as symbolic are likely to be felt symbolically related to one another—they are felt, aesthetically, to fit together even if this remains implicit.

The organizers of the first Holocaust memorial ceremonies decided that a proper ritual of remembrance should include at least three discrete, taxonomic categories of symbolic activities, without specifying their relationship to one another. These categories were the following: (1) a category of actions mandatory for a religious memorial (the reciting of the mourner's prayer, kaddish, and of "God full of mercy" [*El malei rachamim*]); (2) an "artistic" category (consisting of appropriate music and song); and (3) a category of speeches and readings. Music and songs, readings and speeches, were then mixed together and synchronized through alternation: a song followed a speech or reading, and so forth; while the religious practices were clustered towards the end of the ritual. In keeping with bureaucratic logic, these three categories were defined arbitrarily, yet their conjunction produced an aesthetically clean-cut alternation between words and song that felt right—perhaps in that it maintained the discreteness of speech and music, even as it brought them into conjunction. Furthermore, these secular practices were kept together in a broader category, separated from the category of religious practices, most of which were used to close the ritual.

Bureaucratic Aesthetics: Exactitude, Itemization, Modularity

Bureaucratic aesthetics insists on the exactitude of definitions of categories, their borders cleanly demarcated in relation to one another, demonstrating their differences. In keeping with the aesthetics of exactness in division, the sequence of ritual action was divided into segments of measured time, to produce as perfect a synchronization as possible between these parts within ritual space. This aesthetics of exact division and combination, of parts fitting together as if in a machine, is what, above all, enabled the performers to be in the right place at the right time. In a way, this exactness of synchronization was the primary integrating force in this ritual, holding together pieces that otherwise might have little or no sense of connectivity with one another. Much of the logic of integration of this ritual is in the construction of time and space as formats, without which many of the parts marshaled for the ritual might well fly off symbolically in all directions, or trip over one another.

Crucial to this construction of integration is the role of the announcer. In the performance itself, one of the tasks of the announcers is to report the condition of synchronization in the ritual, by telling the audience which segment will perform next. This fully expresses the bureaucratic logic that informs the event, since the announcing of each segment is simultaneously an enunciation of the demarcation of its bounded modularity. The announcer does coordinate the ritual from within its own enactment—but, since the ritual is not organized systemically, the announcer (unlike the commander of the military envelope) has no capacity to modify its course. The announcer may be more a representation of integration within the ritual, than a generating force that produces integration.

In this kind of event it is the extreme modularity of the contents or parts of the ritual that enables its construction and integration as a whole; and, so too, the capacity of its organizers to add and subtract modules almost at will. This is true, of course, for the arbitrariness of much of the practice of everyday life in social orders organized by bureaucratic logic, aesthetics, and apparatuses. There are then powerful continuities and similarities between the organization of the gathering and the organization of the everyday.

The 1991 Memorial Gathering: Sequencing

In the 1991 gathering, there were twenty discrete segments. Their sequencing (and the time of each in minutes) was as follows:

(1) the entry of the Honor Guard five minutes before the start of the ritual;

(2) the entry of the president of the state (2:00);
(3) lowering the state flag to half-mast (2:30);
(4) lighting the central memorial beacon by the president (3:00);
(5) song by choir (2:00);
(6) speech by the chairman of the Yad Vashem directorate (2:00);
(7) song by choir (2:00);
(8) speech by the director of Yad Vashem (2:00);
(9) song by cantor, "God, God, why did you forsake us?" accompanied by the choir (3:00);
(10) speech by the representative of partisans' organizations (3:00);
(11) speech by the prime minister (5:00);
(12) reading of poem by an announcer (2:30);
(13) song by choir (2:00);
(14) lighting the six beacons (8:00, including the introductions of the announcer and accompanying music);
(15) reading by an announcer of a text of the "live witnessing" (*eydoot chai*) of the massacre of Jews in the area of Pinsk, during World War II (3:00);
(16) readings of psalms by the Sephardic chief rabbi of the state (2:00);
(17) recitation of kaddish, the mourner's prayer for the dead (2:00);
(18) song by cantor, *Yizkor*, the prayer of remembrance (6:00);
(19) songs by choir (2:00);
(20) singing of the national anthem, *Hatikvah* (The Hope) (2:00).[9]

The total time formally allocated to the ritual is one hour and thirty seconds.

Like the tableau placed through space along the Wall, the sequence of acts through time is categorical, segmentary, and modular. Parts or segments can be inserted or extracted with ease. The logic of connectivity among these modules and the sense of rightness of their performance apparently must be external to the ritual itself. That is, the ritual has no internal dynamics that are organic to it. Most segments have been rehearsed, and it is through this that participants learn about their roles in connection to other segments; but they have no mandate, say, for ad hoc improvisation if something should go wrong with the organization of time/space in performance. The bureaucratic logic and aesthetics of performance seems to require that, in their entirety, segments be externally administered by a director or organizer—in a functional sense, by bureaucrats who ensure that the performers of every category be in the right place at the right time for the correct duration.

Especially notable in the tableau of categories of persons and segments of practice is just how little kinesic movement there is by the performers and when there is motion, just how contained and restricted it is. Some categories of persons are glued in place throughout the event (Honor Guard, choir, orchestra). Others move very short distances (from the front row of the audience) to take fixed positions temporarily on the podia and behind the beacons. The contents of the taxonomic categories take up their assigned positions and remain rigidly in place. At all times the entire tableau is overt and visible to the gaze of the audience—and, of course, to the television camera that need hardly shift position in order to telecast the performance.[10] The performer is the (near) perfect embodiment of his category of membership in the performance—he neither expands nor restricts this, nor plays with this. Instead he always contributes to the vision of overall perfected taxonomic ordering. All of this speaks to a regime of discipline in aesthetic presentation that is beyond the nationalist and the statist, but is closest to the bureaucratic ordering of people and things.

Framing

Despite the segmented character of performance modules, there is some framing of sequence at the beginning and the end of the ritual. Yet this framing, too, is highly categorical and modular. As the representation of the protective might of the state, the IDF Honor Guard takes up position first, to await the entry of the president and prime minister, the ranking citizens of the state. Within the ritual, the Honor Guard, the military, anticipates the arrival of the civil state. The state flag is lowered to half-mast, signifying the entry of state and citizenry into mourning. The central memorial beacon is lit, signifying the entry of the people into remembrance. Though none of these symbolic acts are essential to such an event, their sequencing demonstrates the logic of the state's protective encompassment of the performance.

Thus, the people do not enter into remembrance until the state first enters into mourning. In these terms, the state controls, coordinates, and synchronizes the remembrance of the Holocaust. State control is practiced through the presentation, in sequence, of a taxonomy of categories of power (the Honor Guard), of authority (the president and prime minister), and of peoplehood (the central beacon). So, too, the end of the event is practiced by the collective singing (by performers and audience members) of the national anthem—the ritual does not end until the state grants it closure. Though this framing signifies the control and power of the state throughout the ritual, the logic of categorization and connection in presentation is that of the bureaucratic. In other words, it is the way in which the bureaucratic mind-set organizes the event as it does that enables the ritual to signify the control and power of the state as it does.

In this aesthetics of presentation the taxonomic categories are displayed and activated, one by one—each is a segment, discrete and quite self-contained, lacking dynamics of design that generate any organic momentum of performance. Just as each category of controlled and constrained formulaic action is added to the next, so, too, the event can be deconstructed into these segments without doing much violence to the event as a whole. Despite the variety of physical postures of the different categories of performers—standing on guard, sitting and holding musical instruments, standing and lighting a beacon, standing and orating, standing and singing—the very immobility and functionality of their embodiments, their movements, suggest that like proper functionaries they could all be seated behind a desk or stood behind a wicket. This ceremonial montage points to the resonance generated by bureaucratic logic in modern social orders like that of Israel with the ordering of society beyond the ritual site, almost without needing any inflection, let alone transformation.

Lighting the Memorial Beacons

The taxonomics of bureaucratic logic and aesthetics organize the lengthiest segment of the ritual, its dramatic highlight, the lighting of the six memorial beacons. Each year a Yad Vashem committee chooses one or more themes to commemorate in the Memorial Gathering, the categories of persons who will represent this theme, and the actual persons who will embody these categories by igniting the beacons in the name of the theme. In 1991 the theme chosen was the fiftieth anniversary of the destruction of the Jewries of the Soviet Union, Yugoslavia, and Bukovina. In its deliberations, the committee emphasized that the Holocaust lives of those chosen had to be unique and striking, so as to attract the media. In the 1991 ritual, the beacon lighters numbered eleven (three beacons were each lit by two persons in unison, and another by three in unison). They had been military heroes, partisans, survivors of ghettos and escapees from concentration camps, children during the Holocaust (one, now a Supreme Court justice, hidden by a "peasant savior of souls"), the mother of a young child slaughtered at Babi Yar whose own mother had been murdered there, and a "righteous gentile" who made his home in Israel.[11] Each of these represented a particular segment of the destroyed Jewries of the themes, and each segment was declared as such by the announcers.

Despite the qualifications of heroism and suffering of the beacon lighters, and despite the death and pain they commemorated, this was enunciated in the announcers' texts as the enumeration of a precise anatomy of horror and as a trait list of its attributes and locations.[12] Thus, the first beacon lighter was introduced by the following text (given here in part): "A full fifty years after the extermination of the Jews in the Soviet territories conquered by the Nazis, in memory of the Jews of Lithuania, Latvia, Estonia, and Byelorussia who were murdered ... the murder of Ponar—near Vilna, the nine in Kovno, Rombli—near Riga, Malitrostiniech—near Minsk, and many other places, ascending first to light the beacon is a new immigrant from the Soviet Union who was in a prisoner camp in the Minsk Ghetto, escaped and joined the partisans in the forests ... one of the survivors of the concentration camp, Sergiosko."

This trait listing, together with those of other texts, seems to practice the premise that an enumeration of details at the microlevel of Nazi actions will produce a comprehensive vision of the multitude of catastrophes that today we call the Holocaust. (In this regard, see the critical comment by Jay [1992b, 103].) This kind of listing by categories that are cross-indexed, as it were, with other categories is precisely one of the attitudes of bureaucratic logic, enabled by a bureaucratic aesthetic, which equates the addition and enumeration of mass with a holistic totality. This logic and its aesthetic of every detail in its proper place are commonplace in the organization of our lifeworlds.

Conclusions

If events like the Memorial Gathering are organized through bureaucratic logic and the aesthetics of practice, then this makes a difference in the kinds of messages that the event can communicate. From the perspective of the state, the organizers, and the audience, the Memorial Gathering is a moral project of the state, carried out in the name of the Jewish people. Given that the state is a Jewish one, the moral duty of its representatives is to remember the evils of the past—evils that fragmented and threatened the Jewish people—and to protect these fragments, as a whole, from threats in the present. This whole is, of course, more than the sum of its values. Crucial to this moral project is the practice of remembering the past. Here, remembering is cast as an itemization, an accounting of the past, occurrence by occurrence, point by point—perhaps an aesthetic double-entry bookkeeping of remembrance. Nonetheless, holism in turn requires ways of communicating its totalistic and comprehensive visions, ones that encompass the discrete itemizations of remembering.

I have argued throughout this work (and elsewhere) that bureaucratic logic is pervasive in the modern world and that it dominates what I call events of presentation. The practice of bureaucratic logic is enabled by the bureaucratic aesthetics of lineal organization, arithmetic modularity, exclusivist classification, and exactitude in itemization; and, for that matter, the invention of all these modalities. Thus, these logical and aesthetic qualities of taxonomization dominate public events that are organized in ways similar to the Memorial Gathering. In the case of the gathering, the power of taxonomizing is brought home more clearly by the ways in which the military envelops the event through its own taxonomies. But the premises of taxonomy used by the military are no different from those used to organize the gathering, and, for that matter, both are quite similar to ones that are powerful, if more camouflaged, in the practice of daily life in social orders with prominent bureaucratic infrastructures. To no small degree, in keeping with taxonomic logic and aesthetics, the relationships between the practices of the ritual and the practices of daily life are fractal.

The elements used in the gathering are without a doubt highly symbolic—nevertheless, the practice of this kind of event depends on connections within and among taxonomies rather than on relationships that are organic, dynamic, and transforming. The bureaucratic message is made explicit in the visible tableau of the gathering. This message stresses the practice of exclusivist classification, fragmentation, and itemization, at the expense of the holism of the vision of remembrance. The state's holistic, moral project is shaped, modified, and fragmented by its passage through the organizing media of bureaucratic logic and aesthetics. The vision and feeling of the Holocaust stand rigidly at attention, open to minute inspection, petrified in place. The vision shifts towards the totalitarian in its presentation.

Ironically, bureaucratic logic and aesthetics contribute to separating the Jewish Holocaust from all other atrocities and to classifying it as the unique, historical occurrence of the planned extermination of an entire people—a category with a single member (indeed, a category that paradoxically is a member of itself and is therefore self-sealing and quite resistant to surrendering its self-referentiality, which augments its power exponentially). This exclusivist patterning, with all its inherent dangers (see, for example, Ophir 1987) resonates with the taxonomic treatment of profound tragedy that characterizes the Memorial Gathering. In this instance, bureaucratic logic and aesthetics support (indeed, nourish) the exclusivist state, nationalism, and remembrance that recursively gather themselves within themselves, an in-gathering that separates the Holocaust from too many other instances of human catastrophe.

In Israel, many persons both identify with and feel alienated from these state rituals. Part of our identification (even as this may repel us) is because we ourselves often are both the practitioners and the targets of bureaucratic logic and aesthetics in everyday life. The kinds of classification used, and the practice of their enabling, are common-sensically obvious to us in the way we live much of our lives. We are not reflexive about our practice of this logic nor about its aesthetic enablement—about our practice of practice. Another reason for our lack of reflexivity is the way in which scholars, in particular, philosophers and art historians, have framed off, classified, and separated aesthetics from its role in the practice of everyday life. It is this separation of aesthetics as a realm apart, one dominated by values of beauty and truth, by genres of art, literature, music, and so forth, that has focused scholarly and elitist reflexivity almost exclusively on aesthetics per se, as a discrete domain of culture. In so doing, the intimate enabling of virtually all practice that aesthetics does, is lost.

The final point I will make points to intimations of lawfulness in the use of bureaucratic logic and aesthetics. One scholar, Michael King, has argued that in Western legal systems, law depends for its ontology on a binary code of lawful/unlawful, legal/illegal, and the like. To carry this a step further, law is a prime way of classifying everyday acts within exclusivist taxonomies, with great authority, and with powerful social and personal consequences. Legal systems operate to generate decisions that clarify conditions of vagueness, overlapping rights, allocations of responsibility, and so forth; and legal systems underwrite these decisions with lineal, ontological sanctification. King (1993, 223) suggests further that "any act or utterance that codes social acts according to this binary code of lawful/unlawful may be regarded as part of the legal system." In other words, this logic of the legal system is much more embracing and totalizing than the formal system as such. Yet even more than this, the binary meets the criteria of exclusivist taxonomic classification. Therefore, this kind of taxonomic classification, which has a much broader range than the binary as such, can be substituted for the latter. Now, I have argued that the operation of such exclusivist logic points to the presence of bureaucratic logic. In my terms, then, the operation of bureaucratic logic in Western societies continually implicates the presence of lawfulness. Indeed, bureaucratic logic is itself authorized ontologically to a degree by a sense or feeling of lawfulness in producing and practicing the kind of lineal, taxonomic classification that it does. There is then an aesthetics, itself imbued with a sense of lawfulness, indeed, of rightness, that enables the practice of bureaucratic logic in everyday life. This is one modern version of aesthetics that enables practice—and one, I think, that helps to explain why the bureaucratic logic of classification used in the Memorial Gathering and in everyday life works on so many of us aesthetically. However, it might also explain why we may be so ambivalent to the practice of such classification, yet without knowing exactly and precisely why.

Notes

1. In other words, it is done like this because it is done like this—this is how it is felt to be done when one does it.
2. For my purposes here the difference between mundane practice and performance is that the latter is that of practice writ large, consciously and self-reflexively. Therefore, mundane practice slips in and out of performance, apart from the conscious shift into ritual, in which performance becomes the mundane.
3. This is so despite claims for the sacralizing qualities of all manners of ritual, including, for example, "secular ritual" (Moore and Myerhoff 1977). Not a few of the studies in that volume, with their focus on "ritual," would have benefited from being analyzed in terms of bureaucratic logic.
4. The ethos of bureaucratic framing conditions all statist rituals in Israel. For an example of the collision between bureaucratic logic and popular sentiment, see the discussion of the funeral of the Israeli Prime Minister, Menachem Begin, in Bilu and Levy (1993).
5. In later years, a second state flag has been placed atop the Wall, above the bas-relief, as a symbol of the statist, national encompassment and transcendence of the sorrow symbolized by the suffering Jews, beneath.
6. In later years, a large video screen has been hung on the Wall, above the Honor Guard, and is used for audiovisual contextualizations, for example, to personalize the introductions of

the beacon lighters through autobiographical narratives of these persons, which were taped beforehand.

7. The Hebrew term for Jewish immigration to Israel is *aliyah*, literally, ascent.

8. Binyamin Arnon, interviewed at Yad Vashem by Noemi Lerner, 24 July 1991.

9. By 1995, some of the speeches by functionaries had been taken out of the program.

10. One may argue that the stronger sense of movement, of dynamics—archetypal, historicist—is located in the poetics of rhetoric, song, and prayer, which I do not discuss here. Nonetheless, the speeches are stilted; the songs, often old favorites; and the psalms and prayers, generic insertions into ritual.

11. The honor of "righteous gentile" is bestowed by Yad Vashem (in the name of the state) on non-Jews who endangered their own lives by rescuing Jews during World War II.

12. In this respect, the form of these introductions resembled the *yizkor* prayer of remembrance that can be expanded to include a limitless listing of attributes to be remembered.

References

Astley, W. Graham. 1985. "Administrative Science as Socially Constructed Truth." *Administrative Science Quarterly* 30: 497–513.

Ben-Amos, Avner, and Eyal Ben-Ari. 1995. "Resonance and Reverberation: Ritual and Bureaucracy in the State Funerals of the French Third Republic." *Theory and Society* 24: 163–91.

Bilu, Yoram, and Andre Levy. 1993. "The Elusive Sanctification of Menachem Begin." *International Journal of Politics, Culture and Society* 7: 297–328.

Bourdieu, Pierre. 1977. *Outline of a Theory of Practice*. Cambridge: Cambridge University Press.

Brown, Richard Harvey. 1978. "Bureaucracy as Praxis: Toward a Political Phenomenology of Formal Organizations." *Administrative Science Quarterly* 23: 365–82.

Dufrenne, Mikel. 1973. *The Phenomenology of Aesthetic Experience*. Evanston, Ill.: Northwestern University Press.

Feldman, Jackie. 2000. "It Is My Brothers Whom I Am Seeking": Israeli Youth Voyages to Holocaust Poland." Ph.D. thesis, Hebrew University of Jerusalem.

Foucault, Michel. 1973. *The Order of Things*. New York: Vintage.

———. 1979. *Discipline and Punish*. New York: Vintage.

Friedlander, Saul, and Adam Seligman. 1994. *The Israeli Memory of the Shoah: On Symbols, Rituals, and Ideological Polarization*. In *HereNow: Space, Time and Modernity*, ed. R. Friedland and D. Boden, 356–71. Berkeley: University of California Press.

Garfinkel, Harold. 1967. *Studies in Ethnomethodology*. Englewood Cliffs, N.J.: Prentice-Hall.

Geertz, Clifford. 1983. *Local Knowledge*. New York: Harper Colophon.

Handelman, Don. 1995. "Cultural Taxonomy and Bureaucracy in Ancient China: *The Book of Lord Shang*." *International Journal of Politics, Culture and Society* 9: 263–93.

———. 1998. *Models and Mirrors: Towards an Anthropology of Public Events*. New York and Oxford: Berghahn Books.

———. 2004. *Nationalism and the Israeli State: Bureaucratic Logic in Public Events*. Oxford: Berg

Handelman, Don, and Lea Shamgar-Handelman. 1993. "Aesthetics versus Ideology in National Symbolism: The Creation of the Emblem of Israel." *Public Culture* 5: 431–49.

———. 1996. "The Presence of Absence: The Memorialism of National Death in Israel." In *Grasping Land: Space and Place in Contemporary Israeli Discourse and Experience*, ed. E. Ben-Ari and Y. Bilu, 85–128. Albany: SUNY Press.

Hardin, Kris L. 1993. *The Aesthetics of Action: Continuity and Change in a West African Town*. Washington, D.C.: Smithsonian Institution Press.

Inglis, David, and John Hughson. 2000. "The Beautiful Game and the Proto-aesthetics of the Everyday." *Cultural Values* 4: 279–97.

Jay, Martin. 1992a. "Scopic Regimes of Modernity." In *Modernity and Identity*, ed. S. Lash and J. Friedman, 178–95. Oxford: Blackwell.

———. 1992b. "Of Plots, Witnesses, and Judgements." In *Probing the Limits of Representation*, ed. S. Friedlander. Cambridge: Harvard University Press.

Katz, Jack. 1999. *How Emotions Work*. Chicago: University of Chicago Press.

Kidron, Carole. 2000. "Amcha's Second Generation Holocaust Survivors: A Recursive Journey into the Past to Construct Wounded Carriers of Memory." M.A. thesis, Hebrew University of Jerusalem.

Kimmerling, Baruch, in collaboration with Irit Backer. 1985. *The Interrupted System: Israeli Civilians in War and Routine Times*. New Brunswick, N.J.: Transaction Books.

King, Michael. 1993. "The 'Truth' about Autopoeisis." *Journal of Law and Society* 20: 218–36.

Melossi, Dario, and Massimo Pavarini. 1981. *The Prison and the Factory*. London: Macmillan.

Moore, Sally F., and Barbara Myerhoff, eds. 1977. *Secular Ritual*. Assen, Netherlands: Van Gorcum.

Morgan, Gareth. 1986. *Images of Organization*. Beverly Hills, Calif.: Sage.

Ophir, Adi. 1987. "On Sanctifying the Holocaust: An Anti-theological Treatise." *Tikkun* 2, no. 2: 61–67.

Polanyi, Michael. 1962. *Personal Knowledge: Towards a Post-Critical Philosophy*. New York: Harper Torchbooks.

———. 1967. *The Tacit Dimension*. London: Routledge & Kegan Paul.

Sheets-Johnstone, Maxine. 2000. "Kinetic Tactile-Kinesthetic Bodies: Ontogenetical Foundations of Apprenticeship Learning." *Human Studies* 23: 343–70.

Shamgar-Handelman, Lea, and Don Handelman. 1991. "Celebrations of Bureaucracy: Birthday Parties in Israeli Kindergartens." *Ethnology* 30: 293–312.

Simmel, Georg. 1994a. "Bridge and Door." *Theory, Culture and Society* 11: 5–10.

———. 1994b. "The Picture Frame: An Aesthetic Study." *Theory, Culture and Society* 11: 11–17.

Wyschogrod, Edith. 1985. *Spirit in Ashes: Hegel, Heidegger, and Man-Made Mass Death*. New Haven: Yale University Press.

Young, James. 1989. "The Biography of a Memorial Icon: Nathan Rapoport's Warsaw Ghetto Monument." *Representations* 26: 69–106.

———. 1990. "When a Day Remembers: A Performative History of Yom Ha-Shoah." *History and Memory* 2, no. 2: 54–75.

Chapter Ten

COMPASSION FOR ANIMALS, INDIFFERENCE TO HUMANS
Non- and Misperceptions among Circus Audiences in 1970s Britain

Yoram S. Carmeli

My chapter centers on two of the queries I came up against during field-work conducted in Gerry Cottle's Circus in Britain in 1975–79. The first concerns circus animal performances. The second relates to human performances and performers in the circus.

In the mid- and late 1970s, Cottle's Circus, like most other British trav-eling shows, presented alongside performances involving humans a vari-ety of animal acts. So did the prestigious stationary circuses in Blackpool and Great Yarmouth, the winter circus productions that performed in halls, and the celebrated televised presentations of circus on Christmas morning. Animal acts in Cottle's circus equaled human acts in number and were prominent on Cottle's posters. They were featured on the front and back covers of the circus's 'souvenir program' and were loudly ap-plauded throughout the performance.

During this same period, animal performances in British circuses in-creasingly came under attack. Protests and legal initiatives against circus animal presentations were lodged by the elitist Royal Society for the Pre-vention of Cruelty to Animals (RSPCA), already active in the final decades of the nineteenth century; later, other organizations joined this opposi-tion. Historical research into the perception on the part of the RSPCA and other protest groups of cruelty towards animals in the circus reflects, gen-erally speaking, the growing sense of both dominance over and nostalgia for Nature and the rising concern about the treatment and fate of animals

References for this chapter begin on page 229.

that has been common among the urban middle class since the mid-nineteenth century (e.g., Ritvo 1990; Turner 1980; Thomas 1984). Vis-à-vis the circus, a major argument of protest groups centered on the animals' suffering, brought about—so they claimed—through the training the animal were subjected to and the circus acts themselves they were forced to perform. Pictures of allegedly torturous training tools and "unnatural" performing postures were distributed among the general public whenever Cottle's circus came to town. The RSPCA held demonstrations in different towns in front of the circus entrance, at which its protesters carried banners showing photographs of injured animals and revealing what was presumably the circus's back stage 'real' treatment of the animals. Shouts of protests were occasionally heard inside the big top during performances. Local council delegates and journalists of various papers often appeared on the circus grounds. Cottle himself began experiencing mounting difficulties in renting public and even private grounds for his circus performances. Soon the accusations and protests by groups opposing cruelty to animals became for the circus a question of survival.

The popularity of, and yet the objection to, animal acts, the closeness between trainer and animal and yet the perceptions of 'cruelty' to animals among the circus public is one concern of this chapter.

But the compassion for animals and the 'cruelty' accusations prompted another puzzling question. During the mid- and late 1970s, what contrasted so remarkably with the high level of concern for the plight of circus animals was the relative indifference to the fate of human circus performers.

In the expectations of circus spectators, as well as the general public, performances by humans in the circus entailed danger as well as bodily abjection. A trapeze performer would hang high in the air, without safety devices. A high-wire act by the 'Cimmaro brothers', which occurred twice every evening in the Cottle circus, climaxed in the daring feat of one man, blindfolded and hooded, carrying his brother on his shoulders while walking across a tight rope. In 1975, the performer atop this human pyramid fell from the tight rope, and had to be hospitalized with eighteen fractures in his wrist, but the accident became a local news sensation and the circus tent was packed the following nights.

Another human act in Cottle's circus was that of a bald 'Fakir', which showed the performer lying on a "bed of swords," then having a "bed of nails" placed on top of him with the nails facing his body. This act, culminated in a man, "our twelve stone Big Brian," standing on top of the Fakir's bed of nails. The routine was announced by the circus's ringmaster as "the human sandwich."

A dwarf with a professional name of Wee Bean was included in Cottle's program and dwarves appeared almost routinely in the programs of other established shows. In different circus productions the dwarf took part in clowning acts, interacted and talked with ordinary human clowns (he is the little one who outwits the others; he is also a Jack-in-the-Box, a music stand, etc.). During the intermission Cottle's dwarf would sell circus souvenir flags (and so earned a few more pounds weekly). He was approached by children who would point at him and ask their parents whether this was a real person.

Last but not least, among human participants in circus acts was the man in the lions' den. A story, generic among circus folks and fiction writers in England, tells of a lady who, following a lethal accident in a 'big cats' act, in all innocence asked whether all this was part of the show.

In the highly unionized and strongly welfare-oriented mid-1970s Britain, no one seemed to care much about human circus performers. The artists union (Equity) was hardly involved in their lives. No one inspected or cared to know the daily conditions of their employment. No insurance protected the human performers in case of accident (except their own families and, to a certain, practical and limited extent, circus owners). For an outside observer, the contrast between these features and the growing sensitivities to animals was striking: Why does the public just giggle at the sight of a dwarf in the ring, the tortured body of a man lying on swords, a man stumbling on the high wire, someone dragged through the lions' tunnel? How come these acts were all just 'expected' to happen and simply and 'traditionally' applauded?

The responses that one would hear when directly posing these questions during the mid-1970s (not only to 'blind' circus fans but also to the moralist Animal Rights protesters) were couched in terms of the circus being a "family thing" and "a way of life" for the acrobats and the lion tamer, "a way of making a living" for a dwarf. However, as I could establish through my research, even when true to life, these 'justifications' in the case of the dwarf and the acrobat were not anchored in any close acquaintance with and knowledge of the circus. Encouraged by the circus's own self-presentation, they were rather part of the public's own lore of the circus. They constituted a folk understanding, a folk construction and participation in the performance of circus, participation that bracketed and suspended, rather than evoked, any moral considerations (see below).

Another, somewhat similar and more frequently heard line of reasoning for the public's indifference, was that "[unlike animals] these people are rational free human beings.... They make their [own] choices." However, this pseudo-liberal argument hardly provides a good enough alibi for the public's indifference. One notes that while liberal tenets were indeed generally at the core of the country's moral and political creed, the state was often found to interfere or activate their legal paternalism to protect people from "harm to self," or from putting themselves in danger (e.g., Feinberg 1986).

So why care about circus animals (are circuses particularly 'cruel' to animals?) but not care about circus humans? Why not interfere with the performers' self-harming performance, protect them from 'their own family tradition', 'their own way of making a living'?

In the following I will try to approach these fieldworker's queries via probing into the epochal significance of circus, i.e., via the public's epochal expectations, as well as perceptions and construction of circus. This approach, via the circus's epochal significances, necessarily entangles one into historical and thus more general contexts through which the circus and its performance have been crystallized. Briefly put, the circus, as observed through the 1970s, emerged during the eighteenth and nineteenth centuries, which makes some general themes of experience and perception concomitant with modernity paradigmatic for the construction of circus significance. Nature's rationalization, the experience of 'loss of Nature' and its 'objective' ontological grounds, the social fragmentariness, commodification and alienation are seen as contexts for the emergence of a spectacle of social and ontological apartness, embodied by the circus. As I suggest, through the performance of the circus's particular marginality, an experience of totality is illusorily conjured for the public—a totality of which the circus is apart. In this totality, nature's objectivity, social time, community, family and biography—all experientially lost in modernity— are illusorily (reflexively) evoked and resurrected by nostalgic spectators.

Within this concept of circus, compassion to animals and 'cruelty' accusations become modalities of anxiety and of longing and the public's indifference to circus humans—a mode of dramatic exclusion and illusory self subjectification. The chapter's initial queries and the concept of marginality within which these queries are 'resolved', are thereby considered as encapsulating order in transformation, the circus offering a particular vantage point for the study of modernity.

Historically, one of the main origins of the traveling circus was the fair (Disher 1942; Speaight 1980; Kwint 1995; Assa'el 1998; Stoddart 2000). For the visitors to the premodern and early modern fair, which traveled on holy days, the acrobatic performances, the freaks ("world wonders," "curiosities"), the menageries' ("exotic") animals, all encapsulated the margins: the characters at the fair were auratic boundary signs of the human and the social. In these characters' exclusion, as well as in the fair's liminal, exterritorial disorder, visitors ritualized community, morality, and their own human identity (e.g., Malcolmson 1973; Cunningham 1980).

The circus emerged with the rise of an industrialized, commoditized urban order when fairs began to be controlled and regulated and their amusements eventually mechanized. Circus travelers gradually became distinguished from the "rogue and vagabond," and legally acknowledged as ordinary human performers (1935). The circus now began to travel according to its own itinerary rather than mainly on holy days. Instead of performing for a whole day (as the fair did), circuses gave two performances a day during the public's leisure time, after work.

Still, in the early twentieth century and even into the mid-1970s, the traveling circuses in Britain carried much of the significance of the old fairs. Circus memory books and autobiographies are full of accounts of the liberties taken by local townsfolk in abusing the travelers and invading their temporary performance grounds. In the mid- and late 1970s, it was often argued that the circus created disorder as it damaged the town's 'common' grounds which they rented for their parking, and its travelers behaved indecently in town. Although these beliefs had serious effects on the real-life conditions of the travelers they were, during this period, 'traditional', expected images that were dramatized and performed by both sides, the travelers and the public: with the emergence of circus, the encounter between the marginal travelers and the townsfolk turned from ritual into play, and nomadism became encapsulated in its self-display of the "traveler."

I shall now turn to an analysis of circus performances, beginning with animal acts. Set in deep-rooted opposition animals complemented humans in constituting the circus as cosmological display. In the Judeo-Christian tradition, animals are seen as inferior to human beings. Animals, and Nature embodied in them, are the "other" through which human identity and superiority are established. The Cartesian secular cosmology, at the dawn of modernity, considers animals a living machine, while man is body and mind. At the same time, through its "objectivity," Nature, in the post-religious era, provided humans with ontological grounds. Further down the road of modernity, Nature is studied and rationalized, occupied and processed. Nature as other, as ground, is shaken and replaced by a threat, the anxiety about the loss of Nature. Moreover, the cosmologically based opposition of Human and Animal (Culture and Nature) has by now been shattered by Darwinian scientific theory (e.g., Evernden 1992). These fears were both encapsulated and playfully, illusorily, transcended at the circus, the margin of society.

During the mid- to late 1970s, Gerry Cottle's Circus used horses, elephants, lions, and tigers in its performances. Occasionally llamas and zebras were included. In the menageries typical of fairs in the early nineteenth century, some of these animals represented the remote and exotic places from which they had allegedly been imported. They represented the vastness of the Empire and the wilderness of Nature, captured and controlled by the imperial race.

Unlike in the old menageries, where Nature, with its variety of species, was perceived as caged, cosmically marginalized, yet still represented, in the circus Nature achieves a different role. In the circus of the 1970s, animals were presented in a ring and—in most acts—with the help of various accessories. There was nothing in the human-made ring, in the blue, modular lions' cage, in the red and white elephants' pedestals, that belonged in the animals' "original" habitat; there was nothing of Nature and wilderness: in the circus the animals were decontextualized and in this sense de-natured(e.g., Berger 1980).

Performances opened with the animals being led around the ring, displayed to the audience. This human-made ring constrained the animals' movements. As the animals were being shown, with the circus ring imposing their circular, mechanical movement, Nature displayed was also experientially played. This play by the human was further articulated for the public in the performance of the different routines. As the public has come to expect, the animals perform culturally conceived configurations (such as pyramids), humanlike body postures, and anthropomorphic imitations of human behavior. Throughout the performance these forms and configurations are perceptually completed through the public's eye. The forms' anticipated completion—the moment the elephant is "finally" "standing" on one front leg, the moment the lions are "finally" frozen in a pyramid—provides the measure for the "accomplishment" of the routine and signals the start of the public's applauding the trainer. Still, Nature as embodied and represented in the animals is always present. Her presence is manifested by the occasional disorder that occurs in the act, by the imperfect distance between animals when circling the ring, by the live motion with which they spoil the pyramid, and by the animals occasional erupting into wildness (which is itself often staged). The circus—as constituted between performers and spectators—thus always shifts between Nature as presence and Nature as played.

Before continuing with this analysis, I would like to comment on Animal Rights protesters, their sensitivity to animals, and their perceptions about "cruelty" in the circus. As stated earlier, one of the stronger arguments of RSPCA was that, in the circus, animals are "tortured" in that they are forced to perform against their nature. Based on fieldwork observations, I can confidently say that only rarely were the animals really tortured in the circus (see also Kiley-Worthington 1990). I suggest that far more than actually suffering or being tortured, Cottle's animals were perceived, seen, and experienced by spectators as being tortured because they were perceived as played: they were experienced—and claimed—as tortured because they were playfully and symbolically denatured. That is, in their performance Nature, embodied in them, was experientially transgressed and deconstructed. Unlike the fair, in which Nature was represented as real, in the circus tamed animals were playfully made to embody an undermining of Nature's ontological 'realness'.

For circus spectators and protesters, Nature's otherness, its rawness and 'objective', 'real', morally right presence were playfully caused to deteriorate, and the spectators' own Nature-mirrored, animal-opposed, Human self was thereby textualized. Much of the Animal Rights protests against circus originated from the way the public's perceptions were shaped through the general epochal predicament, dramatically and playfully encapsulated on society's edges (Carmeli 1997, 2003).

However, 'cruelty' does not exhaust the circus experience of other people, that is, the circus public inside the tent. I look again at the eager spectators watching the animals being led and displayed in the ring. I follow how they applaud when perceiving a circus routine accomplishing a form.

For a brief moment the animal's natural body is perceived as totally engulfed by its cultural display, that is the animal is perceptually constituted as totally played by the play it has been taught to play. Nature, fully denatured and designified, is experienced as momentarily fully derealized.

Under the circus spotlight, the circus animals and their different "Natural" categories appeared as emptied images, as ephemeral embodiments of Nature's transcendence. In the circus of mid-1970s this was the moment of completion, of applause, of phantasm. In this moment it was not only the 'cruel' transgression and deconstruction of Nature, and of their own everyday Nature-grounded selves, that the circus spectators were ratifying. It was rather that "final" momentous disclosure of the ephemeral embodiment of a Nature-transcending ontology, induced through their own eyes. Driven and shaped by the context of modernity's anxieties, circus perception has become a condensed constitutive act. Through the play of the animal's nature in a circus act, the public playfully disintegrated Nature and their own daily grounds. But in totalizing this play, in the consumption and spectacularization of Nature, modernity's lost Nature is nostalgically, illusorily overcome. A higher order is conjured for the public, a Lacanian mirror-image for an illusionary totalized self.

In the mid-1970s circus performance, this structure was repeated time and time again in each of the routines of the animal act. It was furthered through the separation, the relation-of-disrelation between the routines and through the structure of the disrelations between acts throughout the show. As all circus animals were played and objectified, and as all were equalized in their objectification and disrelation, Nature's constituting species were experientially erased in the circus, and all species were denatured and aestheticized, in the experience of circus fans, into 'trans-species', circus repertoire objects.

I now turn to circus human performers and their acts. From the wide variety of human performances, I shall concentrate on acrobatics. The trapeze act in Gerry Cottle's Circus started with the female performer stepping into the ring. The performer walked around the ring in order to be seen, waving to and communicating with the public. Unlike in the fair, where human rope dancing or juggling performers were conceived in terms of "wonders" and esoterica, the waving circus performer is perceived as intentional and intersubjective. The performer is an ordinary human, like the public. However, the circus performer did not talk. She was dressed, as expected, in shining satin, and decorated with "diamonds and spangles." By waving her hand she displayed her own presence. An ordinary human being, like the public, was playing and being displayed. A certain ambiguity emerged in the public's experience as to whether she was performing or was the object of her own performance. As the spectators expected, their own ordinariness, their ordinary selves, were experienced as played. They themselves were playfully forced into an epistemic and ontological unease.

At the same time, something else happened to the spectators. Through their very perception of the person playing and being displayed, the spectators experientially conferred a quality of image-transparency to the acrobat's body. Transparency was already encapsulated in the perception of the overlap of play and display in the early appearance of the trapeze performer. As she then walked around the ring, the circus make-up and the spotlight designified and sterilized her particular subjective features. She smiled, but her smile was frozen, devoid of subjective mood. The shining material of her costuming mirrored and thus discommunicated her subjective presence to the public. The transparency thereby effected a certain derealization and dissociation of the performing acrobat. Unlike the fair's "wonders" and its ritualization of the visitors' human selves, the traveling circus explicated modernity's predicament of body objectification, the loss of the subject in body mechanization and consumption.

The performers' routines in the act intensified this experience. The circus acrobat was perceived as a subject in control while also being controlled, that is, as shifting between playing and being played through her performance. The moment the trapeze performer started the swinging movement, she was perceived as simultaneously being played through the momentum she herself sustained. The man on the wire was perceived as shifting between balancing and being balanced, objectified through an anticipated fall. The circus trampoline performer not only controlled his own movements (as in a sport) but was also bumped into the air by his prop. The epistemological and ontological discomfort facing spectators at the beginning of the acrobatic act was intensified in the more encompassing play as the circus performer, a living human being like themselves, was played, perceived as objectified and deconstructed.

It is in this context that the significance of the danger in the acrobat's act can be understood. Danger was a prerequisite of all aerial performances in Cottle's circus. In danger, the human circus performer, perceptually objectified, embodying the tensed deconstruction and the rupture of unity of object and subject, was about to be staged as stripped of "being" itself, as metaphorized by "being's" strongest metaphor—life. Danger as metaphor crystallized the public's own experience of anxiety, their sense of their own deconstruction, through the circus.

A sense of rupture, anxiety, and occasional laughter were all elements of the experience and drama the public anticipated and looked for in an acrobatic performance at Cottle's circus. But, as with the animal performances, these too did not completely exhaust the spectators' expectations. The moments the public applauded a circus acrobatic act were when the endangered playing performer was perceptually constituted as if engulfed in her own self-referential movement. It was that moment in which the trapeze performer, hanging by her teeth, was perceived by the public as totally enrolled in and by the movement she herself had created, when an impossible unity of play and display was visually embodied and conceptualized in a transparent acrobating body. In Gerry Cottle's Circus in the 1970s, this was a nostalgic moment of a totally objectified subject being disclosed, a body in which the categories of "ordinary" and "real" are not only deconstructed but transcended, a human body that is dissociated from social time, from relations. This visual experience was not constituted by a fixed form, external to the public's eye (see Krauss 1988). Through the anticipation and expectations of the circus spectators themselves, their own eyes conjured up in the circus this embodiment of social and cosmic outsideness. For the spectators the acrobat's body was a body to be gazed at, to be experienced by the encounter with its spectacle. Faced by a surreal or even 'trans'-real body, excluded and external to history and community, the public's own ordinary, every-day self, fragmented and objectified in the realm of modernity, and playfully disrupted in the course of the circus acrobatic act, was now illusorily subjectified. Through the performance of a circus body the spectators disclosed their own mirror-image and thereby their total "really real" selves.

Acrobatics was but one category of human performance. Humans' display, play of self, and body objectification were at the center of other performances in Cottle's circus, evoking experiences not only of transcendence but also of transgression, objectification, and abjection.

To discuss briefly other examples, consider again the circus dwarf. Unlike in the nineteenth century fair, where the dwarf was a "wonder of nature" exhibited by a showman, the circus dwarf in the modern circus is perceived as human and reflexive. Thus, the dwarf, the freak, is human, and thus the human spectators, the public, are also possibly freaks (e.g., Fiedler 1978). However, through the 1970s circus performance, which entailed a play of the displayed human dwarf, his deformity became exposed. As expected by the spectators, in the circus the freak was feared, yet he was also an abject figure, deprived of his auratic shelter, playfully sacrificed by the spectators.

The man lying on a bed of nails was an imperialistic presentation imported in the late nineteenth century fair. His "mystic East" origins suggest that he was the embodiment of Oriental magical power. In the circus, the Fakir performer has been clearly identified as an ordinary human being through his own and the ringmaster's various ironic gestures. During the intermission, he used to walk among the public, selling the raffle tickets, his real self being recognized as he loudly proclaimed the raffle in a cockney accent. Systematically corrupted by nails and swords, a human body was offered to the 1970s public as a "human sandwich," the macabre metaphor of a most common industrial meat product, packed and ready for consumption. Circus performance may well have touched here on some modern or postmodern experience of the abjected body (so central, for instance in the works of Francis Bacon).

And last I mentioned the human performer in the den. A man in the circus lion's cage, vis-à-vis the animals he rules, displays his own kind—the

Human. Like the wild animals on display, he was also played by his exemplification of the Human species. The danger to life in which the trainer makes himself get caught is real, yet in the spectators' expectations, it also dramatizes an allegorical quality—the performer, who is now reduced to a sign of man, is derealized through enacting his own type (the 'circus trainer'), deconstructed through the sacrifice of real life.

His play is totalized, it is expanded beyond the ring. In Cottle's circus, in the course of the "big cats" performance (Bournemouth, 1979), the seventy-year-old lion trainer suddenly had a blackout and was hastily helped out of the ring by his daughter. The next day, a national newspaper, the *Daily Mirror*, proclaimed on page 7, "Fainting Lion Man Saved by the Band." ("They struck up the tune Tiger Rag—the signal for the lions to leave the ring.")

This expansion of the play (as in the case of the lion tamer or, as described earlier, of the acrobats' fall from the wire or of the dwarf who sells flags during the show's interval) is not incidental. It was a most salient and, to a certain extent, unique characteristic of British "big top" shows that the encounter between travelers and townsfolk was not limited to the circus ring and to the two hours of show time. Rather, as 'traditionally' expected by the public, and as one could follow time and again in every town in this type of circus, the performance—a performance of the play of the real—was extended 'offstage', beyond the tent and into everyday real life.

To start with, circus performers did not have a backstage to which they can resign. While the theater player (or any player of this or that social role) goes home at the end of his or her performance, the circus traveler can only retire to the caravan. The difference is not exhausted by the caravan's mobility. It is rather that the home of the circus performer was itself positioned in the line of circus caravans that constituted an exhibit to be peered into, the travelers' private realm turned into an object of the townsfolk's voyeurism. The display was further extended beyond the circus grounds through the expectations and pressures of the townsfolk in their daily interactions with performers. In the local pub or at the laundry, or when exchanging a word with the fish-and-chips lady, traveling performers were expected to flaunt their presence, always playing "circus," always distanced and depersonalized, and made objects of play by their own self display.

When the circus comes to town "for a few days only," the circus" children are legally obliged to attend the local schools. They are supposed to join the class that corresponds to their age, carrying with them a notebook from town to town in which local teachers indicate the last lesson they studied. However, when children from Cottle's circus attended local classes, their visits had turned into school events and publicity stunts as well. The Fakir's son Tony was pictured in the local newspaper, lying on a bed of nails, with a child performer standing on his stomach, surrounded by happy local school kids and their properly tie-clad, giggling teacher. The photograph's captioned reads, "School has its good points." When Gerry Cottle started a school in his circus, located in a converted double-decker bus, the colorfully painted vehicle and the school soon generated much publicity and interest for local newspapers' photographs (one of them captioned "There is no school like it").

During my fieldwork period, a circus performer, the son of a cyclists' family, married his fiancée, also a performer. The ceremony took place in the local registrar's office in Bournemouth. The *Dorset Evening Echo* of 13 August 1977 described the event on its front page, "For when Roland and Anne came down the Town Hall steps from the Registry Office there was an archway of unicycles waiting for them—not to mention a camel, a baby elephant and two monkeys and a pony... [the] marriage brought colour to the Town Hall surroundings and staff stopped work to watch the camera-clicking scene from the office windows. After the wedding Roland and Anne moved off—not surprisingly using the camel and elephant for transport."

As expected by townsfolk, and performed by travelers, these were all part of the extension of the circus self display, of the objectification of the "circus travelers," part of reifying the circus social/ontological exclusion, of conjuring and validating the townsfolk's circus illusion.

As I noted in the introduction, the 'traveler' and traveling life as a whole, turned performed and object of play between circus people and townsfolk. Travelers would flaunt their entrance and their presence in town as abrupt, "unexpected," "for a few days only." They would display their colorful mobile homes on the ground—not only living instruments but simultaneously props in performing the circus presence. With their homes thus objectified and played, and the travelers' displays in town, actual traveling was faced as a provoking, objectified apartness, the idea of being "in town for few days only" turned the circus traveler's performance into an event outside of social time (Carmeli 1987). (The public's anticipation of the circus's immediate departure was an important part of the performance of this sensation of lying outside of time. If it stays more than a very brief moment, circus 'out-of-time', the performance of its objectification and apartness soon falls into irrelevance and into the townfolks' abuse. Cottle's people themselves were very sensitive to this point.)

Marginalization, distancing, and eventual objectification and play of the 'traveler' prevailed beyond the local encounters, in the societal and institutional layers of British circus discourse. As already partially accounted for, the nomadic circus people were ignored by the union and even more so by the state. Circus arts were not supported by the state or by any public funds. No circus schools, of any kind, existed in Britain (though the circus tent was often packed with expectant spectators, the circus could not be conceived of as a legitimate career or alternative life course). Though protected by law, the travelers remained to a large extent without protection from the abuse of locals or from the harassment of local authorities. They were, de facto, also outside the state's welfare system. No one really cared about little Tony, the "Fakir's" son who was able to lie on a bed of nails, performing for the local school kids, but who at nine years old could neither read nor write. Rather, circus art and circus performers were socially excluded through notions of "different blood," family "breeding" and "family secrets." In the public image, the significance of "family" constituted not only social isolation and a unique particular history but also a definition of actual living performers as tokens, and reduction of subjectivity and living biography into a story: a story replayed and validated via its seemingly unchanging repetitive embodiments. When these different objectified "families" were displayed through their different acts, each with a natural order of gender and age objectified in its image, each with its own costuming (identical yet particular to the "family" alone), the Natural oneness of the Human species was itself played. With the objectifications and loss of species in animal acts, objectified circus Humans and Animals were even closer.

The totality of circus encounter did not evaporate, did not turn 'only play', when the circus left town. Through stories about circus, through circus paraphernalia and various traces the circus left behind, the reification of circus continues to be performed in its absence. A last reference to the circus illusion will concentrate, as an example, on circus literature—circus (mostly middle-class) fans' writings.

A five-volume work, "Circus and Its Allied Arts: A World Bibliography" was compiled by R. Toole-Stott, a British circus fan and book collector (Toole-Stott 1958–71). A large number of its entries deal with the British circus, written by British writers and published mostly in Britain. I have studied only some among the more 'serious' books and among those dealing with the periods before and after World War II (Carmeli 1994). As representations these books share in and reproduce the 'traditional circus' lore. The travelers are described as 'family', the circus, as living apart, as being an object of harassment, but as being always there, 'from the days of Rome' or at least 'from the days of the gleeman'. However, these books (and other circus paraphernalia) are not only representations. In their repetitive stories; in their pages not read but leafed through; in the divisions and fragmentation of their chapters, which, as if followed from, were marked by the fragmentation of the circus show; in their visuality; in their being, in the main, objects of collection on the fan's shelf, these books are as if 'traced' by circus performance. They are 'proofs' that reify the circus's absent presence, a presence of circus apart, 'out there'. This absent presence is then revalidated through the circus's actual appearance, making its arrival 'coming again', its appearance a 'reappearance', confirming again the realness of the 'trans'-real circus 'out there'.

Returning to this chapter's initial queries, I see the historical-cultural roots of the moral blindness to the fate of human circus performers in Britain. In the objectified human body—conjured inside the circus tent, reproduced through encounters between travelers and townsfolk, instituted in regulations, reproduced through prejudices and lore—the play of the real is here totalized and reified. It was not, then, only the travelers' actual historical marginality and origins in the fair but rather this new (modern), total performance of the circus that made the real fate of human performers insignificant, the question of their moral status irrelevant or, more bluntly put, spoiling the game. For its public, the circus was a place of the ridiculous, object-like clown, of the endangered acrobating body, of the wretched dwarf. It is through this total performance, a total play of the human player, that the spectators' illusory total order could be experientially "really" invoked.

More generally, in the new order of modernity, where fragmentariness, objectification and commodification prevail, the performance of humans and animals on the margin both encapsulates the crisis and the public's nostalgic yearning. In the "traditional circus," commodification and fragmentariness were paradoxically transcended through a totalized objectification and commodification. This totalization is experienced as the primordial categories of Nature (animal) and Culture (human)which the circus presents and plays—are both designified, as does their opposition. For its fans the circus embodies a transcendence of the order, as conceived and experienced through these categories (i.e., circus as "world upside down").

So much for British spectators, their perceptions of both circus animal and human performances, and their construction of the circus dream. Yet what about the protesters—those in Britain who seemingly did not share the circus dream, those Animal Rights people who, during the 1970s, believed they had recognized the front and backstage of circus, who 'really' knew the secrets of circus 'realness'?

The analysis I presented concerning the audience experience (of both human and animal performances), enable me to pen some comparative notes on the protesters' position. (1) Starting again with the animals, the play inside the tent is wrongly seems so alien to the position that rejects and charges the circus with cruelty. Animals, by their nature, are Nature. The circus in its performance assumes and reproduces the same cosmology the protesters cherish in their rejection and accusations against the circus. It is by playing and reconstructing Nature that circus performance and experience are invoked. (2) Similar to the circus's consuming Nature in its transcendence, so the compassionate position of the circus critics involves a paradox. By seeking to protect Nature, they lose what for them (and for the circus, too) is Nature's "real" nature. Nature protected is Nature known, it is Nature tamed. (As various writers have observed, at least some of the arguments by Animal Rights activists have a strong anthropocentric and paternalistic bias. They present human beings as protectors/patrons of Nature, constituting their own selves as being above Nature [e.g., Lease 1995].) (3) From the point of view of my argument on the totality of circus play, it is both ironic and instructive to see how, in all their moralist posturing against the state of animals, not only the circus fans but also the Animal Rights protesters themselves show little compassion for the other performing beings—the humans that are played on the circus show. In fact, in their moral claim vis-à-vis the circus, in their accusations and condemnation of the circus, they contribute to the wider "traditional" discourse of circus, totalizing its play and exclusion, performing the objectification and abjection of the circus traveler. To an extent then, and in their own way, the protesters themselves are taking part in the larger play or dream they so detest.

In the post–World War II era, and more recently in the 1980s, the 1990s and the early years of the twenty-first century, there has been a growing refutation of the old Human/Animal distinction that the traditional circus assumes in its performance. Rather than an object of domination or playful textualization, Nature is being looked at for new forms of otherness and mutuality with Culture. The performance of "cruelty" has been stripped of its transformative power. Even more generally, within the context of the postmodern "crisis of representation," the irrelevance of the search for the "really real," and the context of a pluralistic order—the yearning and search for the authentic selves, for the lost totality, which are at the core of circus illusion, lost some of their intensity. Traveling circuses in 1970s and 1980s Britain thrived (and still do so today) to a large extent on British nostalgia, repeatedly referring to their own traditions and "traditional" performance. However, the dream of the "traditional circus" has faded.

This does not mean that there are no new meanings, no new significances to old circus nonsense, upside-downs and "impossibility." In fact, postmodernity offers a new context. While many circuses in Britain have completely stopped their animal performances, circus (especially its 'New' or 'Contemporary' versions) is rediscovered in its relevance to the postmodern centrality of play. In other words, the circus, with its generic play of the real, now moves from the margins of order, to the center of the new (dis)order.

References

Assa'el, B. 1998. "The Circus and Respectable Society in Victorian Britain." Ph.D. diss., University of Toronto.
Berger, J. 1980. *About Looking*. New York: Pantheon Books.
Carmeli, Y. S. 1987. "Why Does the Jimmy Brown's Circus Traveling: A Semiotic Approach to Circus Ecology." *Poetics Today* 8: 219–44.
———. 1994. "Text, Traces and the Reification of Totality: The Case of Popular Circus Literature." *New Literary History* 25, no. 1: 175–205.
———. 1997. "The Sight of Cruelty: The Case of Circus Animal Acts." *Visual Anthropology* 10: 1–15.
———. 2003. "On Human-to-Animal Communication: Biosemiotics and Folk Perceptions in Zoos and Circuses." *Semiotica* 146: 51–68.
Cunningham, H. 1980. *Leisure in the Industrial Revolution*. London: Croom-Helm.

Disher, M. W. 1942. *Fairs, Circuses and Musichalls*. London: William Collins.

Evernden, N. 1992. *The Social Creation of Nature*. Baltimore: Johns Hopkins University Press.

Feinberg, J. 1986. *Harm to Self*. Oxford: Oxford University Press.

Fiedler, L. A. 1978. *Freaks: Myth and Images of the Secret Self*. New York: Simon and Schuster.

Kiley-Worthington, M. 1990. *Animals in Circuses and Zoos*. Harlow, England: Little Eco-Farms Publishing.

Krauss, R. 1988. "The Impulse to See." In *Vision and Visuality*, ed. Hal Foster, 57–78. Seattle: Bay Press.

Kwint, M. 1995. "Astley's Amphitheatre and the Early Circus in England, 1768–1830." Ph.D. diss., University of Oxford.

Malcolmson, R. W. 1973. *Popular Recreation in English Society, 1700–1850*. Cambridge: Cambridge University Press.

Ritvo, H. 1990. *The Animal Estate: The English and Other Creatures in the Victorian Age*. London: Penguin.

Speaight, G. 1980. *A History of the Circus*. London: Tantivy Press.

Stoddart, H. 2000. *Rings of Desire*. Manchester: Manchester University Press.

Thomas, K. 1984. *Man and the Natural World*. Harmondsworth, England: Penguin.

Toole-Stott, R. 1958–71. *Circus and Its Allied Arts: A World Bibliography*. Derby, England: Harper and Sons.

Turner, J. C. 1980. *Reckoning with the Beast: Animals, Pain and Humanity in the Victorian Mind*. Baltimore: Johns Hopkins University Press.

CONTRIBUTORS

Rohan Bastin currently teaches anthropology at James Cook University, Australia. He specializes in the study of temple and ritual aesthetics in Sri Lanka and in the relationship between popular religion, ethnicity, and ethnic conflict. He is the author of *The Domain of Constant Excess: Plural Worship at the Munnesvaram Temples in Sri Lanka* (2002) and co-editor (with Barry Morris) of *Expert Knowledge: First World Peoples, Consultancy and Anthropology* (2004).

William O. Beeman is Professor of Anthropology and of Theatre, Speech, and Dance at Brown University, where he teaches linguistic anthropology and performance studies. He is also a professional opera singer. He is co-author of *The Third Line: The Opera Performer as Interpreter* (1993) and the forthcoming *Die Meistersinger: Artistry and Cultural Identity in a German Opera Theatre.*

Yoram Carmeli is an anthropologist at the Department of Sociology and Anthropology, University of Haifa. He conducted fieldwork in the British circus (1975–1980, 2002–2003) and studied sport, consumption, and cultural aspects of new reproductive technologies in Israel. Among his publications are "The Travelling Circus" (1988), "Text, Traces and the Reification of Totality: The Case of Popular Circus Literature" (1994), and "Lion on Display: Culture, Nature and Totality in a Circus Performance" (2003).

Roberto DaMatta is Emeritus Professor at the University of Notre Dame and Professor at the Catholic University in Rio de Janeiro. A native of Brazil and the recipient of a Guggenheim fellowship, he received his master's and doctoral degrees from Harvard University. He has been a visiting scholar and professor at several institutions, including Cambridge University, the University of California at Berkeley, the Pontifícia Universidade Católica do Rio de Janeiro, the University of São Paulo, the University of

Campinas, in Brazil, and the University of Wisconsin at Madison. Among his many publications are *A Casa & a Rua* (The House and the Street, 1997, 5th ed.); *Carnivals, Rogues and Heroes: An Interpretation of the Brazilian Dilemma* (1991); *Relativizando: Uma Introdução à Antropologia Social* (Relativizing: An Introduction to Social Anthropology, 1987); *O que faz o brasil, Brasil?* (What Makes Brazil, Brazil? 1986); *A Divided World: Apinayé Social Structure* (1982); and *Universo do Carnaval* (*The Universe of Carnival*, 1981). He has been elected a member of the Instituto Histórico e Geográfico Brasileiro, the Brazilian Academy of Science, and the American Academy of Arts and Sciences. He has received the Brazilian medal of Scientific Merit and the Rio Branco medal, and, recently, the Brazilian Anthropological Association awarded him the Roquette-Pinto medal for his contributions to Brazilian anthropology. His field of interest encompasses national rituals, ceremonies, and myths of Latin America, Brazil, and the United States.

Steven M. Friedson is Professor of Ethnomusicology at the University of North Texas. For the past twenty years he has conducted research on music and trance in Africa. He has authored *Dancing Prophets: Musical Experience in Tumbuka Healing* (1996) and produced the video documentary *Prophet Healers of Northern Malawi* (1989), and he is currently finishing a book, *Northern Gods in a Southern Land*, based on research among the Ewe-speaking peoples of the Guinea Coast.

Don Handelman is Sarah Allen Shaine Professor of Anthropology and Sociology Emeritus at the Hebrew University of Jerusalem and a member of the Israel Academy of Sciences and Humanities. He has been a fellow of the Netherlands Institute for Advanced Study, the Swedish Collegium for Advanced Study in the Social Sciences, Collegium Budapest, the Institute for Advanced Studies at The Hebrew University, and the Olof Palme Visiting Professor of the Swedish Social Science Research Council. He is the author of *Models and Mirrors: Towards an Anthropology of Public Events* (1998) and *Nationalism and the Israeli State: Bureaucratic Logic in Public Events* (2004), and the co-author, with David Shulman, of *God Inside Out: Siva's Game of Dice* (1997) and *Siva in the Forest of Pines: An Essay on Sorcery and Self-Knowledge* (2004).

Angela Hobart is an Honorary Research Fellow in the Anthropology Department, University College London, and coordinating lecturer at Goldsmiths' College London University on Intercultural Therapy/Medical Anthropology. She lectures at the British Museum on the Art and Culture of South East Asia. She also works as a psychodynamic therapist at the Medical Foundation for the Care of the Victims of Torture. Her interests span mythology, religion, medical anthropology, ethno-medicine, socio-psychology, therapy, the performing arts, and aesthetics. Presently she is doing research on social suffering and healing rituals in Indonesia, with specific reference to Bali. Her publications include *Dancing Shadows of Bali:*

Theatre and Myth (1987); *The People of Bali: The Peoples of South-East Asia and the Pacific* (1996), written together with Albert Leemann and Urs Ramseyer; and *Healing Performances of Bali: Between Darkness and Light* (2003). She is the director of the Cross Cultural Centre Ascona, which she established twelve years ago in memory of her parents, Dr. Edmund and Margianne Stinnes–von Schulze Gaevernitz.

Bruce Kapferer is Professor of Social Anthropology at the University of Bergen and currently Senior Fellow at the National Humanities Center, North Carolina. He has held major posts in Europe, Australia, and the United States. His major research is on ritual, religion, and nationalism, and on cosmologies of the state, past and present. His books include *A Celebration of Demons* (1991); *The Feast of the Sorcerer* (1997); *Legends of People, Myths of State* (1998); and the edited volume, *Beyond Rationalism* (2002).

Saskia Kersenboom is Associate Professor of Linguistic Anthropology at the University of Amsterdam. Her focus on South India is rooted in a twofold curriculum: on the one hand as an Indologist, studying Sanskrit and Tamil language, literature, and culture, and, on the other, as a performing artist trained in Karnatic music and dance since 1975. Her fieldwork has been mainly with Hindu ritual specialists in temples of Tamilnadu. This constant combination of theory and praxis of culture has led her to investigate more general themes of orality, literacy, problems of representation and performance studies. Her work includes book publications as well as interactive multimedia. As a dancer, she teaches, choreographs, and performs regularly.

David Shulman is Professor of Indian Studies and Comparative Religion at the Hebrew University, Jerusalem. He was trained in Tamil by John Marr at the School of Oriental and African Studies, London. He has published mostly in the field of South Indian philology and religion. Among his works are *Tamil Temple Myths* (1980); *The King and the Clown in South Indian Myth and Poetry* (1985); and, with Don Handelman, *God Inside Out: Siva's Game of Dice* (1997) and *Siva in the Forest of Pines* (2004).

INDEX

Note: Page references with an *f* indicate a figure or photograph on the designated page.

Oddisa, the sacrificer in, 136–37, 139–40, 141, 143*f*, 151, 157n7
position of the victim in, 141, 142*f*, 144, 146*f*, 147, 148, 151–53
in the realms of senses/*maya*, 134–35
Suniyama antisorcery exorcism in, 18, 135–37, 140–41, 142*f*, 143*f*, 144, 145*f*, 146*f*, 147, 157–58nn8–16
value of aesthetic processes in, 131–35
virtuality of ritual in, 130, 134–35, 157n5
Slaats, H., 165
Smith, Frank, 73–74, 80
Sri Lanka
revival of exorcism in, 131, 157n2
Tamil Śaivite temple design in, 89–106
śruti, 46, 48–53
Staal, Frits, 90, 91
statues, structuring of perception with, 9–10
Sundberg, Johan, 28
Suniyama exorcism ritual practices, 18, 135–58
Sutherland, Joan, 33, 33*f*
svara, 46, 48–53
symbolic genres, 1
symbolic potency, 9–10

T

Tambiah, Stanley, 104
Tantric Shaktism, 75
Tocqueville, Alexis de, 185
Toole-Stott, R., 227
trance dancing
animality of, 118–19
of being-away, 17, 114–19
of being-in-between with deities, 112–14, 114*f*
of being-there, 125–26
bell and drum patterns in, 14, 119–20, 120*f*, 121–25, 126–27nn13–14, 126n10
clapping patterns in, 121–22, 122*f*, 123–25, 126–27nn13–14
feeding of the gods in, 115
habitus of listening in, 124–25
possession trance and sleeping, 117–18

practices in West Africa, 109–14, 114*f*, 115–20, 120*f*, 121–22, 122*f*, 123–24, 124*f*, 125–26
rhythm of the crossroads in, 119–20, 120*f*, 121–22, 122*f*, 123–24, 124*f*, 125
spouses of the gods in, 113
Turner, Victor
on aesthetics of rites, 12, 16, 18, 21n4, 24, 66, 67–68, 69, 71, 72, 74, 154–55, 158–59n17, 166
on liminality of ritual dynamics, 130, 131, 134–35
Tyagaraja, 49

V

Van Gennep, Arnold, 11, 71, 82
Vedic ritual, 57
Vienna school, 8–9
Vijayakrishnan, K. G., 65, 66, 77, 80–81
Voorter, Thomas, 79

W

Wall of Remembrance
bureaucratic aesthetics in presentation of, 196–213
sequencing of narrative history on, 202–5
taxonomies of, 202–4, 213–14nn5–6
Warsaw Ghetto Plaza, 202
West Africa
Bangle the soldier in, 112–14, 114*f*
Ewe peoples of, 17, 111, 113–14, 114*f*, 126n3
kola nut gods and shrines in, 113
trance dancing practices in, 109–14, 114*f*, 115–20, 120*f*, 121–22, 122*f*, 123–24, 124*f*, 125–26
Western aesthetic traditions, hegemony of, 14
Wikan, Unni, 164

Z

Zimmer, Heinrich, 9
Zoetmulder, P. J., 168, 178, 181n10

THEATER AND POLITICAL PROCESS

Staging Identities in Tokelau and New Zealand

Ingjerd Hoëm

The Argonauts in the Pacific, famous through Malinowski's work, have not been exempt from general historical developments in the world around them. By focusing on two plays performed by the Tokelau Te Ata, a theater group, the author reveals the self-perceptions of the Tokelau and highlights the dynamic relationship between issues of representation and political processes such as nation building, infrastructural changes and increased regional migration.

It is through an analysis of communicative practices, which the author carried out in the home atolls and in the diasporic communities in New Zealand, that we arrive at a proper understanding of how global processes affect local institutions and everyday interaction.

Ingjerd Hoëm is Head of the Institute for Pacific Archaeology and Cultural History, Kon-Tiki Museum.

2004. 256 pages, bibliog., index
ISBN 1-57181-583-X (Hardback)

CELEBRATING TRANSGRESSION

Method and Politics in Anthropological Studies of Cultures

A book in Honour of Klaus Peter Koepping

Edited by **Ursula Rao** and **John Hutnyk**

Transgression is the stock in trade of a certain kind of anthropological sensibility that transforms fieldwork from strict social science to something more engaging. It builds on Koepping's idea that participation transforms perception and investigates how transgressive practices have triggered the re-theorization of conventional forms of thought and life. It focuses on social practices in various cultural fields including the method and politics of anthropology in order to show how transgressive experiences become relevant for the organisation and understanding of social relations.

This book brings key authors in anthropology together to debate and transgress anthropological expectations. Through transgression as method, as discussed here, our understanding of the world is transformed, and anthropology as a discipline becomes dangerous and relevant again.

Ursula Rao is Lecturer in Anthropology in the University of Halle, and is now involved in writing about the problem of fieldwork in dispersed and postmodern settings. **John Hutnyk** is Senior Lecturer in Anthropology and a member of the Centre for Cultural Studies at Goldsmiths College, University of London.

2005. 256 pages, bibliog., index
ISBN 1-84545-025-6 (Hardback)

orders@berghahnbooks.com   www.berghahnbooks.com

IMAGES OF POWER

Iconography, Culture and the State in Latin America

Edited by **Jens Andermann** and **William Rowe**

In Latin America, where even today writing has remained a restricted form of expression, the task of generating consent and imposing the emergent nation-state as the exclusive form of the political, was largely conferred to the image. Furthermore, at the moment of its historical demise, the new, 'postmodern' forms of sovereignty appear to rely even more heavily on visual discourses of power. However, a critique of the iconography of the modern state-form has been missing.

This volume is the first concerted attempt by cultural, historical and visual scholars to address the political dimension of visual culture in Latin America, in a comparative perspective spanning various regions and historical stages. The case studies are divided into four sections, analysing the formation of a public sphere, the visual politics of avant-garde art, the impact of mass society on political iconography, and the consolidation and crisis of territory as a key icon of the state.

Jens Andermann is a Lecturer in Latin American Studies at Birkbeck College, London, and co-editor of the *Journal of Latin American Cultural Studies*.
William Rowe is Anniversary Professor of Poetics at Birkbeck College, London.

2004. 320 pages, 68 ills, bibliog., index
ISBN 1-57181-533-3 (Hardback)

DAY OF THE DEAD

When Two Worlds Meet in Oaxaca

Shawn D. Haley and **Curt Fukuda**

"This is an extremely appealing book ... the photography is absolutely outstanding ... The care taken to integrate the photos with the text and ensure the reader does not get a misleading impression from the visuals is remarkable. The book really is a model of how to use professional quality visual material to enrich an ethnographic account rather than simply to delight the eye."

—**John Gledhill,
University of Manchester**

The Day of the Dead is the most important annual celebration in Oaxaca, Mexico. Skillfully combining textual information and photographic imagery, this book begins with a discussion of the people of Oaxaca, their way of life, and their way of looking at the world. It then takes the reader through the celebration from the preparations that can begin months in advance through to the private gatherings in homes and finally to the cemetery where the villagers celebrate together — both the living and the dead.

Shawn D. Haley is an anthropologist and archaeologist who specializes in Latin American and Urban anthropology. **Curt Fukuda** is a writer and artist, who lives in Mountain View, California. Curt has been traveling regularly to Oaxaca, Mexico since 1989.

2004. 169 pages, 150 photographs
ISBN 1-84545-083-3 (Paperback)

Berghahn Books

orders@berghahnbooks.com   ∾   www.berghahnbooks.com

ACADEMIC ANTHROPOLOGY AND THE MUSEUM

Back to the Future

Edited by **Mary Bouquet**

"...focuses on anthropologists, but the consideration given to the relations between academic and museum worlds will be useful to any scholar with current affiliations or aspirations to engage with museum culture. In terms of the volume's original intent, as a work responding to the needs of those teaching and studying anthro-museology, it is an impressive accomplishment."

—Anthropologica

"The book's central argument is well made."

—Museum National

The museum boom, with its accompanying objectification and politicization of culture, finds its counterpart in the growing interest by social scientists in material culture, much of which is to be found in museums. Not surprisingly, anthropologists in particular are turning their attention again to museums, after decades of neglect.

However, the (re-)invention of museum anthropology presents a series of challenges for academic teaching and research, as well as for the work of cultural production in contemporary museums - issues that are explored in this volume.

Mary Bouquet teaches Cultural Anthropology and Museum Studies at Utrecht University College.

2001. 256 pages, 30 ills, bibliog., index
ISBN 1-57181-321-7 (Paperb ack)
ISBN 1-57181-825-1 (Hardback)

SCIENCE, MAGIC AND RELIGION

The Ritual Processes of Museum Magic

Edited by **Mary Bouquet** and **Nuno Porto**

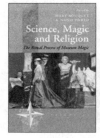

For some time now, museums have been recognized as important institutions of western cultural and social life. The idea of the museum as a ritual site is fairly new and has been applied to the art museums in Europe and the United States so far. This volume expands it by exploring a range of contemporary museums in Europe and Africa.

The case studies examine the different ways in which various actors involved in cultural production dramatize and ritualize such sites. It turns out that not only museum specialists, but visitors themselves are engaged in complex performances and experiences that make use of museums in often unexpected ways.

Mary Bouquet teaches Cultural Anthropology and Museum Studies at Utrecht University College. **Nuno Porto** is Lecturer at the Department of Anthropology, University of Coimbra, where he teaches museology, material culture, and the history of anthropology.

2004. 288 pages, 20 ills, index
ISBN 1-57181-520-1 (HardbacK)

orders@berghahnbooks.com ⁓ www.berghahnbooks.com

RITUAL IN ITS OWN RIGHT

Exploring the Dynamics of Transformation

Edited by **Don Handelman** and **Galina Lindquist**

Historically, canonic studies of ritual have discussed and explained ritual organization, action, and transformation primarily as representations of broader cultural and social orders. In the present, as in the past, less attention is given to the power of ritual to organize and effect transformation through its own dynamics. Breaking with convention, the contributors to this volume were asked to discuss ritual first and foremost in relation to itself, in its own right, and only then in relation to its socio-cultural context. The results attest to the variable capacities of rites to effect transformation through themselves, and to the study of phenomena in their own right as a fertile approach to comprehending ritual dynamics.

Don Handelman is Sarah Allen Shaine Professor of Anthropology & Sociology at the Hebrew University of Jerusalem, and a member of the Israel Academy of Sciences and Humanities. **Galina Lindquist** received her degree at the Department of Social Anthropology, University of Stockholm, for the study of urban shamans in Scandinavia.

2005. 240 pages, ills, bibliog., index
ISBN 1-84545-051-5 (Paperback)

ANTHROPOLOGY & MASS COMMUNICATION

Media and Myth in the New Millennium

Mark Allen Peterson

Anthropological interest in mass communication and media has exploded in the last two decades, engaging and challenging the work on the media in mass communications, cultural studies, sociology and other disciplines. This is the first book to offer a systematic overview of the themes, topics and methodologies in the emerging dialogue between anthropologists studying mass communication and media analysts turning to ethnography and cultural analysis.

Drawing on dozens of semiotic, ethnographic and cross-cultural studies of mass media, it offers new insights into the analysis of media texts, offers models for the ethnographic study of media productio and consumption, and suggests approaches for understanding media in the modern world system. Placing the anthropological study of mass media into historical and interdisciplinary perspectives, this book examines how work in cultural studies, sociology, mass communication and other disciplines has helped shape the re-emerging interest in media by anthropologists.

A former Washington D.C. journalist, **Mark Allan Peterson** is currently Assistant Professor of Anthropology at Miami University, Oxford, Ohio.

304 pages, bibliog.
2003. ISBN 1-57181-277-6 (Hardback)
2004. ISBN 1-57181-278-4 (Paperback)

Berghahn Books

orders@berghahnbooks.com ᵔ www.berghahnbooks.com

BEYOND RATIONALISM
Rethinking Magic, Witchcraft and Sorcery

Edited by **Bruce Kapferer**

"... shows that the discourses on 'occult economies' are multiple ... The presented essays are an excellent illustration of their variety of forms and constitute a valuable contribution to their understanding."
— **Anthropos**

 This book seeks a reconsideration of the phenomenon of sorcery and related categories. The contributors to the volume explore the different perspectives on human sociality and social and political constitution that practices typically understood as sorcery, magic and ritual reveal. In doing so the authors are concerned to break away from the dictates of a western externalist rationalist understanding of these phenomena without falling into the trap of mysticism.

The articles address a diversity of ethnographic contexts in Africa, Asia, the Pacific and the Americas.

Bruce Kapferer is Professor of Social Anthropology at the University of Bergen, Adjunct Professor at James Cook University and Honorary Professor at University College London.

2003. 288 pages, bibliog., index
ISBN 1-57181-418-3 (Paperback)

HEALING PERFORMANCES OF BALI
Between Darkness and Light

Angela Hobart

"What the book accomplishes, in an engaging style ..., is what is announced in the title, i.e. to demonstrate and explain the richness of the performatory aspects of the healing systems."
—**Aseasuk News**

"...an invaluable study for anyone interested in holistic medicine and local healing and sorcery rituals in Indonesia. It would be a useful introduction for undergraduates and postgraduates."
—**Asian Affairs**

Contemporary western societies have tended to proclaim a separation between the scientific and artistic, or the human and non-human. In Bali, these dimensions are intertwined as this study shows.

The healing performances discussed in this book take into account healing by spirit mediums and scholarly healers, the masked ritual drama, and the shadow theater. These animated performances take place during the annual religious festival that is aimed at individual well being as well as social regeneration, brought to life in this volume through rich illustrative material.

Angela Hobart is Honarary Research Fellow in the Anthropology Department, University College London, and coordinating lecturer of Intercultural Therapy [Medical Anthropology]. She also lectures at the British Museum on the Art and Culture of South East Asia.

2005. ISBN 1-84545-121-X (Paperback)
2003. ISBN 1-57181-480-9 (Hardback)
292 pages, photos, maps, diagrams and tables, bibliog., index

orders@berghahnbooks.com ~ www.berghahnbooks.com